THE
OVERCOMING
LIFE

THE
OVERCOMING
LIFE

BY

DWIGHT L. MOODY

Bridge-Logos
Orlando, FL 32822 USA

Bridge-Logos

Orlando, FL 32822 USA

The Overcoming Life
by Dwight L. Moody

Edited by Gene Fedele

Library of Congress Catalog Card Number: 2007930455
International Standard Book Number: 978-0-88270-400-5

Scripture quotations are from the *King James Version* of the Bible.

G163.316.N.m706.35250

CONTENTS

CHRISTIAN LOVE

PRACTICAL DIRECTIVES FOR PASTORS AND TEACHERS
(QUESTIONS AND ANSWERS WITH D. L. MOODY)

EFFECTIVE EVANGELISM

GEMS FROM D. L. MOODY

PREFACE

"Some day you will read in the papers that D.L. Moody, of East Northfield, is dead. Don't you believe a word of it! At that moment I shall be more alive than I am now, I shall have gone up higher, that is all; out of this old clay tenement into a house that is immortal—a body that death cannot touch; that sin cannot taint; a body fashioned like His glorious body. I was born of the flesh in 1837. I was born of the Spirit in 1856. That which is born of the flesh may die, that which is born of the Spirit will live forever."

Though more than one hundred biographies have been published and enjoyed by thousands of readers over the past 108 years since his death, this short statement is the extent of the autobiography of D. L. Moody. Yet, it truly expresses the heart of this eminent 19th-century American preacher and evangelist who preached the gospel with humility, simplicity and power to a lost and dying world—leading sinners to the Savior, equipping them as His disciples, and preparing them for the world to come.

It hadn't been since the days of George Whitefield and John Wesley, a century earlier, that the world had seen an evangelist who could move two continents for Christ, as did D. L. Moody. It is fair to say that one could scarcely find a Christian today who has never heard of the name D. L. Moody. During his travels between Europe and America, Moody personally witnessed to over 750,000 people, preached to more than 100 million, and led over a million into a personal relationship with Jesus Christ. But Moody's labors and influence were not limited to his preaching. He saw to the erecting of numerous churches, and he founded educational institutions including the Northfield School for boys and girls and the Chicago Evangelism Society, today operating as the Moody Bible Institute. He also began a publishing company, Moody Publishing, which is still producing fine Christian literature.

His dear friend and fellow laborer, R. A. Torrey, wrote of Moody: "The first thing that accounts for God's using D. L. Moody so mightily was that *he was a fully surrendered man.* Every ounce of that two-hundred-and-eighty-pound body of his belonged to God; everything he was and everything he had, belonged wholly to God."

D. L. Moody was a man who was always about the work of spreading the gospel message. In his book *To the Work, To the Work,* he gives an exhortation to believers to consider the solemn responsibility, given by God, to influence Christian revival throughout the world. Mr. Moody said that "he would rather wake up a slumbering church than a slumbering world," and that "the man who does the most good in the world is not the man who works himself, but the man who sets others to work."

Though his focus was on the spoken word more than the written, Moody penned one of his finest works, *The Overcoming Life* in 1896, to encourage believers in the daily struggle of Christian warfare. Now, for the first time in many years, the editors of Bridge-Logos Publishing are bringing back into print this great Christian classic as part of its Pure Gold Classics library. *The Overcoming Life* is a book of encouragement and inspiration to the believer in Christ. Moody's simple, practical, and anecdotal writing style, like his preaching, is engaging and easily understood by all readers. Moody expresses, with passion and conviction, the inexpressible joy a Christian can experience through victory in the daily warfare against sin, flesh, the world, and the devil. To the unconverted this book is a call—a call to come to Christ, enlist in His army, fight the battle, and gain the victory in this life and in the life to come.

In his book, Moody said of the Christian life, "The world, the flesh, and the devil are too much for any man. But if we are linked to Christ by faith, and He has formed in us the hope of glory, then we shall get the victory over every enemy. It is the believers who are the overcomers. Through Christ we shall be more than conquerors."

The health, wealth, and prosperity gospel is not the Gospel of the Bible, and Moody knew that better than most. He says, "If we are to gain a crown, we must work for it." He also says, "The most glorious triumphs of the Church have been won in times of persecution ... they were the years of growth and progress. Hear the words of Christ, 'In this world ye shall have tribulation: but be of good cheer, for I have overcome the world.' It is a battle all the time, but we have this to encourage us; we are assured of victory in the end. We are promised a glorious triumph."

In addition to *The Overcoming Life*, we are including a book that Moody wrote in 1884, *The Way to God*. In this companion work, he lovingly instructs Christians on how to draw nearer to God, through love of Christ, in the power of the Holy Spirit. He opens the book with these words: "If I could only make men understand the real meaning of the words of the apostle John—'God is Love' (1 John 4:8), I would take that single text, and would go up and down the world proclaiming this glorious truth. If you can convince a man that you love him you have won his heart. If we could really make people believe that God loves them, how we should find them crowding into the kingdom of heaven!" He also relates some poignant warnings against backsliding.

In his biography of Moody, R. A. Torrey relates, "Most of you have heard, I presume, the story President Wilson used to tell about D. L. Moody. Ex-President Wilson said that he once went into a barbershop and took a chair next to the one in which D. L. Moody was sitting, though he did not know that Mr. Moody was there. He had not been in the chair very long before, as ex-President Wilson phrased it, he 'knew there was a personality in the other chair,' and he began to listen to the conversation going on. He heard Mr. Moody tell the barber about the Way of Life, and President Wilson said, 'I have never forgotten that scene to this day.' When Mr. Moody was gone, he asked the barber who he was. When he was told that it was D. L. Moody, President Wilson said, 'It made an impression upon me I have not yet forgotten.'"

These works, along with a riveting biography, dozens of photos, and numerous shorter works of Moody, comprise a truly compelling addition to our Pure Gold Classics library of great Christian books.

The biography of D. L. Moody is a unique combination of biographical writings from his two sons, William and Paul, on the life and ministry of their father. Also included are a number of excerpts from the biographies of his dear friends, Arthur Percy Fitt and Ruben Archer Torrey. Together the reader will come to know the man Moody, as well as the pastor and evangelist.

Though these writings of D. L. Moody are not as well known as other great Christian classic titles, I am confident you will blessed and encouraged to learn about and lead an overcoming life in Christ Jesus.

Gene Fedele
Editor
May 2007

BIOGRAPHY OF

DWIGHT L. MOODY
1837-1899

Through his early training D. L. Moody was religious, but he had not, to the tender age of seventeen, experienced the regenerating work of God's Spirit by a personal acceptance of Jesus Christ. In the spring of 1854, in the Mount Vernon Sunday school, his Bible-class teacher had been gradually leading the young Moody to a fuller knowledge of God's plan of salvation. He needed only an additional personal interview to bring him to that place in his life of seeing God's provision for overcoming sin and entering into harmony with Himself. The opportunity for this interview was not a chance event, but one carefully and prayerfully sought by Mr. Kimball, who thus relates the story of Dwight L. Moody's conversion:

1

"I was determined to speak to him about Christ and about his soul, and started down to Holton's shoe store (where Moody worked). When I was nearly there I began to wonder whether I ought to go in just then during business hours. I thought that possibly my call might embarrass the boy, and that when I went away the other clerks would ask who I was, and taunt him because of my efforts in trying to make him a good boy. In the meantime, I had passed the store, and discovering this, I determined to make a dash for it and have it over at once. I found Moody in the back part of the building wrapping up shoes. I went up to him at once, and putting my hand on his shoulder, I made what I afterwards felt was a very weak plea for Christ. I don't know just what words I used, nor could Mr. Moody tell. I simply told him of Christ's love for him and the love Christ wanted in return. That was all there was. It seemed the young man was just ready for the light that then broke upon him, and there, in the back of that store in Boston, he gave himself and his life to Christ."

From the moment that Moody accepted Christ his whole life changed. The merely passive religious life that suffered the restrictions of the moral law suddenly became a life of joyful service. Whereas church attendance had been observed simply because it was a duty, from this time forth for nearly 45 years he found his greatest joy in the service of his God. "Before my conversion," as he himself used to express it, "I worked *towards* the Cross, but since then I have worked *from* the Cross; then I worked to *be* saved, now I work because I *am* saved."

Forty years afterward, preaching in Boston, he thus described the effect of his conversion upon his life:

"I can almost throw a stone from here at Tremont Temple to the spot where I found God over forty years ago. I wish I could do something to lead some of you young men to that same God. He has been a million times better to me than I have been to Him.

"I remember the morning on which I came out of my room after I had first trusted Christ. I thought the old sun shone a good deal brighter than it ever had before—I thought that it was just smiling upon me; and as I walked out upon Boston Common and heard the birds singing in the trees I thought they were all singing a song to me. Do you know I fell in love with the birds. I had never cared for them before. It seemed to me that I was in love with all creation. I had not a bitter feeling against any man, and I was ready to take all men to my heart. If a man has not the love of God shed abroad in his heart, he has never been regenerated. If you hear a person get up in the prayer meeting and he begins to find fault with everybody, you may doubt whether his is a genuine conversion; it may be counterfeit. It has not the right ring, because the impulse of a converted soul is to love, and not to be getting up and complaining of every one else and finding fault."

Moody's wish to be used by God to lead some of the youth to Christ came true in a most special way. Bread cast upon the waters returns again, and the Bible-class teacher received a blessing in his own household, seventeen years later, in the conversion of his own son. Mr. Kimball's eldest son was visiting an uncle in Worcester, Massachusetts, while Mr. Moody was conducting a mission in that city. After one of the services young Kimball introduced himself to Mr. Moody as the son of his old Bible-class teacher.

3

"What! Are you the son of Mr. Edward Kimball, of Boston? What is your name?"

"Henry."

"I am glad to see you. Henry, are you a Christian?"

"No, sir, I do not think I am."

"How old are you?"

"I am seventeen."

"Henry, when I was just seventeen, and you were a little baby in the crib, your father came to me and put his hand on my shoulder and asked me to be a Christian, and he was the only man that ever came to me and talked to me, because he loved my soul; and now I want you, my boy, to be a Christian. Henry, don't you want to be a Christian?"

"Yes, sir. I think I do," said the boy.

They sat down together, and Mr. Moody opened his Bible, the boy listening attentively to the words that impressed him more and more, till at length they brought him to where Moody himself had been led so long ago.

Moody's Family History
The earliest records of the Moody family in America date from the landing of John Moody in 1633. Settling first in Roxbury, he moved later to the Connecticut Valley, where he became one of the original proprietors of Hartford; from there he moved to Hadley, Massachusetts. At the beginning of the nineteenth century Isaiah Moody and his sons were

Birthplace of D.L. Moody at Northfield, Massachusettes.

settled in Northfield; and the eldest of these boys was Edwin, the father of Dwight L. Moody.

Mr. Moody received a goodly heritage of Puritan stock; the Holton's antedating the Moody's in America by three years. They landed in 1630, and were among the first settlers of Northfield, where for more than two hundred years they have been residents. They cherish a natural pride in the fact that, from the date of the original grant from the British Crown, no deed of transfer of the old Holton homestead has ever been recorded. This farm, beautiful in its situation, lies on the west bank of the Connecticut River, a mile or two from Northfield Street, adjoining the commanding site, purchased by Mr. Moody, upon which is built the well-known Mount Hermon School.

Betsy Holton and Edwin Moody were married on January 3, 1828. It had been arranged that the ceremony should take place on New Year's Day, but the Connecticut River had little regard for the lovers, and unexpectedly rose above its banks after a sudden thaw. Although the young people's homes were but four miles apart, in those days before bridges spanned the river the swollen stream was an insurmountable obstacle even to so resolute a character as Edwin Moody, and only by making a detour of many miles was the marriage celebrated without a still longer postponement. The bride was 23 years old and her husband 28 when they left the old Holton homestead that January evening to make a new home in Northfield.

It was a true love match between the reckless, dashing, and openhanded young man and his pretty wife, and for twelve and a half years they enjoyed their happiness. God blessed their union with seven children during this time, and by the skill and industry of his trade the father provided amply for his family support. Dwight Lyman, the sixth child, was born February 5, 1837.

Death of Moody's Father

It was foreign to the disposition of Edwin Moody to give much thought to the future, and so it is not strange that he made little or no provision for the contingency of his sudden death. When, therefore, he was stricken down without a moment's warning at the early age of 41, the widow was left with practically no means of support. The homestead itself was encumbered with a mortgage, and but for the merciful provision of the law securing dower rights, the widow would have been left without even a shelter for the family. The creditors took everything that they could secure, to the very kindling wood in the shed, and left the widow with her seven children in the utmost straits. It was at this time that one of Mrs. Moody's brothers ministered most opportunely and generously to the needs of the family. The supply of firewood had been completely exhausted, and the children had been told that they must stay in bed till school time to keep warm. It was then that "Uncle Cyrus" Holton came to the rescue with a load of wood, and as the good Samaritan that he was, sawed and split it for immediate use.

"I remember," said Mr. Moody in later years, "just as vividly as if it were yesterday, how I heard the sound of chips flying, and I knew someone was chopping wood in our wood-shed, and that we should soon have a fire. I shall never forget Uncle Cyrus coming with what seemed to me the biggest pile of wood I ever saw in my life." It was such remembrances as these that always made his heart vibrate with peculiar sympathy for those who were in want.

The birth of twins after her husband died added greatly to the cares and difficulties of her position, and during the long summer that followed there were many times when it seemed that the burden was too great for human endurance.

A less determined and courageous heart than the resolute widow's would have been overcome by the dark prospect for the future, but that true soul had inherited the sturdy strength and undaunted courage that had distinguished her early ancestors as pioneers in the new world, and with a strong faith in God she faced the conflict with poverty.

With the sole care of so large a family one would think that religious instruction in the home would suffer, but Mrs. Moody instructed her children in the true religion of the heart that seeks first God and His righteousness.

"Trust in God" was the brief creed of his mother's simple Christian faith, and early in life the children learned to love that God and pray to Him who is the strength of the fatherless and the widow. Many evidences of the thoroughness with which this lesson was taught to Dwight and his brothers are found in their early experiences.

Mrs. Moody was tender hearted, and the children early learned the privilege of giving from their scanty possessions. The hungry were never turned away from her door, and on one occasion when the provision for the evening meal was very meager it was put to the vote of the little ones whether they should give of their small supply to a poor beggar who appealed for aid. The children begged that he should be aided and offered to have their own slices cut thinner.

Church attendance was not a debatable question in the family, but was as inevitable as a law of nature. And Sabbath's rest, beginning with sundown on Saturday and

Betsy Holton Moody, D.L.'s mother, in 1867.

ending at the same time Sunday evening, was Mrs. Moody's most welcome respite.

In later years Mr. Moody looked back with gratitude to this strict requirement of church attendance. Those hours in the village church, tedious as they were, listening as he must to sermons that he could not understand, he came to look upon as a blessing because they fixed upon him the habit of attending God's house.

"I remember blaming my mother for sending me to church on the Sabbath," he once said. "On one occasion the preacher had to send some one into the gallery to wake me up. I thought it was hard to have to work in the field all the week, and then be obliged to go to church and hear a sermon I didn't understand. I thought I wouldn't go to church any more when I got away from home; but I had got so in the habit of going that I couldn't stay away. After one or two Sabbaths, back again to the house of God I went. There I first found Christ, and I have often said since: 'Mother, I thank you for making me go to the house of God when I didn't want to go.'"

Mr. Moody could never speak of those early days of want and adversity without the tenderest references to that brave mother whose self-sacrifice and devotion had sacredly guarded the home entrusted to her care. When, at the age of 90, her life-voyage ended and she entered the Haven of Rest; her children, her children's children, and an entire community rose up to call her blessed. And well she deserved the praise they gave her, for she had wisely and discreetly discharged the duties God had placed upon her, and entering the presence of her Master, could render a faithful account of the stewardship of motherhood. To rule a household of seven sturdy boys and two girls, the eldest twelve years old, required no ordinary tact and sound judgment, but so discreet was this loyal mother that to the very end she made "home" the most loved place on earth to her family, and so trained her children as to make them a blessing to society.

"For nearly fifty years I have been coming back to Northfield," said Mr. Moody long after that little circle had been broken up, "and I have always been glad to get back. When I get within fifty miles of home I grow restless and walk up and down the car. It seems as if the train will never get to Northfield. When I come back after dark I always look to see the light in Mother's window."

Boyhood Years

Dwight's early life was not much different from other New England boys. He went to school during the fall and winter. In the summer, he worked on a neighbor's farm turning out the cows to pasture, receiving one penny a day for his labors.

Moody was of a fun-loving nature and full of practical jokes—a characteristic he carried with him his entire life; and one that also contributed to his developing qualities of leadership in his latter career.

Dwight, always the ringleader in mischief, was one of the first to break the rules. The teacher asked him to stay behind. Since it was the school's custom to administer the cane to such unruliness, Moody was preparing himself and was in a fighting mood. The teacher took him alone and began to talk to him kindly. That was worse than the cane to him. She said, "I have made up my mind that if I cannot control my class by love, I will give it up. I will have no punishment. If you love me, then keep the rules." Love conquered him that day!

When Dwight grew older he found employment, like his brothers, in neighboring towns. His first experience was never forgotten, and the homesickness that came with the first separation from his family left a lasting impression. In describing this he said:

"There were nine of us children, and my widowed mother had very great difficulty in keeping the wolf from the door. My next older brother had found a place for me to work during the winter months in a neighboring village about thirteen miles away, and early one November morning we started out together on our dismal journey. Do you know, November has been a dreary month to me ever since? As we passed over the river and up the opposite side of the valley we turned to look back for a last view of home. It was to be my last for weeks, for months, perhaps forever, and my heart very well broke at the thought. That was the longest journey I ever took, for thirteen miles was more to me at ten than the world's circumference has ever been since.

"When at last we arrived in the town I had hard work to keep back my tears, and my brother had to do his best to cheer me. Suddenly he pointed to some one and said: 'There's a man that'll give you a cent. He gives one to every new boy that comes to town.' He was a feeble, old, white-haired man, and I was so afraid that he would pass me by that I planted myself directly in his path. As he came up to us my brother spoke to him, and he stopped and looked at me. 'Why, I have never seen you before. You must be a new boy,' he said. He asked me about my home, and then, laying his trembling hand upon my head, he told me that, although I had no earthly

11

father, my Heavenly Father loved me and sent His Son, Jesus Christ, down here and He died for me. He only talked for about five minutes, but he took me so captive that I forgot about the penny. Then he put his hand into his pocket and pulled out a bright new cent, and gave it to me. I do not remember what became of that cent, but that old man's blessing has followed me for over fifty years, and to my dying day I shall feel the kindly pressure of that hand upon my head. A loving deed costs very little, but done in the name of Christ it will be eternal."

In 1854, Dwight decided he wanted to go to Boston. "I'm tired of this! I'm not going to stay around here any longer. I'm going to the city." The family had been strongly opposed to his going to Boston, as no one believed that he had any special

Dwight L. Moody at the time of his leaving home for Boston.

qualification for a successful career in the city. The cities were full of young men looking for positions. While at Northfield he was at least assured of steady work on the farms. But young Moody had made up his mind that the one thing for him to do was to go to Boston and, in spite of all obstacles, make a career for himself.

Relating one day his rough early days on his own, Moody

recalls, "It seemed as if there was room for every one else in the world, but none for me. For about two days I had the feeling that no one wanted me. I never have had it since, and I never want it again. It is an awful feeling. It seems to me that must have been the feeling of the Son of God when He was down here. They did not want Him. He had come to save men, and they did not want to be saved. He had come to lift men up, and they did not want to be lifted up. There was no room for Him in this world, and there is no room for Him yet."

Young Moody had little acquaintance with city ways and city manners, but it soon became evident that he was by natural wit and brightness one of the best salesmen. With his keen perception and irrepressible energy he became quite a success. He was not satisfied with the ordinary methods of the salesman, and, like the merchants of old, he sold his wares door-to-door, and actually went out into the street to persuade uninterested passers that they wanted to buy. Nothing delighted him so much as a success of this kind, and that he had many is not surprising.

His new occupation, far from lessening his love of practical joking, seemed to make it keener. Always on the lookout for some one whom he could tease, he found a tempting victim in a cobbler who worked in the store. One day in his absence young Moody, with a sharp knife, made a clean slit in the leather seat of the cobbler's box. Then taking a pan of water, he set it under the box so that the cobbler's weight would bring the seat in contact with the water, which, of course, would rise through the cut.

Having set his trap, the joker awaited the result. Presently the cobbler came in and sat down. One can imagine the effect. The victim took his seat only to jump up hurriedly, but as soon as the leather was relieved of his weight the hole closed, and after wiping the seat dry he again seated himself to begin his work. It was not till the third or fourth time that he discovered the trouble, and Moody had to make a hurried escape.

This was the nonsense of a lively boy of seventeen, but from that harmless love of fooling the happy geniality of the mature man was to result. This sense of humor, this healthy appreciation of the ridiculous, is the very salt of a great temperament. Such a man, however intense, can never be a fanatic, and the people—the men in the street—feel this instantly.

Coming to Christ

In accordance with the agreement by which he entered his uncle's employment, Moody became a regular attendant of the Mount Vernon Congregational Church. He was also enrolled as a member of the Sunday school, where he was assigned to a young men's Bible class conducted by Mr. Edward Kimball.

The Bible was not a familiar book to the new student, for in his home, though he had always lived in a truly Christian atmosphere, there was only one copy of God's Word, and that a ponderous family Bible, too sacred for the inquisitiveness of the little children, and too uninviting in its massive appearance for the older ones

On one occasion, seventeen-year-old Dwight, as a member of a young men's Bible class in Boston, was bewildered by the request to turn to a simple Scriptural reference. He didn't know how to find the gospel of John in the Bible, and the other students who took opportunity to embarrass him readily detected his ignorance. It is doubtful that any of his amused companions were more thoroughly established in "pure religion and undefiled before God" than he. Certainly none was purer and more innocent in heart than the keen, awkward country boy. It was not till after he left home that his actual personal conversion occurred, but it was to a tender conscience and an open heart that the gospel invitation was given in that precious Sabbath-school class, and a soul already trained to love and honor God readily accepted His offer of salvation.

After his conversion young Moody was no less energetic and ambitious in the interests of the Kingdom of God than he had been in business. His vigorous and irrepressible spirit was looked upon with misgivings by some of the elder members of the church. In the first glad joy of his Christian experience he longed for some channel into which he might direct his energies and share in the forwarding of the Kingdom. He did not have to wait long.

Move to Chicago

Young Moody arrived in Chicago in the early autumn of 1856. At first he encountered the same difficulty in securing employment that had so tried his fortitude two years before in Boston. In two days, however, he secured a position that promised greater opportunities than the one he left, and from the very first his energy and keen business judgment was rewarded by a steady increase in responsibility and income.

The same earnest Christian spirit that had shown itself in Boston dominated his life in Chicago, and on his arrival, as his letters prove, he promptly associated himself with Christian people. Writing to his mother under date of September 25, 1856, he says:

D. L. Moody during his early years in Chicago.

Mr. Moody at age 27: Sunday school worker.

"I reached this far-famed city of the West one week ago tonight ... I went into a prayer meeting last night, and as soon as I made myself known, I had friends enough. After meeting they came to me and seemed to be as glad to see me as if I were their earthly brother. God is the same here as He was in Boston, and in Him I can find peace."

The great religious revival that swept over the country in 1856 had reached to Chicago, and young Moody heartily enjoyed the opportunities and blessings it brought. Writing to his mother in 1857, he expressed great delight in the interest that was awakened, introducing the phrases current at the time.

"I have nothing to write that will interest you unless it is that there is a great revival of religion in this city. I go to meeting every night. Oh, how I do enjoy it! It seems as if God was here Himself. Oh, Mother, pray for us. Pray that this work may go on until every knee is bowed. I wish there could be a revival in Northfield that many might be brought into the fold of Christ. Oh, Mother, keep the family away from the Spiritualists' meetings, for I am afraid they may be led astray."

Moody became very successful in business, but his heart was increasingly yearning for something more. In a letter to his mother he writes:

"If I have my health and my God is with me, I shall succeed better here in Chicago than I ever thought. Mother, I hope you will not forget to pray for your son here in the West, surrounded by temptations on all sides. I never worked in a place since my conversion where there were so many young men as here. I hope you will plead with God that I may live a consistent Christian before them. I am in hope to live so before them that I may succeed in winning their souls to Christ. Pray for me, dear Mother."

Early Christian Work

Moody was a man who was never content with inactivity, and sought a number of opportunities of service to occupy his time and energies. He settled on establishing the Wells Street Sunday School at the Mission. Here he made the acquaintance of the one who, four years later, became his wife—Emma C. Revell, at this time a girl of fifteen and a teacher in the school.

Feeling that his success in the Wells Street Mission pointed to greater undertakings, Mr. Moody, in the fall of 1858, determined to begin another mission school on a larger scale in another part of the city. The same success attended these efforts, and it was soon found that a large hall would be necessary to accommodate the attendance. Such a place was secured in the North Market Hall, a public hall over one of the large city markets of Chicago. Here, in company with his friends, Mr. Moody began the Sunday school work that developed later into the Illinois Street Church, afterwards the Chicago Avenue Church, in which he held membership during the later years of his life.

At the close of the school each day, Mr. Moody took his place at the door and seemed to know personally every boy and girl. He shook hands and had a smile and a cheery word for each. They crowded about him tumultuously, and his arm must have ached many a time after those meetings.

Illinois Street Church, Chicago. First building erected by Mr. Moody.
Scene of his efforts before the Chicago fire.

It was easy to see the hold he had on those young lives, and why they were drawn to that place week after week.

Full-Time Ministry

In 1860, Mr. Moody was led to give up business and devote all his time to Christian ministry. "The greatest struggle I ever had in my life was when I gave up business," Mr. Moody often said. The steadily increasing duties in his pioneer religious work had not prevented his success in business, and though manager of the largest Sunday school in the country, he could hold this position without detriment to the interests of his employer.

About this time he was actively connected with a Congregational church on the North Side. The meetings were too slow for Moody, and he went to some good brother and asked him if, at the next meeting, he would not get up and be the first to speak. He said he would. Mr. Moody then went to others, and engaged three to be the second speaker and three others to be third. When the first man had spoken the others followed, several rising at once. This unusual sight inspired the meeting with the enthusiasm of a revival, and was really the beginning of a great quickening of spiritual interest in the church.

It was a time of great excitement in the nation. Abraham Lincoln had been nominated and elected President, and, like the young men who were his associates, Mr. Moody was immersed in business and politics, and keenly alive to all the events of the hour. He had an experience at this time, however, that entirely transformed his career and led him to devote himself exclusively to Christian work. All ambitions for wealth were sacrificed, but not until the struggle had lasted three long months. Finally what he felt to be the call of God was triumphant, and he surrendered his own plans for his Father's. How he came to give up business altogether may best be told in his own words:

"I had never lost sight of Jesus Christ since the first time I met Him in the store in Boston, but for years I really believed that I could not work for God. No one had ever asked me to do anything.

"When I went to Chicago I hired four pews in a church, and used to go out on the street and pick up young men and fill these pews. I never spoke to the young men about their soul; that was the work of the elders, I thought. After working for some time like that, I started a mission Sunday school. I thought numbers were everything, and so I worked for numbers. When the attendance ran below one thousand it troubled me, and when it ran to twelve or fifteen hundred I was elated. Still, none were converted; there was no harvest.

"Then God opened my eyes! There was a class of young ladies in the school who were, without exception, the most frivolous set of girls I ever met. One Sunday the teacher was ill, and I took that class. They laughed in my face, and I felt like opening the door and telling them all to go out and never come back.

"That week the teacher of the class came into the store where I worked. He was pale and looked very ill.

"'What is the trouble?' I asked.

"'I have had another hemorrhage from the lungs. The doctor says I cannot live on Lake Michigan, so I am going back to New York State. I suppose I am going to die.'

"He seemed greatly troubled, and when I asked the reason he replied: 'Well, I have never led any of my class to Christ. I really believe I have done the girls more harm than good.'

"I had never heard any one talk like that before, and it set me thinking.

"After a while I said: 'Suppose you go and tell them how you feel. I will go with you in a carriage, if you want to go.'

"He consented, and we started out together. It was one of the best journeys I ever had on earth. We went to the house of one of the girls, called for her, and the teacher talked to her about her soul. There was no laughing then. Tears stood in her eyes before long. After he had explained the way of life, he suggested that we have a word of prayer. He asked me to pray. True, I had never done such a thing in my life as to pray God to convert a young lady there and then. But we prayed, and God answered our prayer.

"We went to other houses. He would go upstairs and be all out of breath, and he would tell the girls what he had come for. It wasn't long before they broke down and sought for salvation.

"When his strength gave out I took him back to his lodgings. The next day we went out again. At the end of ten days he came to the store with his face literally shining.

"'Mr. Moody,' he said, 'the last one of my class has yielded herself to Christ.'

"I tell you we had a time of rejoicing.

"He had to leave the next night, so I called his class together that night for a prayer-meeting, and God kindled a fire in my soul that has never gone out. The height of my ambition had been to be a successful merchant, and if I had known that meeting was going to take that ambition out of me, I might not have gone. But how many times I have thanked God since for that meeting!"

Having a sizable sum saved during his business career, Mr. Moody decided to live on this as long as it lasted. If at the end of this time the Lord continued to reward his labor, thus indicating that it was the right course to continue, he believed that the means for it would be provided. He never again received a regular salary from any source after leaving business.

In his Christian work, as formerly in business, Moody had little regard for strict conventionalities that did not appeal to his very practical judgment as useful or effective, and many a strange position did he find himself in when he undertook to secure his object without consideration of what was the regular but less immediate method. Often he would hail children on the street, inviting them to his Sunday school, and would ask an introduction to their parents to secure their consent to the children becoming members.

Most of the children that attended the North Market Hall came from homes where there was no Christian influence. Mr. Moody felt he had the children for an hour a week and the devil had them the rest of the time. That led him to start Sunday night meetings. It didn't take long to see "the tides coming in" and "converts increasing."

Civil War and His Commission

On his arrival in Chicago in 1861, he joined the Young Men's Christian Association (YMCA), which had recently been organized in that city as one of the results of the revival movement, and took an active interest in its noonday prayer meetings.

After giving up business Moody devoted much of his time to YMCA work (later to become its president), with which he was closely identified at the beginning of the Civil War. He was successful in raising much support for the expansion of the YMCA. He defined their aim:

> "To promote the spiritual instincts and look after the temporal welfare of young men. Each ought to be a nursery of Christian character, a most efficient evangelistic agency, a center of social meetings, and a means of furthering the progress of young men in the general pursuits of life. But along with liberality in your aims you must have thoroughness in details. The spiritual must be distinctly dominant. Do not, however, put the Association in place of the church; it is only a handmaid and a feeder of the church. For every man it must find some work, and use every particle of power in the young convert."

In the days that followed the firing on Fort Sumter, Chicago, like all the other cities in the Union, felt the greatest excitement. Moody's first act of service in the war was to preach to soldiers passing through Chicago on the way to their posts. But the most interesting opportunity followed shortly thereafter, when the Union army captured 9,000 Confederate soldiers and placed them in a camp in Chicago. Moody enlisted his friend Hawley to accompany him to the camp that they might preach the gospel to the prisoners. After much effort convincing the guards to allow the service, Moody finally reached the pulpit. The words of Hawley describe the result:

> "Mr. Moody took charge, and it seemed as though the Spirit of the Lord came down upon these men with great power. They came forward to the altar—twenty, thirty, forty at a time. We closed the meeting and began inquiry work. Moody had the

platform, and God used him wonderfully. The whole audience melted, and we saw strong men in tears. 'God is here!' Moody whispered to me."

Through worship services, prayer meetings, song services, distribution of Bibles, books and tracts, and by personal visitations, he tried to win many soldiers to Christ. He was a great favorite of the soldiers and highly respected for his self-sacrificing labors. Each evening, while at the front, the boys would gather around the blazing campfire and listen to his earnest appeals. It wasn't uncommon to hear his voice rising up in prayer from the tents of the ungodly.

In many ways these war experiences served to prepare him for his larger work. It brought him prominently before the whole country. Mr. Moody learned, in dealing with the dying, just how urgent it is not to delay in matters of eternal salvation.

Marriage to Emma Revell

Dwight L. Moody married Emma Charlotte Revell on August 28, 1862. The Lord blessed them with three beautiful children, Emma (1864), William Revell (1869), and Paul Dwight (1879). In the biography of his father, Paul Moody writes an intimate depiction of their relationship: "If in retrospect our home seemed ideal, the secret was my mother. My father's admiration for her was as boundless as his love. He never ceased to wonder at the miracle of having won the love of a woman he considered so completely his superior. No two people were ever more in contrast. He was impulsive, outspoken, dominant, informal, and with little education at the time they met. She was intensely conventional and conservative, far better educated, fond of reading, with a discriminating taste, and self-effacing to the last degree." Yet in all, the match proved to be wonderful in all respects

Emma and Dwight Moody in 1864 and 1869.

and complimentary to the ministry to which Mr. Moody was called by God.

First Trip to Europe

There were two men in England whom Mr. Moody had a great desire to hear and meet—Charles H. Spurgeon and George Muller, and with the two-fold purpose of affording a beneficial trip for Mrs. Moody, who was suffering from asthma, and making the acquaintance of these leaders in Christian work, he went oversees.

An intimate bond developed between the English and American evangelists, and they had occasion to share of the revival work going on in both continents. Moody tried to induce Spurgeon to come to America, but without success. He was also moved when he visited Muller's great orphan schools. He wrote, "It is amazing to see what God can do with a man of prayer."

Shortly after Charles Spurgeon's death, Mrs. Spurgeon sent to Moody his personal Bible as a gift, with the inscription:

"Mr. D. L. Moody, from Mrs. C. H. Spurgeon, in tender memory of the one gone home to God. This Bible has been used by my precious husband, and is now given with unfeigned pleasure to one in whose hands its blessed service will continue to be extended."

Since that day, Spurgeon's Bible became one of Moody's most precious possessions, and he was in the habit of turning to it first to see what Mr. Spurgeon had to say about whatever text he was studying.

Ira Sankey Joins the Work

Throughout the world, Mr. Moody's name is associated with that of Ira D. Sankey more than any other of his fellow-laborers. To many, the names of Moody and Sankey are inseparable.

The great evangelistic team of D. L. Moody and Ira D. Sankey was first formed in 1870, while the two were attending a YMCA convention in Indianapolis. They had never met, but knew of each other. At the close of the convention it was announced that Mr. Moody would lead an early morning prayer meeting at six o'clock the next day in a neighboring church. There was some difficulty in starting the singing until Mr. Sankey's friend urged him to begin a hymn. He began to sing, "There is a fountain filled with blood," in which all the congregation joined. At the close of the service Mr. Sankey was introduced by his friend, and was immediately recognized by Moody as the leader of the singing. A few inquiries regarding Mr. Sankey's family ties

Bible used by Mr. Moody for many years.

28

and occupation followed; then the evangelist announced in his determined fashion, "Well, you'll have to give that up! You are the man I have been looking for, and I want you to come to Chicago and help me in my work."

Mr. Sankey was somewhat surprised at this sudden suggestion, and assured Mr. Moody that he could not leave his business, but accepted an invitation to lunch with him that day to learn something of the nature of the work proposed. Nothing definite resulted from this conference, although Mr. Sankey promised to give the matter his prayerful consideration.

Later in the day he was given a card asking him to meet Mr. Moody that evening at a certain street corner to assist in an open-air service. In company with a few friends Mr. Sankey met Mr. Moody at the appointed place, and thus describes the informal service that followed:

"Without stopping, Mr. Moody walked into a store on the corner and asked permission to use a large empty box which he saw outside the door. This he rolled to the side of the street, and taking his stand upon it, asked me to sing the hymn, 'Am I a soldier of the Cross?'

"After one or two hymns Mr. Moody began his address. Many workingmen were just then on their way home from the mills, and in a short time a large crowd had gathered. The address that evening was one of the most powerful I had ever heard. The crowd stood spellbound at the burning words, and many a tear was brushed away from the eyes of the men as they looked up into the speaker's honest face."

Mr. Sankey was greatly impressed, and after the convention, went back to Newcastle and told his family of his invitation to Chicago. Some months later he yielded to Mr. Moody's invitation to come for at least a week, and then to decide the question, which he did.

They spent their first day together visiting the sick that were members of Mr. Moody's congregation. Mr. Sankey sang and Mr. Moody read words of comfort from the Word of God and offered prayer for the healing of both body and soul. The following Sunday a large meeting was held in Farwell Hall. At the close of the service a number of persons arose for prayer, and at the close of the "inquiry meeting" Mr. Moody turned to the singer and said, "You are going home tomorrow, but you see I was right in asking you to come and help me in this work, and I hope you will make up your mind to come as soon as possible." This wish was granted, for Mr. Sankey soon resigned his business, went to Chicago, and joined Mr. Moody in his work in the Illinois Street Church and also in that of the Young Men's Christian Association.

Chicago Fire

On October 8, 1871, while preaching at Farwell Hall, Moody felt a great sense of the Holy Spirit and closed his words with, "I wish you would take this text home with you and turn it over in your minds during the week, and next Sabbath we will come to Calvary and the cross, and we will decide what to do with Jesus of Nazareth." But the call to the people would never be realized. For that night Farwell Hall and a great deal of the city of Chicago would burn to the ground. In an address 22 years later, Moody relates the lessons he learned:

"I have never dared to give an audience a week to think of their salvation since. If they were lost they

Ira D. Sankey

might rise up in judgment against me. I have never seen that congregation since. I have to work hard to keep back the tears today. I have looked over this audience, and not a single one is here that I preached to that night. I have a great many old friends and am pretty well acquainted in Chicago, but twenty-two years have passed away, and I have not seen that congregation since, and I never will meet those people again until I meet them in another world. But I want to tell you of one lesson I learned that night, which I have never forgotten, and that is, when I preach, to press Christ upon the people then and there, and try to bring them to a decision on the spot. I would rather have that right hand cut off than to give an audience now a week to decide what to do with Jesus. I have often been criticized; people have said: 'Moody, you seem to be trying to get people to decide all at once: why do you not give them time to consider?'

Moody's Tabernacle. First building erected after the Chicago fire.

"I have asked God many times to forgive me for telling people that night to take a week to think it over, and if He spares my life, I will never do it again. This audience will break up in a few moments—we may never meet after today.

"Ever since that night of the great fire I have determined as long as God spares my life to make more of Christ than in the past. I thank God that He is a thousand times more to me today than He was twenty-two years ago. I am not what I wish I was, but I am a good deal better than I was when Chicago was on fire."

Spiritual Awakening in Scotland and England

The success of the American evangelists in the North of England led to an investigation of their methods, and after some hesitation they were invited to Edinburgh, and held their first service in the Music Hall, the largest in the city, Edinburgh, on Sunday, November 23, 1873.

The ministry of Moody and Sankey had a great impact on the spiritual condition of the people of the city. Many were awakened to realize the importance of eternal things and burdened with the sense of sin and a longing to obtain salvation. For hundreds of years only Psalms had been sung in the churches with no musical instruments. Now with Sankey "singing the Gospel" the people were packing out the auditoriums.

After a number of services and revivals *The Edinburgh Daily Review* had this to say:

"The part of the service toward which all the rest tends, and in which the power culminates is the address of Mr. Moody, in which, in simple figures and telling language, he holds up before men the truth as it is in Jesus and makes most earnest and powerful appeals to heart and conscience. Mr. Moody is strikingly free from all pretense and parade. He speaks as one who thoroughly believes what he says and who is in downright earnest in delivering his message. His descriptions are characterized by a remarkable vividness and graphic power. He has a great wealth of illustration, and his illustrations are always apposite, bringing into the clearest light the point that he intends to illustrate, and fixing it forever into the memory. There is very little excitement; there is no extravagance; but the effect of the services is seen in the manifest impression produced on the audience, generally in the anxious inquirers (varying in number from about forty to upward of seventy), who remain for spiritual conversation and prayer after every meeting. Not a few also profess to have been brought out of darkness into marvelous light, and to be going on their way rejoicing."

Many ministers and laymen of the various evangelical denominations in Edinburgh, Glasgow, Dundee, and Leith gladly welcomed Mr. Moody on his arrival in the city, and threw themselves heartily into the work. Others who at first had difficulties and stood somewhat aloof found their objections melting away with personal contact, and identified themselves cordially with the work. It was delightful to witness the unbroken unity and brotherly love that prevailed among all engaged in the movement. Denominational differences were for the time lost sight of.

Dr. Horatius Bonar thus referred to the meetings not long after they were started:

"There has been not a few awakened of late, and the interest is deepening. The ministers of all denominations take part most cordially. Men are coming from great distances to ask the way of life, awakened to this concern by no directly human means, but evidently by the Holy Spirit, who is breathing over the land. It is such a time, as we have never had in Scotland before. The same old Gospel as of aforetime is preached to all men; but now the Gospel is preached '*with the Holy Ghost sent down from Heaven,*' and amid all this the enemy is restrained. Surely it is the time to seek the Lord that He may rain righteousness upon us."

The final meeting was held in the Botanical Gardens. Mr. Sankey found his way into the building and began the service with more than six thousand, who were crushed together inside. But so great was the crowd outside, estimated at twenty or thirty thousand people, that Mr. Moody himself could not get inside. Standing on the coachman's box of the carriage in which he was driven, he asked the members of the choir to sing. They found a place for themselves on the roof of a low shed near the building, and after they had sung Mr. Moody preached for an hour on "Immediate Salvation." So distinct was his voice that the great crowd could hear him without difficulty. Writing of this, a witness said:

"We thought of the days of Whitefield, of such a scene as that mentioned in his life, when, in 1753 at Glasgow, twenty thousand souls hung on his lips as he bade them farewell. Here there were thirty thousand eager hearers, for by this time the thousands within the Crystal Palace had come out, though their numbers quietly melting into the main body did not make a very perceptible addition to the crowd; and many onlookers who knew something of such gatherings were inclined to estimate the number much higher."

He used lecture halls, theaters, and even the streets as his pulpits, crossing over entrenched denominational lines. He was able to reach the masses that otherwise would not visit a church or listen to the claims of the gospel. His popularity grew quickly.

One of the most successful and blessed services was held in Spurgeon's Tabernacle. It was designed for the benefit of the students of Mr. Spurgeon's college and the Baptist ministers in town, but the scope of the meeting was widened and tickets were issued to the Sunday congregation. In his address Mr. Moody was dwelling on the passage, *"Prepared unto every good work,"* and he said:

"I wonder how many of you would rise if I should ask every man and woman to do so who is ready to go and speak to some anxious soul. I wonder how many would rise and say, 'I am ready for one.'" He paused. "Someone behind me says, 'Try it,' but I am rather afraid." He paused again. "Well, suppose we do try it. How many of you are ready to go and talk to some soul?'"

The students and ministers on either side of the platform at once rose in a body, and members throughout the congregation quickly followed their example. Equal to the occasion, Mr. Moody said, "Well, now you have risen, I want to tell you that the Lord is ready to send you. Nothing will wake up London quicker than to have the Christians going out and speaking to the people. The time has come when it should be done. We have been on the defensive too long."

With reference to Moody and Sankey's work in England, the late Rev. Dr. Philip Schaff, of New York, made the following remarks in an address in London some years ago:

"One of the most interesting and remarkable facts in the history of these days is the wonderful effect produced among you by the efforts of two laymen from America. It was a greater marvel to us than to you, and the only way to account for it is to refer it at once to the grace of God! Such a movement the world has not seen since the days of Whitefield and Wesley, and it is wider in its results than the work of those two honored men. It is most unsectarian in its character, and, I may add, the most unselfish movement known in our common history. It was for the purpose of winning souls to Christ and of extending His Kingdom, without regard to denominational boundaries, that these two men came to England, and every church may reap the benefit … We in America had no idea these two men could have produced such a commotion among you all; but it is just the old, old story of the simple fishermen of Galilee over again."

Subsequently he said of his countrymen:

"They have proved the power of elementary truths over the hearts of men more mightily than all the learned professors and eloquent pastors of England could do. As the Methodist revival, more than a hundred years ago stopped the progress of deism, so these plain laymen from America turned the tide of modern materialism and atheism. It is the grace of God behind these men that explains the extraordinary religious interest they have awakened all over Scotland and England."

The return of Moody and Sankey to America in 1875 was received with great anticipation. They left the States as those known only in Chicago and among a small group of friends and fellow ministers; but came home to carry forth the work of revival so successful in England, Scotland and Ireland. Campaigns were conducted all over the country and in major cities such as New York, Philadelphia, Boston, Denver, St. Louis, San Francisco, Baltimore, and Chicago.

Interior of Old Pennsylvania Railroad Depot in Philadelphia.
Scene of the great meetings in Philadelphia.

38

The late George H. Stuart thus spoke of the Philadelphia meetings a few weeks after their close:

"In October last we attempted a great work for God in our city. Some had high expectations that it would redound largely to the glory of Heaven. They saw a deep spirit of prayer among the clergymen and members of the churches; and what has been the result? It has far exceeded the highest hopes of the most sanguine. We had little thought to see a hall filled to overflowing day after day with from seven thousand to thirteen thousand people who came to hear the old, old story of Jesus and His love."

SCHOOLS FOR GIRLS AND BOYS

Northfield Seminary for Young Women
Northfield, MA

"You know," said Moody, "that the Lord laid it upon my heart some time ago to organize a school for young women in the humbler walks of life, who never would get a Christian education but for a school like this. I talked about this plan of mine to friends, until a number of them gave money to start the school. Some thought I ought to make it for boys and girls, but I thought that if I wished to send my daughter away to school I should prefer to send her to an institution for girls only. And now as we dedicate this building to God, I want to read you the motto of this school." Then, turning to Isaiah 27:3, he read: "'I the Lord do keep it; I will water it every moment lest any hurt it, I will keep it night and day.'"

And it would seem that this promise has been more than fulfilled, for during the 20 years which have elapsed since then the Seminary has been remarkably blessed.

In the cornerstone of each of the school buildings has been placed a copy of the Scriptures. This is symbolic of the place that God's Word holds in the life of the schools. It is, indeed, foundation, cornerstone, and capstone of Mr. Moody's whole system. He recognized that all studies have their value, but believed their importance is increased if pursued in right relation to central truths.

It was not the idea of the Seminary to pay exclusive attention to the training of the mind and soul, but rather to develop a symmetrical womanhood.

Mount Hermon School for Men—New Haven, CT

No sooner was the Seminary under way than a corresponding school for boys suggested itself. Mount Hermon School for Young Men was therefore started on similar principles. The first purchase of property was made in November 1879, when Mr. Moody secured a farm of 175 acres. When, a little later, Mr. Hiram Camp, of New Haven, Conn., agreed to contribute $25,000, some adjoining land was bought, and the school started with an estate of about 275 acres and two farmhouses. At Mr. Camp's suggestion the name Mount Hermon was adopted, *"for there the Lord commanded the blessing, even life for evermore"* (Psalm 133:3).

Rev. Alexander McGaffin, of Brooklyn, a former student in the school, thus writes of the spirit of the place, which he terms *hermonology:*

Northfield Seminary buildings on the Connecticut River.

"I went to Mount Hermon as a mere boy without any particular aim in life or any serious religious convictions. There I came upon a species of Christianity altogether new to me, and an educational training tempered by an earnest religious spirit. One did not study merely for learning's sake, nor was one religious merely for religion's sake. A great purpose was constantly held up, towards which we boy learners were to struggle, and pure motives were inculcated as the ever-present power of our lives. We were taught that the present was the means and the future the end; that in that future dwelt God and humanity, and that our work would have to do with them."

The Bible Institute for Home and Foreign Missions
East Northfield, MA.

"I believe we have got to have 'gap-men'—men who are trained to stand between the laity and the ministers," was a common expression of Mr. Moody's. He felt the great need for more lay Christian workers. On the one hand he found many consecrated men and women ready and anxious to do God's will, and on the other hand he saw that there was plenty of opportunity for them to go to work if they only had the necessary skill and training. His effort was to solve this problem, and he made urgent appeals for funds wherewith to open a training school. Responses to this appeal came heartily, the money was pledged, the preliminary steps were taken, and the new enterprise was chartered under the name of "The Chicago Evangelization Society."

On December 31, 1886, Mr. Moody began a four-month campaign of evangelistic services in Chicago, going from one church to another, and utilizing the great roller-skating rinks. Every noon a large meeting was held in old Farwell Hall, the audience room of the Young Men's Christian Association building, which had been the scene of many former experiences in Mr. Moody's life. Each Monday noon reports were heard from the various churches and missions.

The Institute was formally opened with a week's conference, beginning September 26, 1889. The Rev. Mr. R. A. Torrey, superintendent of the Congregational City Missionary Society of Minneapolis, a graduate of Yale College and Seminary, was called to the position of superintendent.

While spiritual exposition was emphasized, all was based upon the most careful and scholarly study of the Word. Two years of twelve months each were required for the course, but, as it proceeded in a circle, students could enter at any time and by remaining two years complete the full course.

Mr. Moody always recognized the power of gospel song, and no education for Christian service would be complete in his eyes without it. Hence a musical department was a necessity. Those gifted in that direction received careful training in the art of singing the Gospel, a branch of vocal culture to which special attention is not usually given.

Visit to the Holy Land

In 1887, one of Moody's life-long desires to visit the Holy Land was fulfilled. Taking his wife and his son Paul, he went from Paris to Rome, where he was to join Mr. McKinnon's party. His interest in everything about him was intense, and, as usual, it centered particularly in the people and their methods of life. Paul Moody relates:

"He had long talked about a visit to Palestine, but it was little more than a dream in the back of his mind. In 1892, however, the McKinnons of Scotland invited my father and mother to be their guests on a trip to the Holy Land, and I was taken with them.

"On Easter Sunday father preached at the request of the missionaries on the summit of what is supposed to have been Calvary. He unconsciously gave offense to devout Mohammedans, for inadvertently he had preached in the center of a Moslem burying ground.

"One experience is most vivid to me. We were being shown through the Mosque of Omar and in accordance with their custom had to either remove our shoes or put over them slippers furnished by the authorities to prevent non-Moslem feet from treading on holy ground. One of mine came off, unnoticed by anyone at first, and I profaned some yards of the sacred carpet before it was discovered. Then a terrible hubbub arose and Arab eloquence was poured out in every direction while I stood on one foot, not a little scared, as were my parents. The slipper was finally retrieved, the ears of the erring attendant who had carelessly fastened it duly boxed, and we went on amid the muttering of scandalized Moslems. We were all relieved to get out.

"The sight of Moslem guards at the Holy Sepulchre and at the Church of the Nativity at Bethlehem to keep Christians from fighting deeply wounded my father. He did so hate differences among Christians."

The Colportage Library

Like all the institutions and organizations that owe their birth to Mr. Moody, the Bible Institute Colportage Association grew out of a need that he observed as he traveled to and fro in his evangelistic work. He was holding meetings in a Western town in the fall of 1894 and wanted some books to give away. He called at a local bookstore, but, although the shelves were loaded with fiction of all kinds, not a single religious book could be had.

Determined to do something to fill the gap that he had discovered, he returned to Chicago and consulted prominent Christian workers, who said, "People won't buy religious books; they are too expensive." "Then their price must come down," said Mr. Moody. The only way to reduce the price, without working on a charity basis, would be by printing large editions, and Mr. Moody organized a colportage department in connection with the Bible Institute, his Chicago school for the training of Christian workers.

It was felt that, before the work could become in any way extensive, a class of books must be secured that it was impossible at that time to obtain. The Colportage Library was therefore planned to combine these important features:
- Popular, readable style
- Well-known authors, or books of existing reputation
- Strictly non-denominational
- First-class workmanship
- Low price

An order for 100,000 copies of one book—*The Way to God*—was given at once. Equally large editions of other books have been ordered since.

So rapid was the growth of this work that in four years Mr. Moody saw it spread over not only the whole continent, but to foreign lands. In addition to the English editions, there are in the library books in German, Danish, Norwegian, and Swedish, and there are requests on file for translations in Spanish, Polish, Bohemian, Dutch, French, and other languages.

One of his early publications was entitled *Heaven*. One day on the railroad train he heard the newsboy, with a bundle of books under his arm, shouting, "Here you are, *Ingersoll on Hell!*" He caught the boy, and placed a copy of his own book in his hand, saying, "Here, my lad, here is another book; give them that at the same time." The boy went on through the car, shouting, "*Ingersoll on Hell; Moody on Heaven! Ingersoll on Hell; Moody on Heaven!*"

"Don't be afraid to borrow or lend Bibles," he used to say. "Some time ago a man wanted to take my Bible home to get a few things out of it, and when it came back I found these notes in it:

"'Justification, a change of state, a new standing before God.

"'Repentance, a change of mind, a new mind about God.

"'Regeneration, a change of nature, a new heart from God.

"'Conversion, a change of life, a new life for God.

"'Adoption, a change of family, a new relationship toward God.

"'Sanctification, a change of service, separation unto God.

"'Glorification, a change of condition, at home with God.'

"In the same handwriting I found these lines:

"'Jesus only:
"'The light of Heaven is the face of Jesus.
"'The joy of Heaven is the presence of Jesus.
"'The melody of Heaven is the name of Jesus.
"'The harmony of Heaven is the praise of Jesus.
"'The theme of Heaven is the work of Jesus.
"'The employment of Heaven is the service of Jesus.
"'The fullness of Heaven is Jesus Himself.
"'The duration of Heaven is the eternity of Jesus.'"

Capacity for the Work

"The reward of faithful service is more service" was a favorite saying of Mr. Moody's, and indeed, it perfectly indicates his life's work.

To those who knew Mr. Moody closely it was not difficult to understand the secret of his capacity for hard work. The magnificent constitution with which he was endowed enabled him to undertake work that demanded continued exertion and special effort. But, beyond this, he was able to throw off all burden of mind when he had done his utmost. "It's worry that kills," he would say, and after the most exacting work he would be able to relieve his mind of all anxiety and rest as quietly as a child. He believed that God would carry on His own work, and after doing all in his power he would cast his burden on the Lord.

A man of such energetic spirit as Mr. Moody found very little opportunity for holidays. He sacredly tried to observe one day in seven as a rest day, but otherwise he was almost constantly occupied except when journeying—and even then people recognized him and sought his spiritual advice, and were not denied. In later years, with the multiplication of his schools, conferences, and other organizations for promoting the cause of Christ, there was less and less opportunity for withdrawing for any length of time from active participation in their control.

As a preacher D. L. Moody was much criticized from the standpoint of academic homiletics. Nor would any think of defending his preaching method on that ground. But the fact that for thirty-five continuous years, in the centers of culture and of active practical thought in the English-speaking world, this self-taught preacher drew the greatest audiences which have faced any modern speaker on any theme—this fact,

Interior of the Moody Auditorium at Northfield.

one would say, should suggest to teachers of homiletics that possibly they might learn something from him.

One can only ask the question, "What is the magic power which draws together these mighty multitudes and holds them spellbound?" Is it the worldly rank or wealth of learning or oratory of the preacher? No, for he is possessed of little of these. It is the simple lifting up of the cross of Christ—the holding forth the Lord Jesus before the eyes of the people in all the glory of His Godhead, in all the simplicity of His manhood, in all the perfection of His nature, for their admiration, for their adoration, for their acceptance.

It must not be supposed that Mr. Moody was entirely free from criticism. The infidel in the street and an occasional editor in his office vented his spite against religion by attacking those who came to proclaim it. As the crowds gathered for the opening service, false handbills were distributed, pretending to describe the sermons that were about to be delivered. The "Vanity Fair" outside the great hall in the evening as described by an eyewitness:

"Many policemen to keep the way; multitudes of young men full of fun and joking; multitudes also of evil women and girls, gaily dressed, joining in the ribaldry; the two together forming a mass of well-dressed but disreputable blackguardism, proving to demonstration that the American evangelists had come at last exactly where they were sorely needed. Busmen, cabmen, tramcar-men, board-men, and loafers of every description took part in the universal carnival. Oaths, jests, slang, and mockery were all let loose together; but not one serious face, not one thoughtful countenance, not an idea of God's judgment or of eternity in all the vast changing multitude outside."

"Of Mr. Moody's power," says Horatius Bonar, "I find it difficult to speak. It is so real and yet so unlike the power of ordinary preachers that I hardly know how to analyze it. Its reality is indisputable. Any man who can interest and impress an audience of from three to six thousand people for half an hour in the morning and for three-quarters of an hour in the afternoon, and who can interest a third audience of thirteen or fifteen thousand people for three-quarters of an hour again in the evening, must have power of some kind. Of course, some people listened without caring much for what he said, but though I generally sat in a position that enabled me to see the kind of impression he produced, I rarely saw many faces that did not indicate the most active and earnest interest.

"The people were of all sorts, old and young, rich and poor, tradesmen, manufacturers, and merchants, young ladies who had just left school, cultivated women, and rough boys who knew more about dogs and pigeons than about books. For a time I could not understand it—I am not sure that I understand it now. At the first meeting Mr. Moody's address was simple, direct, kindly, and hopeful; it had a touch of humor and a touch of pathos; it was lit up with a story or two that filled most eyes with tears, but there seemed nothing in it very remarkable. Yet it told. A prayer meeting with an address at eight o'clock on a damp, cold January morning was hardly the kind of thing—let me say it frankly—that I should generally regard as attractive, but I enjoyed it heartily; it seemed one of the happiest meetings I had ever attended: there was warmth and there was sunlight in it."

His character could bear a rigid examination; as one of his closest friends said, "Doubtless he had faults, but I never saw them." If his preaching was persuasive in the pulpit while addressing thousands, it was in the quiet seclusion of his home life, or in the companionship of a few warm friends, that he was most truly eloquent. Impulsive, energetic, and resolute by nature, he yet possessed in a great degree the quiet strength of patience, sympathy, and unselfishness. To the stranger his most prominent characteristic was enthusiasm. Like the Apostle Paul, he could say, "*For me to live is Christ,*" and as a result of that life his gain came at the end of earth's career. "*This one thing I do*" was the key to his life of service. Nothing could swerve him from this deep-rooted purpose of his life, and in all the various educational and publishing projects to which he gave his energy there was but one motive—the proclamation of the Gospel through multiplied agencies.

Absorbed in his correspondence.

But all this enthusiasm was perfectly controlled by what was perhaps his most remarkable quality, quoted before as "his consecrated common sense." While his enthusiasm prompted him to seize every available opportunity for work, it was his keen insight into the conditions of any occasion that enabled him to judge of its fitness for his special effort. For this reason he frequently stood out against the advice of his friends, not that he did not welcome advice and appreciate it, but its value to him was chiefly suggestive, and if no new view of the matter was offered it was not likely to be followed.

Dr. C. I. Scofield, writing of Mr. Moody as an evangelist, calls attention to his strength and faithfulness under the trial of temptation:

"Three supreme testings await strong men in this life," he says—"the testing of poverty and obscurity,

51

The Moody home at Northfield.

Mr. and Mrs. Moody with their grandchildren.

of prosperity and applause, and of suffering. Many, who enter life conscious, even though dimly, of great latent capacities turn sour and bitter under neglect, narrow circumstances, and lack of appreciation. Others who pass that first trial successfully are corrupted or enfeebled by success and adulation. Many who stand erect alike in obscurity and success fail utterly under the testing of suffering. By God's grace Mr. Moody passed unscathed through them all. Perhaps it has happened to few men, suddenly lifted into the fellowship of the noble and famous of the earth, to be so little moved from the serenity of their minds, the even tenor of their ways."

The home, above all other places, is where a man most truly reveals himself, and here Mr. Moody was at his best. Home was the sweetest place upon earth to him, and had he chosen only his own comfort and pleasure, he would have devoted his last years to work at Northfield, in connection with his schools, without heeding the calls to service in the outer world. Entering into all the plans and interested in everything that demanded the attention of the members of his family, he made their life his own. A child's pleasures afforded him keen enjoyment, the student's school or college experience enlisted his hearty sympathy, and his advice in business affairs or even domestic problems was most highly valued. Nothing was too trifling for his notice, and in the home and community he became the great burden-bearer.

Many of his earlier sermons contained effective illustrations suggested by the daily life of his children, and his influence upon the lives of the children in other homes was great. No work was so important as to make him neglect his family duties and privileges. He took keen interest in the experiences of his sons at school and college, and shared their joys and entered into the excitement of their sports with the zest of a fellow student. The slightest matter that caused sorrow or pain to any member of his family, even the youngest, engaged at once his personal concern, and no drudgery of house or farm was beneath his notice or sympathetic interest. He had learned the secret of being a confidant of all, sharing others' burdens, weeping with the sorrowing and rejoicing with those glad of heart.

As a grandfather he seemed to experience a special joy, and entered into sweetest and happiest relations with the little ones who laid hold of his heart.

God had ordained something other than unbroken joy for the happy grandfather, though. His only grandson and namesake, who was born on November 7, 1897, was taken home on November 30, 1898, while Mr. Moody was absent in Colorado. In a letter to the parents, written from Colorado Springs, he said:

> "… I know Dwight is having a good time, and we should rejoice with him. What would the mansions be without children? He was the last to come into our circle, and he is the first to go up there! So safe, so free from all the sorrow that we are passing through! I do thank God for such a life. It was nearly all smiles and sunshine, and what a glorified body he will have, and with what joy he will await your coming! God does not give us such strong love for each other for a few days or years, but it is going to last forever, and you will have the dear little man with you for ages and ages, and love will keep increasing. The Master had need of him, or He would not have called him; and you should feel highly honored that you had anything in your home that He wanted."

The next few months were filled with anxiety as his oldest grandchild, little Irene, was slowly recovering from a protracted and unusually persistent attack of pneumonia. Later it was found that the germs of consumption had become implanted in the weakened system, and after a few weeks' wasting illness she joined her little brother, just four months before their grandfather followed them.

Though the deaths of these precious babes affected Moody more than he could ever imagine, his deep affliction in the bereavement was hidden from the parents in his unselfish efforts to cheer and comfort them. At the funeral service of little Irene, unannounced and unexpectedly, he arose and paid the following tribute to the little life he loved so dearly: "Irene has finished her course; her work was well wrought on earth. She had accomplished more than many in their threescore years and ten. We would not have her back, although her voice was the sweetest voice I ever heard on earth. She never met me once, since she was three months old, until the last few days of pain, without a smile. But Christ has some service for her above. My life has been made much better by her ministry here on earth. She has made us all better."

From Mortal to Immortal

In view of the approaching end, the following paragraphs from one of the last sermons in Kansas City are significant:

> "I have no sympathy with the idea that our best days are behind us," and he smiled as he related the impression that he had a year before when he saw in the papers that "Old Moody is in town." "Why," he said, "I am only sixty-two; I am only a baby in comparison with the great eternity which is to come.

Mr. Moody as he appeared in 1886.

"We say this is the land of the living! It is not. It is the land of the dying. What is our life here but a vapor? A hearse is the most common sight. Families broken into. Over there is one who has lost a father, there a mother, there is a place vacant, there a sister's name is no more heard, there a brother's love is missed. Death stalks triumphant through our midst, in this world."

On Thursday, December 21, he had seemed rather more nervous than usual, but nevertheless spoke cheerfully about himself. Asked if he was comfortable, he said: "Oh, yes! God

56

is very good to me—and so is my family." No man loved his family and lifework more devotedly, and he had often said: "Life is very sweet to me, and there is no position of power or wealth that could tempt me from the throne God has given me."

To the world, Friday, December 22, was the shortest day of all the year, but for Dwight L. Moody its dawn ushered in that day that knows no night. For 46 years he had been a partaker of the divine life, and the transition from the seen world to the unseen, from the sphere of the temporal to that of the eternal, was no interruption in the life with which his friends were familiar.

About 6 o'clock he quieted down, and soon fell into a natural sleep, from which he awoke in about an hour. Suddenly he was heard speaking in slow and measured words. He was saying, when he came to the close of life:

"Earth recedes; Heaven opens before me. I have been beyond the gates. God is calling. Don't call me back." I cannot but think he must have caught a sight of the future glory. "It is beautiful. It is like a trance. If this is death, it is sweet. There is no valley here. God is calling me, and I must go."

Meanwhile the nurse was summoning the family and the physician, who had spent the night in the house. Mr. Moody continued to talk quietly, and seemed to speak from another world his last message to the loved ones he was leaving. "I have always been an ambitious man," he said, "ambitious to leave no wealth or possessions, but to leave lots of work for you to do. Will, you will carry on Mount Hermon. Paul will take up the Seminary, when he is older; Fitt will look after the Institute, and Ambert (his nephew) will help you in the business details." Then it seemed as though he saw beyond the veil, for he exclaimed: "This is my triumph; this is my coronation day! I have been looking forward to it for years." Then his face lit up, and he said in a voice of joyful rapture: "Dwight! Irene! —I see the children's faces," referring to the two little grandchildren God had taken from his life in the past year. Then, as he thought he was losing consciousness he said, "Give my love to them all." Turning to his wife, he exclaimed, "Mamma, you have been a good wife to me!" and with that he became unconscious. Shortly after that, the great evangelist left this world to finally meet his Savior and join the heavenly throng in glory.

D. L. Moody has been gone from this world for over a century, but his words of life still speak to us—filling our hearts with encouragement, grace, and peace.

THE
OVERCOMING
LIFE

Chapter 1

THE CHRISTIAN'S WARFARE

"Whatsoever is born of God overcometh the world: and this is the victory that overcometh the world, even our faith. Who is he that overcometh the world, but he that believeth that Jesus is the Son of God?" (1 John 5:4-5)

When a battle is fought, all are anxious to know who are the victors. In these verses we are told who is to gain the victory in life. When I was converted I made the mistake of thinking the battle was already mine, the victory already won, the crown already in my grasp. I thought that old things had passed away and that all things had become new. I thought that my old corrupt nature, the Adam life, was gone. But I found out, after serving Christ for a few months, that conversion was only like enlisting in the army, that there was a battle on hand, and that if I was to get a crown, I had to work for it and fight for it.

Salvation is a gift, as free as the air we breathe. It is to be obtained, like any other gift, without money and without price. There are no other terms. "To him that worketh not, but believeth" (Romans 4:5). But on the other hand, if we are to gain a crown, we must work for it.

For other foundation can no man lay than that is laid, which is Jesus Christ. Now if any man build upon this foundation gold, silver, precious stones, wood, hay, stubble; Every man's work shall be made manifest: for the day shall declare it, because it shall be revealed by fire; and the fire shall try every man's work of what sort it is. If any man's work abide which he hath built thereupon, he shall receive a reward. If any man's work shall be burned, he shall suffer loss: but he himself shall be saved; yet so as by fire. (1 Corinthians 3:11-15).

We see clearly from this that we may be saved, yet all our works burned up. I may have a wretched, miserable voyage through life, with no victory, and no reward at the end; saved, yet so as by fire, or as Job puts it, "with the skin of my teeth." I believe that a great many men will barely get to heaven as Lot got out of Sodom, burned out, nothing left, works and everything else destroyed.

It is like when a man enters the army, he is a member of the army the moment he enlists. He is just as much a member as a man who has been in the army ten or twenty years. But enlisting is one thing and participating in a battle another. Young converts are like those just enlisted. It is folly for any man to attempt to fight in his own strength. The world, the flesh, and the devil are too much for any man. But if we are linked to Christ by faith, and He has formed in us the hope of glory, then we shall get the victory over every enemy. It is believers who are the overcomers, "Thanks be unto God, which always causeth us to triumph in Christ" (2 Corinthians 2:14). Through Him we shall be more than conquerors.

I wouldn't think of talking to unconverted men about overcoming the world, for it is utterly impossible. They might as well try to cut down the American forest with their penknives. But a good many Christian people make the mistake of thinking that the battle is already fought and won. They have an idea that all they have to do is to put the oars down in the bottom of the boat, and the current will drift them into the ocean of God's eternal love. But we have to cross the current. We have to learn how to watch and fight, and how to overcome. The battle has only just begun. The Christian life is a conflict and warfare, and the quicker we find it out the better.

There is not a blessing in this world that God has not linked to Himself. All the great and higher blessings God associates with Himself. When God and man work together, then there is going to be victory. We are coworkers with Him. You might take a mill, and put it forty feet above a river, and there isn't capital enough in the States to make that river turn the mill; but get it down about forty feet, and away it works. We want to keep in mind that if we are going to overcome the world, we have got to work with God. It is His power that makes all the means of grace effectual.

The story is told that Frederick Douglass, the great slave orator, once said in a mournful speech when things looked dark for his race, "The white man is against us, governments are against us, the spirit of the times is against us. I see no hope for the colored race. I am full of sadness." Just then, a woman rose in the audience and said, "Frederick, is God dead?"

My friend, it makes a difference when you count God in. Now many a young believer is discouraged and disheartened when he realizes this warfare. He begins to think that God has forsaken him, and that Christianity is not all that it professes to be. But he should rather regard it as an encouraging sign. No sooner has a soul escaped from his snare than the great

Adversary takes steps to ensnare it again. He puts forth all his power to recapture his lost prey.

The fiercest attacks are made on the strongest forts, and the fiercer the battle the young believer is called to fight; the surer evidence there is of the work of the Holy Spirit in his heart. God will not desert him in his time of need, any more than He deserted His people of old when they were hard-pressed by their foes.

The Only Complete Victor

"Ye are of God, little children, and have overcome them: because greater is He that is in you than he that is in the world" (1 John 4:4). The only man that ever conquered this world—was complete victor—was Jesus Christ. When He shouted on the cross, "It is finished!" it was the shout of a conqueror. He had overcome every enemy. He had met sin and death. He had met every foe that you and I will meet, and had come off victor. Now if I have the Spirit of Christ, if I have that same life in me, then it is that I have a power that is greater than any power in the world, and with that same power I overcome the world.

Notice that everything human in this world fails. Every man, the moment he takes his eye off God, has failed. Every man has been a failure at some period of his life. Abraham failed. Moses failed. Elijah failed. Take the men that have become so famous and that were so mighty—the moment they took their eye off God, they were weak like other men. And it is very poignant that those men failed on the strongest point in their character.

I suppose it was because they were not on the watch. Abraham was noted for his faith, and he failed right there—he denied his wife. Moses was noted for his meekness and humility, and he failed right there—he became angry. God kept him out of the Promised Land because he lost his temper. I know he was called "the servant of God," and that he was a mighty man and had power with God, but humanly speaking he failed and was kept out of the Promised Land. Elijah was noted for his power in prayer and for his courage, yet he became a coward. He was the boldest man of his day and stood before Ahab and the royal court and all the prophets of Baal; yet when he heard that Jezebel had threatened his life, he ran away to the desert and under a juniper tree prayed that he might die. Peter was noted for his boldness, and a little maid scared him nearly out of his wits. As soon as she spoke to him, he began to tremble, and he swore that he didn't know Christ. I have often said to myself that I'd like to have been there the day of Pentecost alongside of that maid when she saw Peter preaching.

"Why," I suppose she said, "What has come over that man? He was afraid of me only a few weeks ago, and now he stands up before all Jerusalem and charges these very Jews with the murder of Jesus." The moment he got his eye off the Master he failed. Every man, I don't care who he is, that doesn't have Christ in him, is a failure. John, the beloved disciple, was noted for his meekness; and yet we hear him wanting to call fire down from heaven on a little town because it had refused the common hospitalities.

Triumphs of Faith

Now, how are we to get the victory over all our enemies? We read in Galatians 2:20, "I am crucified with Christ: nevertheless I live; yet not I, but Christ liveth in me: and the life which I now live in the flesh I live by the faith of the Son of God, who loved me, and gave himself for me." We live by faith. We get this life by faith and become linked to Immanuel—"God with us." If I have God for me, I am going to overcome. How do we gain this mighty power? —by faith. The next passage I want to call your attention to is Romans 11:20. "Because of unbelief they were broken off, and thou standest by faith." The Jews were cut off on account of their unbelief, and we were grafted in on account of our belief. So here notice—we live by faith, and we stand by faith.

Next, we walk by faith. "For we walk by faith, not by sight" (2 Corinthians 5:7). The most faulty Christians I know are those who want to walk by sight. They want to see the end—how something is going to come out. That isn't walking by faith at all—that is walking by sight.

I think the characters that best represent this difference are Joseph and Jacob. Jacob was a man who walked with God by sight. You remember his vow at Bethel, "If God will be with me, and will keep me in this way that I go, and will give me bread to eat, and raiment to put on, so that I come again to my father's house in peace; then shall the Lord be my God." And you remember how his heart revived when he saw the wagons Joseph sent him from Egypt. He sought after signs. He never could have gone through the temptations and trials that his son Joseph did. Joseph represents a higher type of Christian. He could walk in the dark. He could survive thirteen years of misfortune, in spite of his dreams, and then ascribe it all to the goodness and providence of God.

Lot and Abraham are a good illustration. Lot turned away from Abraham and tented on the plains of Sodom. He got a good stretch of pastureland, but he had bad neighbors. He was a weak character, and he should have stayed with Abraham to become strong. A good many men are just like that. As long as their mothers are living, or a godly person bolsters them up, they get along very well; but they can't stand alone. Lot walked by sight, but Abraham walked by faith; he went out in the footsteps of God. "By faith Abraham, when he was called to go out into a place which he should after receive for an inheritance, obeyed; and he went out, not knowing whither he went. By faith he sojourned in the land of promise, as in a strange country, dwelling in tabernacles with Isaac and Jacob, the heirs with him of the same promise: For he looked for a city which hath foundations, whose builder and maker is God." (Hebrews 11:8). And again, we fight by faith. "Above all, taking the shield of faith, wherewith ye shall be able to quench all the fiery darts of the wicked" (Ephesians 6:16). Every dart Satan can fire at us we can quench by faith. By faith we can overcome the Evil One. To fear is to have more faith in your antagonist than in Christ.

Some of the older people can remember when our war broke out. Secretary Seward, who was Lincoln's secretary of state—a longheaded and shrewd politician—prophesied that the war would be over in ninety days; and young men in thousands and hundreds of thousands came forward and volunteered to go down to Dixie and whip the South. They thought they would be back in ninety days, but the war lasted four years and cost about half a million lives. What was the matter? Well, the South was a good deal stronger than the North supposed. Its strength was underestimated. Jesus Christ makes no mistake of that kind. When He enlists a man in His service, He shows him the dark side. He lets him know that he must live a life of self-denial. If a man is not willing to go to heaven by the way of Calvary, he cannot go at all. Many men want a religion in which there is no cross, but they cannot enter heaven that way. If we are to be disciples of Jesus Christ, we must deny ourselves and take up our cross and follow Him.

So let us sit down and count the cost. Do not think that you will have no battles if you follow the Nazarene. No, many battles are before you. Yet if I had ten thousand lives, Jesus Christ would have every one of them. Men do not object to a battle if they are confident that they will have victory, and, thank God, every one of us may have the victory if we will.

The reason so many Christians fail all through life is that they underestimate the strength of the enemy. My dear friend, you and I have a terrible enemy to contend with. Don't let Satan deceive you. Unless you are spiritually dead, it means warfare. Nearly everything around tends to draw us away from God. We do not step clear out of Egypt onto the throne of God. There is the wilderness journey, and there are enemies in the land.

Don't let any man or woman think all he or she has to do is join the church. That will not save you. The question is, are you overcoming the world, or is the world overcoming you? Are you more patient than you were five years ago? Are you more amiable? If you are not, the world is overcoming you, even if you are a church member. That epistle that Paul wrote to Titus says that we are to be sound in patience, faith, and charity. We have a good many Christians who are good in some areas, but mighty poor in others. Just a little bit of them seems to be saved, you know. They are not rounded out in their characters. It is just because they haven't been taught that they have a terrible foe to overcome.

If I wanted to find out whether a man was a Christian, I wouldn't go to his minister. I would go and ask his wife. I tell you, we want more home piety just now. If a man doesn't treat his wife right, I don't want to hear him talk about Christianity. What is the use of his talking about salvation in the next life if he has no salvation in this? We want a Christianity that goes into our homes and everyday lives. Some men's religion just repels me. They put on a whining voice and a sort of a religious tone and talk so sanctimoniously on Sunday that you would think they were wonderful saints. But on Monday they are quite different. They put their religion away with their clothes, and you don't see any more of it until the next Sunday. You laugh, but let us look out that we don't belong to that class.

My friends, we have got to have a higher type of Christianity, or the church is gone. It is wrong for men or women to profess what they don't possess. If you are not overcoming temptations, the world is overcoming you. Just get on your knees and ask God to help you. My friends let us go to God and ask Him to search us. Let us ask Him to wake us up, and let us not think that just because we are church members we are all right. We are all wrong if we are not getting victory over sin.

Chapter 2

INTERNAL FOES

Now if we are going to overcome, we must begin inside. God always begins there. An enemy inside the fort is far more dangerous than one outside. Scripture teaches that in every believer there are two natures warring against each other. Paul says, in his epistle to the Romans:

> *"For we know that the law is spiritual: but I am carnal, sold under sin. For that which I do I allow not: for what I would, that I do not; but what I hate, that do I. If then I do that which I would not, I consent unto the law that it is good. Now then it is no more I that do it, but sin that dwelleth in me. For I know that in me (that is, in my flesh), dwelleth no good thing: for to will is present with me; but how to perform that which is good I find not. For the good that I would I do not: but the evil, which I would not, that I do. Now if I do that I would not, it is no more I that do it, but sin that dwelleth in me. I find then a law that, when I would do good, evil is present with me. For I delight in the law of God after the inward man: but I see another law in my members, warring against the law of my mind, and bringing me into captivity to the law of sin which is in my members"* (Romans 7:14-23).

Again, in the epistle to the Galatians, he says, "For the flesh lusteth against the Spirit, and the Spirit against the flesh: and these are contrary the one to the other: so that ye cannot do the things that ye would" (Galatians 5:17). When we are born of God, we get His nature, but He does not immediately take away all the old nature. Each species of animal and bird is true to its nature. You can tell the nature of the dove or canary bird. The horse is true to his nature; the cow is true to hers. But a man has two natures, and do not let the world or Satan make you think that the old nature is extinct, because it is not. "Reckon ye yourselves dead," but if you were dead, you wouldn't need to reckon yourselves dead, would you? The dead self would be dropped out of the reckoning. "I keep my body under"; if it were dead, Paul wouldn't have needed to keep it under. I am judicially dead, but the old nature is alive, and therefore if I don't keep my body under and crucify the flesh with its affections, this lower nature will gain the advantage, and I would be in bondage.

Many men live all their lives in bondage to the old nature, when they could have liberty if they would only live this overcoming life. The old Adam remains corrupt. "From the sole of the foot even unto the head there is no soundness in it; but wounds, and bruises, and putrefying sores have not been closed, neither bound up, neither mollified with ointment."

A gentleman in India once caught a tiger cub and tamed it so that it became a pet. One day when it had grown up, it tasted blood, and the old tiger nature flashed out, and it had to be killed. So it is with the old nature in the believer. It never dies, though it is subdued. Unless he is watchful and prayerful it will gain the upper hand and lead him into sin. Someone has pointed out that "I" is the center of S-I-N. It is the medium through which Satan acts. And so the worst enemy you have to overcome, after all, is yourself. At the time Captain T. became converted in London, he was a great society man. After he had been a Christian some months, he was asked, "What have you found to be your greatest enemy since you began to be a Christian?"

After a few minutes of deep thought he said, "Well I think it is myself."

"Ah," said the lady, "the King has taken you into His presence, for it is only in His presence that we are taught these truths."

"I have had more trouble with D. L. Moody than with any other man who has crossed my path. If I can only keep him right, I wouldn't have any trouble with other people. A good many have trouble with servants. Did you ever think that the trouble lies with you instead of the servants? If one member of the family is constantly snapping, he will have the whole family snapping. It is true whether you believe it or not. You speak quickly and snappishly to people and they will do the same to you."

APPETITE

Now take *appetite*. That is an enemy inside. How many young men are ruined by an appetite for strong drink! Many a young man has grown up to be a curse to his father and mother instead of a blessing. Not long ago the body of a young suicide was discovered in one of our large cities. In his pocket was found a paper on which he had written, "I have done this myself. Don't tell anyone. It is all through drink." An intimation of these facts in the public press drew 246 letters from 246 families, each of whom had a prodigal son who, it was feared, might be this suicide.

Strong drink is an enemy, both to body and soul. It is reported that Sir Andrew Clarke, the celebrated London physician, once made the following statement, "Now let me say that I am speaking solemnly and carefully when I tell you that I am considerably within the mark in saying that within the rounds of my hospital wards today, seven out of every ten that lie there in their beds owe their ill health to alcohol. I do not say that seventy in every hundred are drunkards. I do not know if one of them is, but they use alcohol. As soon as a man begins to take one drop, the desire begun in him becomes a part of his nature. That nature, formed by his acts, inflicts curses inexpressible when handed down to the generations that aspire to follow him as part and parcel of their being. When I think of this I am disposed to give up my profession—to give up everything—and to go forth upon a holy crusade to preach to all men, 'Beware of this enemy of the human race!'" It is the most destructive agency in the world today. It kills more than the bloodiest wars. It is the fruitful parent of crime and idleness and poverty and disease. It spoils a man for this world and damns him for the next. The Word of God has declared, "Be not deceived: neither fornicators, nor idolaters, nor adulterers, nor effeminate, nor abusers of themselves with mankind, nor thieves, nor covetous, nor drunkards, nor revilers, nor extortioners, shall inherit the Kingdom of God" (1 Corinthians 6:9-10).

How can we overcome this enemy? Bitter experience proves that man is not powerful enough in his own strength. The only cure for the accursed appetite is regeneration—a new life—the power of the risen Christ within us. Let a man that is given to strong drink look to God for help, and He will give him victory over his appetite. Jesus Christ came to destroy the works of the devil, and He will take away that appetite if you will let Him.

TEMPER

Then there is *temper.* I wouldn't give much for a man that doesn't have temper. Steel isn't good for anything if it doesn't have temper. But when temper gets the mastery over me I am its slave, and it is a source of weakness. It may be made a great power for good all through my life and help me, or it may become my greatest enemy from within and rob me of power. The current in some rivers is so strong as to make them useless for navigation.

Someone has said that a preacher will never miss the people when he speaks of temper. It is astonishing how little mastery even professing Christians have over it. A friend of mine in England was out visiting, and while sitting in the parlor heard an awful noise in the hall. He asked what it meant and was told that it was only the doctor, throwing his boots downstairs because they were not properly polished. "Many Christians," said an old divine, "who bore the loss of a child or all their property with the most heroic Christian fortitude are entirely vanquished by the breaking of a dish or the blunders of a servant."

Many people have said to me, "Mr. Moody, how can I get control of my temper?" If you really want to get control, I will tell you how, but you won't like the medicine. Treat it as a sin and confess it. People look upon temper as a sort of misfortune, and one lady told me she inherited it from her father and mother. Supposing she did. That is no excuse for her. When you get angry again and speak unkindly to someone, and when you realize it, go and ask that person to forgive you. You won't get mad at that person for the next twenty-four hours. You might do it in about forty-eight hours, but go the second time; and after you have done it about a half dozen times, you will get out of the business, because it makes the old flesh burn.

A lady said to me once, "I have got so in the habit of exaggerating that my friends accuse me of exaggerating so that they don't understand me." She said, "Can you help me? What can I do to overcome it?"

"Well," I said, "the next time you catch yourself lying, go right to that party and say you have lied, and tell them you are sorry. Say it is a lie. Stamp it out, root and branch; that is what you want to do." "Oh," she said, "I wouldn't like to call it lying." But that is what it was. Christianity isn't worth a snap of your fingers if it doesn't straighten out your character. I have got tired of all mere gush and sentiment. If people can't tell when you are telling the truth, there is something radically wrong, and you had better straighten it out right away. Now, are you ready to do it? Bring yourself to it whether you want to or not.

Do you find someone who has been offended by something you have done? Go right to him and tell him you are sorry. You say you are not to blame. Never mind, go right to him and tell him *you* are sorry. I have had to do it a good many times. An impulsive man like myself has to do it often, but I sleep all the sweeter at night when I get things straightened out. Confession never fails to bring a blessing. I have sometimes had to get off the platform and go down and ask a man's forgiveness before I could go on preaching. A Christian man ought to be a gentleman every time; but if he is not, and he finds he has wounded or hurt someone, he ought to go and straighten it out at once.

You know there are a great many people who want just enough Christianity to make them respectable. They don't think about this overcoming life that gets the victory all the time. They have their blue days and their cross days, and the children say, "Mother is cross today, and you will have to be careful." We don't want any of these touchy blue days, these ups and downs. If we are overcoming, that is the effect our life is going to have on others, they will have confidence in our Christianity. The reason that many a man has no power is that there is some cursed sin covered up. There will not be a drop of dew until that sin is brought to light. Get right inside. Then we can go out like giants and conquer the world if everything is right within.

Paul says that we are to be sound in faith, in patience, and in love. If a man is unsound in his faith, the clergy take the ecclesiastical sword and cut him off at once. But he may be ever so unsound in charity, in patience, and nothing is said about that. We must be sound in faith, in love, and in patience if we are to be true to God. How delightful it is to meet a man who can control his temper! It is said of William Wilberforce that a friend once found him in the greatest agitation, looking for a dispatch he had mislaid, for which one of the royal family was waiting. Just then, as if to make it still more trying, a disturbance was heard in the nursery.

"Now," thought the friend, "surely his temper will give way." The thought had hardly passed through his mind when Wilberforce turned to him and said, "What a blessing it is to hear those dear children! Only think what a relief, among other hurries, to hear their voices and know they are well."

COVETOUSNESS

Take the sin of *covetousness*. There is more said in the Bible against covetousness than against drunkenness. I must get it out of me—destroy it, root and branch—and not let it have dominion over me. We think that a man who gets drunk is a horrid monster, but a covetous man will often be received into the church and put into office. Yet, he is as vile in the sight of God as any drunkard.

The most dangerous thing about this sin is that it is not generally regarded as very heinous. Of course we all have contempt for misers, but all covetous men are not misers. Another thing to be noted about this sin is that it grabs hold of the old more so than the young. Let us see what the Bible says about covetousness:

> "*Mortify therefore your members ... covetousness, which is idolatry*" (Colossians 3:5).

> "*... nor covetous man, who is an idolater, hath any inheritance in the kingdom of Christ and of God*" (Ephesians 5:5).

> "*They that will be [that is, desire to be] rich fall into temptation and a snare, and into many foolish and hurtful lusts, which drown men in destruction and perdition*" (1 Timothy 6:9).

> "*For the love of money is the root of all evil: which while some coveted after, they have erred from the faith, and pierced themselves through with many sorrows*" (1 Timothy 6:10).

"For the wicked boasteth of his heart's desire, and blesseth the covetous, whom the LORD abhorreth" (Psalm 10:3).

Covetousness enticed Lot into Sodom. It caused the destruction of Achan and all his house. It was the iniquity of Balaam. It was the sin of Samuel's sons. It left Gehazi a leper. It sent the rich young ruler away sorrowful. It led Judas to sell his Master and Lord. It brought about the death of Ananias and Sapphira. It was the blot in the character of Felix. What victims it has had in all ages!

Do you say, "How am I going to check covetousness?" Well, I don't think there is any difficulty about that. If you find yourself becoming covetous, miserly, wanting to gain every possession you can, just begin to scatter. Just say to covetousness that you will strangle it and rid it out of your disposition.

A wealthy farmer in New York State, who had been a noted miser, a very selfish man, was converted. Soon after his conversion a poor man came to him one day to ask for help. He had been burned out of his home and had no provisions. This young convert thought he would be liberal and give him a ham from his smokehouse. He started toward the smokehouse, and on the way the tempter said, "Give him the smallest one you have." He struggled all the way as to whether he would give a large one or a small one. In order to overcome his selfishness, he took down the biggest ham and gave it to the man.

The tempter said, "You are a fool."

But he replied, "If you don't keep still, I will give him every ham I have in the smokehouse."

If you find that you are selfish, give something. Determine to overcome that spirit of selfishness and to keep your body under, no matter what it may cost.

Mr. Durant told me he was engaged by Goodyear to defend the rubber patent, and he was to have half of the money that came from the patent, if he succeeded. One day he woke up to find that he was a rich man, and he said that the greatest struggle of his life then took place as to whether he would let the money be his master, or he be the master of money; whether he would be its slave, or make it a slave to him. At last he gained the victory, and that is how Wellesley College was built.

Are you jealous or envious? Go and do something good for that person of whom you are jealous. That is the way to cure *jealousy*; it will kill it. Jealousy is a devil; it is a horrid monster. The poets imagined that Envy dwelt in a dark cave, being pale and thin, looking asquint, never rejoicing except in the misfortune of others, and hurting himself continually.

There is a fable of an eagle that could fly swifter than another, and the other didn't like it. The latter saw a sportsman one day and said to him, "I wish you would shoot down that eagle." The sportsman replied that he would if he only had some feathers to put into the arrow. So the eagle pulled one out of his wing. The arrow was shot, but didn't quite reach the rival eagle; it was flying too high. The envious eagle pulled out more feathers and kept pulling them out until he lost so many that he couldn't fly. Then the sportsman turned around and killed him. My friend, if you are jealous, the only one you can hurt is yourself.

There were two businessmen-merchants who had a great rivalry between them, and a great deal of bitter feelings. One of them was converted. He went to his minister and said, "I am still jealous of that man, and I do not know how to overcome it."

"Well," he said, "if a man comes into your store to buy goods, and you cannot supply him, just send him over to your neighbor."

He said he wouldn't like to do that.

"Well," the minister said, "you do it, and you will kill jealousy."

He said that he would, and when customers came into his store for goods that he did not have, he would tell them to go across the street to his neighbor's store. Then soon enough the other began to send his customers over to this man's store, and the breach was healed.

PRIDE

Then there is *pride*. This is another of those sins which the Bible so strongly condemns, but which the world hardly thinks of as a sin at all. "A high look and a proud heart" are sin. "Everyone that is proud in heart is an abomination to the Lord; though hand join in hand, he shall not be unpunished."

Christ included pride among those evil things that proceed out of the heart of a man and defile him. People have an idea that it is just the wealthy who are proud. But go down some of the back streets, and you will find that some of the very poorest are as proud as the richest. It is the heart, you know. People that haven't any money are just as proud as those that have. We must crush it out of our hearts. It is an enemy. You needn't be proud of your face, for there is not one of you that after ten days in the grave the worms would be eating your body. There is nothing to be proud of—is there?

Let us ask God to deliver us from pride. You can't fold your arms and say, "Lord, take it out of me," but just go and work with Him. Mortify your pride by cultivating humility. "Put on therefore," says Paul, "as the elect of God, holy and beloved ... humbleness of mind." (Colossians 3:12) "Be clothed with humility," says Peter. (1 Peter 5:5) "Blessed are the poor in spirit." (Matthew 5:3)

Chapter 3

EXTERNAL FOES

What are our enemies without? What does James say? "Know ye not that the friendship of the world is enmity with God? Whosoever therefore will be a friend of the world is the enemy of God" (James 4:4). "Love not the world, neither the things that are in the world. If any man love the world, the love of the Father is not in him" (1 John 2:15).

Now, people want to know what is *the world*. When you talk with them they ask, "Well, when YOU say 'the world,' what do you mean?" Well, here we have the answer in the next verse: "For all that is in the world, the lust of the flesh, and the lust of the eyes, and the pride of life, is not of the Father, but is of the world. And the world passeth away, and the lust thereof: but he that doeth the will of God abideth for ever" (1 John 2:16,17).

"The world" does not mean nature around us. God nowhere tells us that the material world is an enemy to be overcome. On the contrary, we read; "The earth is the Lord's, and the fullness thereof; the world, and they that dwell therein" (Psalm 24:1). "The heavens declare the glory of God; and the firmament [showeth] His handiwork" (Psalm 19:1).

It means "human life and society as far as alienated from God, through being centered on material aims and objects, and thus opposed to God's Spirit and kingdom." Christ said, "If the world hate you, ye know that it hated me before it hated you ... but because ye are not of the world ... therefore the world hateth you" (John 15:18,19).

Love of the world means the forgetfulness of the eternal future by reason of love of passing things. How can the world be overcome? Not by education, not by experience, only by faith. "This is the victory that overcometh the world, even our faith. Who is he that overcometh the world, but he that believeth that Jesus is the Son of God?" (1 John 5:4,5)

WORLDLY HABITS AND FASHIONS

For one thing, we must fight *worldly habits and fashions.* We must often go against the customs of the world. I have great respect for a man who can stand up against the whole world for what he believes is right. He who can stand alone is a hero. Suppose it is the custom for young men to do certain things you wouldn't like your mother to know about—things that your mother taught you are wrong. You may have to stand up alone among all your companions.

They will say, "You can't get away from your mother, eh? Tied to your mother's apron strings!" But you just say, "Yes! I have some respect for my mother. She taught me what is right, and she is the best friend I have. I believe that is wrong, and I am going to stand for what is right." If you have to stand alone, then stand. Enoch did it, and Joseph, and Elisha, and Paul. God has kept such men in all ages.

Someone says, "I move in society where they have wine parties. I know it is rather a dangerous thing because my son is apt to follow me. Now, even though I know I can stop just where I want to, perhaps my son hasn't the same power as I have, and he may go over the dam. But it is the custom in the society where I move."

Once I got into a place where I had to get up and leave. I was invited to a home, and they had a late supper, and there were seven kinds of liquor on the table. I am ashamed to say they were Christian people. A deacon urged a young lady to drink until her face was flushed. I rose from the table and left. I felt that it was no place for me. They considered me very rude. They thought I was going against the custom. But I was entering a protest against such an infernal thing. Let us go against custom when it leads us astray.

I was told that, in a southern college some years ago, no man was considered a first-class gentleman who did not drink. Of course it is not so now.

PLEASURE

Another enemy is *worldly pleasure*. A great many people are just drowning in pleasure. They do not have any time for meditation. Many a man has been lost to society, and lost to his family, by giving himself up to the god of pleasure. God wants His children to be happy, but in a way that will help and not hinder them.

A lady came to me once and said, "Mr. Moody, I wish you would tell me how I can become a Christian." The tears were rolling down her cheeks, and she was in a very favorable mood. "But," she said, "I don't want to be one of your kind."

85

"Well," I asked, "have I got any peculiar kind? What is the matter with my Christianity?"

"Well," she said, "my father was a doctor and had a large practice, and he used to get so tired that he used to take us to the theater. We were a large family of girls, and we had tickets for the theaters three or four times a week. I suppose we were there a good deal more often than we were in church. I am married to a lawyer, and he has a large practice. He gets so tired that he takes us out to the theater ... I am far better acquainted with the theater and theater people than with the church and church people, and I don't want to give up the theater."

"Well," I said, "did you ever hear me say anything about theaters? There have been reporters here every day for all the different papers, and they are giving my sermons verbatim in one paper. Have you ever seen anything in the sermons against the theaters?"

She said, "No."

Then I asked her, "Well, I have seen you in the audience every afternoon for several weeks and have you heard me say anything against theaters?"

No, she hadn't.

"Well, what made you bring them up?"

"Why, I supposed you didn't believe in theaters."

"What made you think that?" I asked.

"Why," she said, "do you ever go?"

"No," I replied emphatically.

"Why don't you go?" she asked.

"Because I have something better. I would sooner go out into the street and eat dirt than do some of the things I used to do before I became a Christian."

"Why!" she said, "I don't understand."

"Never mind," I said. "When Jesus Christ has the preeminence, you will understand it all. He didn't come down here and say we shouldn't go here and we shouldn't go there, and lay down a lot of rules; but He laid down great principles. Now, He says if you love Him you will take delight in pleasing Him." And I began to preach Christ to her.

The tears started again. She said, "I tell you, Mr. Moody, that sermon on the indwelling Christ yesterday afternoon just broke my heart. I admire Him, and I want to be a Christian, but I don't want to give up the theaters."

"Then please don't mention them again," I said, "I don't want to talk about theaters. I want to talk to you about Christ." So I took my Bible and I read to her about Christ. But she said again, "Mr. Moody, can I go to the theater if I become a Christian?"

"Yes," I replied, "you can go to the theater just as much as you like if you are a real, true Christian and can go with His blessing."

"Well," she said, "I am glad you are not so narrow-minded as some."

She felt quite relieved to think that she could go to the theaters and be a Christian. But I said, "If you can go to the theater for the glory of God, keep on going; only be sure that you go for the glory of God. If you are a Christian you will be glad to do whatever will please Him." I really think she became a Christian that day.

The burden was gone and there was joy, but just as she was leaving me at the door she said, "I am not going to give up the theater."

In a few days she came back to me and said, "Mr. Moody, I understand all about that theater business now. I went the other night. There was a large group of people at our house, and my husband wanted us to go, and we went; but when the curtain lifted, everything looked so different. I said to my husband, 'this is no place for me; this is horrible. I am not going to stay here. I am going home.' He said, 'Don't make a fool of yourself. Everyone has heard that you have been converted in the Moody meetings. If you go out now, our fashionable society will be all through. I beg of you, don't make a fool of yourself by getting up and going out.' But I said, 'I have been making a fool of myself all my life.'"

Now, the theater hadn't changed, but she had something better, and she was going to overcome the world. "They that are after the flesh do mind the things of the flesh; but they that are after the Spirit the things of the Spirit" (Romans 8:5). When Christ has the first place in your heart you are going to get victory. Just do whatever you know will please Him. The great objection I have to these things is that they get the mastery and become a hindrance to spiritual growth.

BUSINESS

It may be that we have got to overcome in *business.* Perhaps it is business morning, noon, and night, and Sundays too. When a man will drive like Jehu all the week and like a snail on Sunday, isn't there something wrong with him?

Now business is legitimate; but I do not think a man is a good citizen that will not go out and earn his bread by the sweat of his brow. He ought to be a good businessman and, whatever he does, do thoroughly. At the same time, if he lays his whole heart on his business and makes a god of it, and thinks more of it than anything else, then the world has come into his heart. It may be very legitimate in its place—like fire, which, in its place, is one of the best friends of man; out of place, is one of the worst enemies of man; —like water, which we cannot live without; and yet, when not in place, it becomes an enemy.

So my friends, that is the question for you and me to settle. Now look at yourself. Are you getting the victory? Are you growing more even in your disposition? Are you getting mastery over the world and the flesh? And bear this in mind: Every temptation you overcome makes you stronger to overcome others, while every temptation that defeats you makes you weaker. You can become weaker and weaker, or you can become stronger and stronger. Sin takes the pith out of your sinews, but virtue makes you stronger. How many men have been overcome by something small! Turn a moment to the Song of Solomon, the second chapter, fifteenth verse: "Take us the foxes, the little foxes that spoil the vines: for our vines have tender grapes." A great many people seem to think these little things—getting out of patience, using little deceits, telling white lies (as they call them), and when somebody calls on you, sending word by the servant that you are not at home—are not important. Sometimes you can brace yourself up against a great temptation and almost before you know it you fall before some little thing. A great many men are overcome by a little *persecution*.

PERSECUTION

Do you know, I don't think we have enough persecution in these days. Some people say we have persecution that is just as hard to bear as in the Dark Ages. I think it would be a good thing if we had a little of the old-fashioned kind of persecution just now. It would bring out the strongest of characters and make us all healthier. I have heard men get up in prayer meetings, say they were going to make a few remarks, and then keep on till you would think they were going to talk all week! If we had a little persecution, people of that kind wouldn't talk so much. Spurgeon used to say some Christians would make good martyrs; they would burn well, because they are so dry. If there were a few stakes for burning Christians, I think it would take all the piety out of some men. I admit they haven't got much, but then if they are not willing to suffer a little persecution for Christ, they are not fit to be His disciples.

We are told: "All that will live godly in Christ Jesus shall suffer persecution" (2 Timothy 3:12). Make up your mind to this: if the world has nothing to say against you, Jesus Christ will have nothing to say for you.

The most glorious triumphs of the church have been won in times of persecution. The early church was persecuted for about three hundred years after the crucifixion, and they were years of growth and progress. But then, as St. Augustine has said, "the cross has passed from the scene of public executions to the diadem of the Caesars, and the downgrade movement began." When the church has joined hands with the state, it has invariably declined in spirituality and effectiveness; but the opposition of the state has only served to purify it of all dross. It was persecution that gave Scotland to Presbyterianism. It was persecution that gave this country to civil and religious freedom.

How are we to overcome in time of persecution? Hear the words of Christ, "In the world ye shall have tribulation: but be of good cheer; I have overcome the world" (John 16:33). Paul could testify that though persecuted, he was never forsaken; that the Lord stood by him, and strengthened him, and delivered him out of all his persecutions and afflictions.

A great many shrink from the Christian life because they fear they will be sneered at. But then, sometimes when persecution won't bring a man down, *flattery* will. Foolish persons often come up to a man after he has preached and flatter him. Sometimes they will say to some worker in the church, "You speak a great deal better than so-and-so," and he then becomes proud and begins to strut around as if he was the most important person in town. I tell you, we have a wily devil to contend with. If he can't overcome you with opposition, he will try flattery or ambition. If that doesn't serve his purpose, perhaps there will come some affliction or disappointment, and he will overcome in that way. But remember that anyone that has Christ to help him can overcome all foes, and overcome them singly or collectively. Let them come. If we have Christ within us, we will overthrow them all. Remember what Christ is able to do. In all the ages, men have stood in greater temptations than you and I will ever have to meet.

Now, there is one more thing on this subject. Either I am going to overcome the world, or the world is going to overcome me. Either I must conquer sin in me—or sin about me—and get it under my feet, or it is going to conquer me. A good many people are satisfied with one or two victories and think that is sufficient. I tell you, my dear friends, we must do something more than that. It is a battle all the time. Yet, we have this to encourage us; we are assured of victory at the end. We are promised a glorious triumph.

EIGHT "OVERCOMES"

Let me give you the eight "overcomes" of Revelation.

The first is: *"To him that overcometh will I give to eat of the tree of life" (Revelation 2:7).* He shall have a right to the tree of life. When Adam fell, he lost that right. God turned him out of Eden lest he should eat of the tree of life and live as he was forever. Perhaps He just took that tree and transplanted it to the Garden above; and through the Second Adam we are to have the right to eat of it.

Second: *"He that overcometh shall not be hurt of the second death" (Revelation 2:11).* Death has no terrors for him. It cannot touch him. Why? Because Christ tasted death for every man. Hence, he is on resurrection ground. Death may take this body, but that is all. This is only the house I live in. We need have no fear of death if we overcome.

Third: *"To him that overcometh will I give to eat of the hidden manna, and will give him a white stone, and in the stone a new name written, which no man knoweth saving he that receiveth it" (Revelation 2:17).* If I overcome, God will feed me with bread that the world knows nothing about, and give me a new name.

Fourth: *"He that overcometh, and keepeth my works unto the end, to him will I give power over the nations"* *(Revelation 2:26).* Think of it! What a thing it is to have power over the nations! A man that is able to rule himself is the man that God can trust with power. Only a man who can govern himself is fit to govern other men. I have an idea that we are down here in training, that God is just polishing us for some higher service. I don't know where the kingdoms are, but if we are to be kings and priests we must have kingdoms to reign over.

Fifth: *"He that overcometh, the same shall be clothed in white raiment; and I will not blot his name out of the book of life, but I will confess his name before my Father, and before his angels"* *(Revelation 3:5).* He shall present us to the Father in white garments, without spot or wrinkle. Every fault and stain shall be taken out, and we will be made perfect. He that overcomes will not be a stranger in heaven.

Sixth: *"Him that overcometh will I make a pillar in the temple of my God; and he shall go no more out: and I will write upon him the name of my God, and the name of the city of my God, which is New Jerusalem, which cometh down out of heaven from my God: and I will write upon him my new name"* *(Revelation 3:12).* Think of it! No more backsliding, no more wanderings over the dark mountains of sin, but forever with the King, and He says, "I will write upon him the name of my God." He is going to put His name upon us. Isn't it grand? Isn't it worth fighting for? It is said when Muhammad came in sight of Damascus and found that all had left the city, he said: "If they won't fight for this city what will they fight for?" If men won't fight here for all this [heavenly] reward, what will they fight for?

Seventh: *"To him that overcometh will I grant to sit with me in my throne, even as I also overcame, and am set down with my Father in his throne"* (Revelation 3:21). My heart has often melted as I have looked at that. The Lord of Glory coming down and saying: "I will grant to you to sit on my throne, even as I sit on my Father's throne, if you will just overcome." Isn't it worth a struggle? How many will fight for a crown that is going to fade away! Yet we are to be placed above the angels, above the archangels, above the seraphim, above the cherubim, away up, upon the throne with Him, and there we shall be forever with Him. May God put strength into every one of us to fight the battle of life, so that we may sit with Him in glory. When Frederick of Germany was dying, his own son would not have been allowed to sit with him on the throne, or to let anyone else sit there with him. Yet we are told that we are joint heirs with Jesus Christ, and that we will one day sit with Him in glory!

And now, the last I like best of all: *"He that overcometh shall inherit all things; and I will be his God, and he shall be my son"* (Revelation 21:7). My dear friends, isn't that a high calling? I used to have my Sabbath school children sing "I want to be an angel," but I have not done so for years. We shall be above angels. We shall be sons of God. Just see what a kingdom we shall come into. We shall inherit all things! Do you ask me how much I am worth? I don't know. The Rothschilds cannot compute their wealth. They don't know how many millions they own. That is my condition. I haven't the slightest idea how much I am worth. God has no poor children. If we overcome we shall inherit all things.

Oh, my dear friends, what an inheritance! Let us then get the victory, through Jesus Christ our Lord and Master.

Chapter 4

RESULTS OF TRUE REPENTANCE

I want to call your attention to what true repentance leads to. I am not addressing the unconverted only, because I am one of those who believe that there is a good deal of repentance to be done by the church before much good will be accomplished in the world. I firmly believe that the low standard of Christian living is keeping a good many in the world and in their sins. When the ungodly see that Christian people do not repent, you cannot expect them to repent and turn away from their sins. I have repented ten thousand times more since I knew Christ than ever before, and I think most Christians have some things to repent of. So now I want to preach to Christians as well as to the unconverted, and to myself as well as to one who has never accepted Christ as his Savior.

There are five things that flow out of true repentance:

1. Conviction
2. Contrition
3. Confession of sin
4. Conversion
5. Confession of Jesus Christ

1. CONVICTION

When a man is not deeply convicted of sin, it is a likely sign that he has not truly repented. Experience has taught me that men who have little conviction of sin sooner or later lapse back into their old life. For the last few years I have been a good deal more anxious for a deep and true working profession in converts than for great numbers. If a man professes to be converted without realizing the heinousness of his sins, he is likely to be one of those stony-ground hearers who don't amount to anything. The first breath of opposition, the first wave of persecution or ridicule, will drag him back into the world again.

I believe we are making a woeful mistake in taking so many people into the church who have never been truly convicted of sin. Sin is just as dark in a man's heart today as it ever was. I sometimes think it is darker. For the more light a man has, the greater his responsibility and therefore the greater his need of deep conviction.

William Dawson once told this story to illustrate how humble the soul must be before it can find peace. He said that, at a revival meeting, a little lad who was used to Methodist ways went home to his mother and said, "Mother, John So-and-so is under conviction and seeking peace, but he will not find it tonight, Mother."

"Why, William?" she said.

"Because he was only down on one knee, Mother, and he will never get peace until he is down on both knees."

Until conviction of sin brings us down on both knees, until we are completely humbled, until we have no hope left in ourselves, we will not find the Savior.

There are three things that lead to conviction:
1. Conscience
2. The Word of God
3. The Holy Spirit.

All three are used by God. Long before we had any Word, God dealt with men through the conscience. That is what made Adam and Eve hide themselves from the presence of the Lord God amongst the trees of the Garden of Eden. That is what convicted Joseph's brethren when they said: "We are verily guilty concerning our brother, in that we saw the anguish of his soul, when he besought us, and we would not hear. Therefore," they said [and remember, over twenty years had passed away since they had sold him into captivity], "therefore is this distress come upon us" (Genesis 42:21). That is what we must use with our children before they are old enough to understand the Word and the Spirit of God. This is what accuses or excuses the heathen.

Conscience is "a divinely implanted faculty in man, telling him that he ought to do right." Someone has said that it was born when Adam and Eve ate of the forbidden fruit, when their eyes were opened and they "knew good and evil." It passes judgment, without being invited, upon our thoughts, words, and actions, approving or condemning according as it judges them to be right or wrong. A man cannot violate his conscience without being self-condemned.

But conscience is not a safe guide, because very often it will not tell you a thing is wrong until you have done it. It needs illuminating by God because it partakes of our fallen nature. Many a person does things that are wrong without being condemned by conscience. Paul said: "I verily thought with myself, that I ought to do many things contrary to the name of Jesus of Nazareth" (Acts 26:9). Conscience itself needs to be educated.

Again, conscience is too often like an alarm clock, which awakens a man at first, but after a time the man becomes used to it, and it loses its effect. Conscience can be smothered. I think we make a mistake in not preaching more to the conscience.

Hence, in due time, conscience was superseded by the law of God, which in time was fulfilled in Christ.

In this Christian land, where men have Bibles, these are the agency by which God produces conviction. The old Book tells you what is right and wrong before you commit sin, and what you need is to learn and appropriate its teachings under the guidance of the Holy Spirit. Conscience compared with the Bible is as a candle compared with the sun in the heavens.

See how the truth convicted those Jews on the day of Pentecost. Peter, filled with the Holy Spirit, preached that "God hath made this same Jesus, whom ye have crucified, both Lord and Christ." Now when they heard this, they were pricked in their heart, and said unto Peter and the rest of the apostles, Men and brethren, what shall we do?" (Acts 2:36,37)

Then, thirdly, the Holy Spirit convicts. I once heard the late Dr. A. J. Gordon expound the passage, "And when he [the Comforter] is come, he will reprove the world of sin, and of righteousness, and of judgment: Of sin because they believe not on me," (John 16:8,9) as follows:

"Some commentators say there was no real conviction of sin in the world until the Holy Ghost came. I think that foreign missionaries will say that that is not true, that a pagan who never heard of Christ may have a tremendous conviction of sin. Notice that God gave conscience first, and gave the Comforter afterward. Conscience bears witness to the law, and the Comforter bears witness to Christ. Conscience brings legal conviction, and the Comforter brings evangelical conviction. Conscience brings conviction unto condemnation, and the Comforter brings conviction unto justification.

"'He shall convince the world of sin, because they believe not on me.' That is the sin about which He convinces. It does not say that He convinces men of sin because they have stolen or lied or committed adultery; but the Holy Ghost is to convince men of sin because they have not believed on Jesus Christ. The coming of Jesus Christ into the world made a sin possible that was not possible before. Light reveals darkness; it takes whiteness to bring conviction concerning blackness. There are a great many people in this world that never knew they were sinful until they saw the face of Jesus Christ in all its purity.

"Jesus Christ now stands between us and the law. He has fulfilled the law for us. He has settled all claims of the law, and now whatever claim it had upon us has been transferred to Him, so that it is no longer the sin question, but the Son question, that confronts us. And, therefore, you notice that the first

101

thing Peter does when he begins to preach after the Holy Ghost has been sent down is about Christ; 'Him being delivered by the determinate counsel of God, ye have taken and by wicked hands have crucified and slain.' It doesn't say a word about any other kind of sin. That is the sin that runs all through Peter's teaching, and as he preached, the Holy Ghost came down and convicted them, and they cried out, 'What shall we do to be saved?'

"Well, but we had no part in crucifying Christ; therefore, what is our sin? It is the same sin in another form. They were convicted of crucifying Christ; we are convicted because we have not believed on Christ crucified. They were convicted because they had despised and rejected God's Son. The Holy Ghost convicts us because we have not believed in the Despised and Rejected One. It is really the same sin in both cases—the sin of unbelief in Christ."

Some of the most powerful meetings I have ever been in were those in which there came a sort of hush over the people and it seemed as if an unseen power gripped their consciences. I remember a man coming to one meeting, and the moment he entered, he felt that God was there. There came a sense of awe upon him, and that very hour he was convicted and converted.

2. CONTRITION

The next thing for our consideration is contrition, deep godly sorrow and humiliation of heart because of sin. If there is not true contrition, a man will turn right back into the old sin. That is the trouble with many Christians.

A man may get angry, and if there is not much contrition, the next day he will get angry again. A daughter may say mean, cutting things to her mother, and then her conscience troubles her, and she says, "Mother, I am sorry. Forgive me." But soon there is another outburst of temper, because the contrition is not deep and real. A husband speaks sharp words to his wife, and then to ease his conscience he goes and buys her a bouquet of flowers. He will not go like a man and say he has done wrong.

What God wants is contrition, and if there is not contrition, there is not full repentance. "The LORD is nigh unto them that are of a broken heart; and saveth such as be of a contrite spirit" (Psalm 34:18). "A broken and a contrite heart, O God, thou wilt not despise" (Psalm 51:17). Many sinners are sorry for their sins, and sorry that they cannot continue in sin; but they repent only with hearts that are not broken. I don't think we know how to repent these days. We need some John the Baptist, wandering through the land, crying: "Repent! Repent!"

3. CONFESSION OF SIN

If we have true contrition, that will lead us to confess our sins. I believe that nine-tenths of the trouble in our Christian life comes from failing to do this. We try to hide and cover up our sins; there is very little confession of them. Someone has said: "Unconfessed sin in the soul is like a bullet in the body."

If you have no power, it may be there is some sin that needs to be confessed, something in your life that needs straightening out. There is no amount of psalm singing, no amount of attending religious meetings, no amount of praying or reading your Bible that is going to cover up anything of that kind. It must be confessed, and if I am too proud to confess I need expect no mercy from God and no answers to my prayers.

The Bible says, "He that covereth his sins shall not prosper" (Proverbs 28:13). He may be a man in the pulpit, a priest behind the altar, a king on the throne; I don't care who he is. Man has been trying it for six thousand years. Adam tried it and failed. Moses tried it when he buried the Egyptian whom he killed, but he failed. "Be sure your sin will find you out." You cannot bury your sin so deep but it will have a resurrection soon enough, if it has not been blotted out by the Son of God. What man has failed to do for six thousand years, you and I had better give up trying to do.

There are three ways of confessing sin. All sin is against God and must be confessed to Him. There are some sins I need never confess to anyone on earth. If the sin has been between God and myself, I may confess it alone in my closet. I need not whisper it in the ear of any mortal. "Father, I have sinned against heaven, and before thee." "Against thee, thee only, have I sinned, and done this evil in thy sight" (Psalm 51:4).

But if I have done some man a wrong, and he knows that I have wronged him, I must confess that sin not only to God but also to that man. If I have too much pride to confess it to him, I need not come to God. I may pray, and I may weep, but it will do no good. First confess to that man, and then go to God and see how quickly He will hear you and send peace. "If thou bring thy gift to the altar, and there rememberest that thy brother hath aught against thee; leave there thy gift before the altar, and go thy way; first be reconciled to thy brother, and then come and offer thy gift" (Matthew 5:23,24). That is the scriptural way.

Then there is another class of sins that must be publicly confessed. Suppose I have been known as a blasphemer, a drunkard, or a reprobate. If I repent of my sins, I owe the public a confession. The confession should be as public as the transgression. Many people will say some mean thing about another in the presence of others and then try to patch it up by going to that person alone. The confession should be made so that all who heard the transgression can hear it. We are good at confessing other people's sins, but if it is true repentance, we will have all we can do to look after our own. When a man or woman gets a good look into God's looking glass, he is not finding fault with other people, he has as much as he can do at home.

"If we confess our sins, he is faithful and just to forgive us our sins, and to cleanse us from all unrighteousness" (1 John 1:9). Thank God for the gospel! Church member, if there is any sin in your life, make up your mind that you will confess it and be forgiven. Do not have any cloud between you and God. Be able to read your title clear to the mansion Christ has gone to prepare for you.

4. CONVERSION

Confession leads to true conversion, and there is no conversion at all until the first three steps have been taken. Now the word *conversion* means two things. We say a man is "converted" when he is born again. But it also has another meaning in the Bible. Peter said, "Repent, and be converted." Paul said, "Repent, and turn." He was not disobedient unto the heavenly vision, but began to preach to Jews and Gentiles that they should repent and turn to God. Some old divine has said, "Every man is born with his back to God. Repentance is a change of one's course. It is right about face."

105

Sin is a turning away from God. As someone once said, it is *aversion* from God and *conversion* to the world. True repentance means conversion to God and aversion to the world. When there is true contrition, the heart is broken *for* sin; when there is true conversion, the heart is broken *from* sin. When we leave the old life, we are translated out of the kingdom of darkness into the kingdom of light. Wonderful, isn't it?

Unless our repentance includes this conversion, it is not worth much. If a man continues in sin, it is proof of an idle profession. It is like pumping away continually at the ship's pumps without stopping the leaks. Solomon said, "If they pray toward this place, and confess thy name, and turn from their sin ..." (1 Kings 8:35). Prayer and confession would be of no avail while they continued in sin. Let us heed God's call. Let us forsake the old wicked way. Let us return unto the Lord and He will have mercy upon us, for He will abundantly pardon.

If you have never turned to God, turn now. I have no sympathy with the idea that it takes six months, or six weeks, or six hours to be converted. It doesn't take you very long to turn around, does it? If you know you are wrong, then you need to change and turn.

5. CONFESSION OF JESUS CHRIST

If you are converted, the next step is to confess openly. Listen, "If thou shalt confess with thy mouth the Lord Jesus, and shalt believe in thine heart that God hath raised him from the dead, thou shalt be saved. For with the heart man believeth unto righteousness; and with the mouth confession is made unto salvation" (Romans 10:9,10).

Confession of Christ is the culmination of the work of true repentance. We owe it to the world, to our fellow-Christians, to ourselves. He died to redeem us, and shall we be ashamed or afraid to confess Him? Religion as an abstraction, as a doctrine, has little interest for the world, but what people can say from personal experience always has weight.

I remember some meetings being held in a locality where the tide did not rise very quickly, and bitter and reproachful things were being said about the work. But one day, one of the most prominent men in the place rose and said, "I want it to be known that I am a disciple of Jesus Christ; and if there is any odium to be cast on His cause, I am prepared to take my share of it."

It went through the meeting like an electric current, and a blessing came at once to his soul and to the souls of others. Men come to me and say, "Do you mean to affirm, Mr. Moody, that I've got to make a public confession when I accept Christ? Do you mean to say I've got to confess Him in my place of business and in my family? Am I to let the whole world know that I am on His side?"

That is precisely what I mean. A great many are willing to accept Christ, but they are not willing to publish it, to confess it. A great many are looking at the lions and the bears in the way. Now, my friends, the devil's mountains are made of only smoke. He can throw a straw into your path and make a mountain of it. He says to you, "You cannot confess and pray before your family; why, you'll break down! You cannot tell it to your co-worker he will laugh at you." But when you accept Christ, you will have the power to confess Him.

There was a young man in the West—it was the West in those days—who had been more or less interested in things concerning his soul's salvation. One afternoon, in his office, he said, "I will accept Jesus Christ as my Lord and Savior." He went home and told his wife (who was a nominal professor of religion) that he had made up his mind to serve Christ; and he added, "After supper tonight I am going to take the company into the drawing room and erect the family altar."

"Well," said his wife, "you know some of the gentlemen who are coming to tea are skeptics, and they are older than you are, and don't you think you had better wait until after they have gone? Or else go out in the kitchen and have your first prayer with the servants?"

The young man thought for a few moments, and then he said, "I have asked Jesus Christ into my house for the first time, and I shall take Him into the best room, not the kitchen."

So he called his friends into the drawing room. There was a little sneering, but he read and prayed. That man afterwards became Chief Justice of the United States Supreme Court. Never be ashamed of the gospel of Christ; it is the power of God unto salvation.

A young man enlisted and was sent to his regiment. The first night he was in the barracks with about fifteen other young men who passed the time playing cards and gambling. Before he retired, he fell on his knees and prayed, and they began to curse him and jeer at him and throw boots at him.

So it went on the next night and the next. Finally the young man went and told the chaplain what had taken place and asked what he should do.

"Well," said the chaplain, "you are not at home now, and the other men have just as much right in the barracks as you have. It makes them mad to hear you pray, and the Lord will hear you just as well if you say your prayers in bed and don't provoke them."

For weeks after, the chaplain did not see the young man again, but one day he met him and asked, "By the way, did you take my advice?"

"I did, for two or three nights."

"How did it work?"

"Well," said the young man, "I felt like a whipped hound, and on the third night I got out of bed, knelt down, and prayed."

"Well," asked the chaplain, "how did that work?"
The young soldier answered, "We have a prayer meeting there now every night, and three have been converted, and we are praying for the rest."

Oh, friends, I am so tired of weak Christianity! Let us be out and out for Christ. Let us give no uncertain sound. If the world wants to call us fools, let them do it. It is only for a little while, for the crowning day is coming. Thank God for the privilege we have of confessing Christ.

Chapter 5

TRUE WISDOM

"They that be wise shall shine as the brightness of the firmament; and they that turn many to righteousness as the stars for ever and ever" (Daniel 12:3).

That is the testimony of an old man, and one who had the richest and deepest experience of any man living on the face of the earth at the time. He was taken down to Babylon when a young man. Some Bible scholars think he was not more than twenty years of age. Who could have imagined that, when this young Hebrew was carried away into captivity, that he would outrank all the mighty men of the day, and that all the generals who had been victorious in almost every nation at that time were to be eclipsed by this young slave! Yet for five hundred years no man whose life is recorded in history shined as this man. He outshone Nebuchadnezzar, Belshazzar, Cyrus, Darius, and all the princes and mighty monarchs of his day. We are not told when he was converted to knowledge of the true God, but I think we have good reason to believe that he had been brought under the influence of Jeremiah the prophet. Evidently some earnest, godly man, and no worldly professor, had made a deep impression upon him. Someone had at any rate taught him how he was to serve God.

We hear people nowadays talking about the hardness of the field where they labor. They say their position is a very peculiar one. Think of the field in which Daniel had to work. He was not only a slave, but he was held captive by a nation that detested the Hebrews. The language was unknown to him. There he was among idolaters, yet he commenced at once to shine. He took his stand for God from the very first, and so he went on through his whole life. He gave the dew of his youth to God, and he continued faithful right on till his pilgrimage was ended.

Notice that all those who have made a deep impression on the world and shined most brightly have been men who lived in a dark day. Look at Joseph; the Ishmaelites sold him as a slave into Egypt; yet he took his God with him into captivity, as Daniel did afterwards. And he remained true to the last. He did not give up his faith because he had been taken away from home and placed among idolaters. He stood firm, and God stood by him.

Look at Moses, who turned his back upon the gilded palaces of Egypt and identified himself with his despised and downtrodden nation. If a man ever had a hard field it was Moses, yet he shined brightly and never proved unfaithful to his God.

Elijah lived in a far darker day than we do. The whole nation was going over to idolatry. Ahab and his queen, Jezebel, and all the royal court were throwing their influence against the worship of the true God. Yet Elijah stood firm and shined brightly in that dark and evil day. How his name stands out on the pages of history!

Look at John the Baptist. I used to think I would like to live in the days of the prophets, but I have given up that idea. You may be sure that when a prophet appears on the scene, everything is dark, and the professing church of God has gone over to the service of the god of this world. So it was when John the Baptist made his appearance.

See how his name shines out today! Eighteen centuries have rolled away, and yet the fame of that wilderness preacher shines brighter than ever. He was looked down upon in his day and generation, but he has outlived all his enemies. His name will be revered and his work remembered as long as the church is on the earth.

Talk about your field being a hard one! See how Paul shined for God as he went out as the first missionary to the heathen, telling them of the God whom he served and who had sent His Son to die a cruel death in order to save the world. Men reviled him and his teachings. They laughed him to scorn when he spoke of the crucified One. But he went on preaching the gospel of the Son of God. He was regarded as a poor tent maker by the great and mighty ones of his day; but no one can now tell the name of any of his persecutors, or of those who lived at that time, unless their names happen to be associated with him and they were brought into contact with him.

Now the fact is, all men like to shine. We may as well acknowledge it at once. Go into business circles and see how men struggle to get into the front rank. Everyone wants to outshine his neighbor and to stand at the head of his profession. Go into the political world and see how there is a struggle going on as to who shall be the greatest. If you go into a school, you find that there is a rivalry among the boys and girls. They want to stand at the top of the class. When a boy does reach this position and outranks all the rest, the mother is very proud of it. She will manage to tell all the neighbors what Johnnie has accomplished and how many prizes he has won.

Go into the army and you find the same thing—one trying to outstrip the other. Everyone is very anxious to shine and rise above his comrades. Go among the young men in their games and see how anxious the one is to outdo the other. So we have all that desire in us. We like to shine above others. And yet there are very few who really shine in the world. Once in a while one man will outstrip all his competitors.

Every four years what a struggle goes on throughout our country as to who shall be the president of the United States. The battle rages on for six months or a year. Yet only one man can get the prize. There are a good many struggling to get the place, but many are disappointed because only one can attain the coveted prize. But in the kingdom of God the very least and the weakest may shine if they so desire. Not only can one obtain the prize, but all may have it if they will.

It does not say in this passage that the statesmen are going to shine as the brightness of the firmament. The statesmen of Babylon are gone and their very names are forgotten. It does not say that the nobility are going to shine. Earth's nobility are soon forgotten. The fame of John Bunyan, the Bedford tinker, has outlived the whole crowd of those who were the nobility in his day. They lived for self, and their memory is blotted out. He lived for God and for souls, and his name is as fragrant as it ever was.

We are not told that the merchants are going to shine. Who can tell the name of any of the millionaires of Daniel's day? They were all buried in oblivion a few years after their death. Who were the mighty conquerors of that day? But few can tell. It is true that we have heard of Nebuchadnezzar, but

114

probably we would not have known very much about him except for his relation to the prophet Daniel. How different it is with this faithful prophet of the Lord. Twenty-five centuries have passed away and his name shines on and on and on, brighter and brighter. And it will continue to shine while the church of God exists. "They that be wise shall shine as the brightness of the firmament; and they that turn many to righteousness as the stars forever and ever" (Daniel 12:3).

How quickly the glory of this world fades away! Eighty years ago the great Napoleon almost made the earth to tremble. How he blazed and shined as an earthly warrior for a little while! A few years passed, and a little island held that once proud and mighty conqueror. He died a poor, broken-hearted prisoner. Where is he today? Almost forgotten. Who in all the world will say that Napoleon lives in their hearts' affections? But look at this despised and hated Hebrew prophet. They wanted to put him into the lions' den because he was too sanctimonious and too religious. Yet see how green his memory is today! How his name is loved and honored for his faithfulness to his God.

Many years ago I was in Paris, at the time of the Great Exhibition. Napoleon III was then in his glory. Cheer after cheer would rise as he drove along the streets of the city. A few short years, and he fell from his lofty estate. He died an exile from his country and his throne, and where is his name today? Very few think about him at all, and if his name is mentioned it is not with love and esteem.

How empty and short-lived are the glory and the pride of this world! If we are wise, we will live for God and eternity. We will get outside of ourselves and will care nothing for the honor and glory of this world. In Proverbs we read, "He that winneth souls is wise" (Proverbs 11:30). If any man, woman, or child by a godly life and example can win one soul to God, his life will not have been a failure. He will have outshined all the mighty men of his day, because he will have set a stream in motion that will flow on and on forever and ever.

God has left us down here to shine. We are not here to buy and sell and get gain—to accumulate wealth, or acquire worldly position. If we are Christians, this earth is not our home. It is up yonder. God has sent us into the world to shine for Him—to light up this dark world. Christ came to be the Light of the World, but men put out that light. They took it to Calvary and blew it out. Before Christ went up on high, He said to His disciples, "Ye are the light of the world" (Matthew 5:14). "Ye are witnesses" (Luke 24:48). Go forth and carry the gospel to the perishing nations of the earth.

So God has called us to shine, just as much as Daniel was sent into Babylon to shine. Let no one say that he cannot shine because he does not have as much influence as some others may have. What God wants you to do is to use the influence you have. Daniel probably did not have much influence when he was in Babylon at first, but God soon gave him more because he was faithful and used what he had.

Remember, a small light will do a great deal when it is in a very dark place. Put one little tallow candle in the middle of a large hall, and it will give a good deal of light. Away out in the prairie regions, when meetings are held at night in the log schoolhouses, the announcement of the meeting is given out in this way: "A meeting will be held by early candlelight." The first man who comes brings a tallow dip with him. It is perhaps all he has, but he brings it and sets it on the desk. It does not light the building much, but it is better than nothing at all. Then the next man brings his candle, and the next family brings theirs. By the time the house is full, there is plenty of light. So if we all shine a little, there will be a good deal of light. That is what God wants us to do. If we cannot all be lighthouses, anyone of us can at any rate be a tallow candle. A little light will sometimes do a great deal.

The city of Chicago was set on fire by a cow kicking over a lamp, and a hundred thousand people were burned out of house and home. Do not let Satan get the advantage of you and make you think that because you cannot do any great thing you cannot do anything at all. Then we must remember that we are to *let* our light shine. It does not say *"Make* your light shine."* You do not have to *make* light to shine; all you have to do is to *let* it shine.

I remember hearing of a man at sea who was very seasick. If there is a time when a man feels that he cannot do any work for the Lord it is then—in my opinion. While this man was sick, he heard that someone had fallen overboard. He was wondering if he could do anything to help to save the man. He laid hold of a light, and held it up to the porthole. The drowning man was saved. When this man got over his attack of sickness, he went on deck one day and was talking with the man who was rescued. The saved man gave this testimony. He said he had gone down the second time and was just going down again for the last time, when he put out his hand. Just then, he said, someone held a light at the porthole, and the light fell on it. A sailor caught him by the hand and pulled him into the lifeboat.

It seemed a small thing to do to hold up the light, yet it saved the man's life. If you cannot do some great thing you can hold the light for some poor, perishing drunkard, who may be won to Christ and delivered from destruction. Let us take the torch of salvation, go into the dark homes, and hold up Christ to the people as the Savior of the world. If the perishing masses are to be reached, we must lay our lives right alongside theirs and pray with them and labor for them.

I would not give much to a man's Christianity if he is saved himself and is not willing to try to save others. It seems to me the basest ingratitude if we do not reach out the hand to others who are down in the same pit from which we were delivered. Who is able to reach and help drinking men like those who have themselves been slaves of the intoxicating cup? Will you not go out this very day and seek to rescue these men? If we were all to do what we can, we would soon empty the drinking saloons.

I remember reading of a blind man who was found sitting at the corner of a street in a great city with a lantern beside him. Someone went up to him and asked what he had the lantern there for, seeing that he was blind and the light was the same to him as the darkness. The blind man replied, "I have it so that no one may stumble over me." Dear friends, let us think of that. Where one man reads the Bible, a hundred read you and me. That is what Paul meant when he said we were to be living epistles of Christ, known and read by all men. I would not give much for all that can be done by sermons, if we do not preach Christ by our lives. If we do not commend the gospel to people by our holy walk and conversation, we shall not win them to Christ. Some little act of kindness will perhaps do more to influence them than any number of long sermons.

A vessel was caught in a storm on Lake Erie, and the passengers were trying to make it to the harbor of Cleveland. At the entrance of that port they had what are called the upper lights and the lower lights. Away back on the bluffs were the upper lights burning brightly enough, but when they came near the harbor they could not see the lights showing the entrance to it. The pilot said he thought they had better get back on the lake again. The captain said he was sure they would go down if they went back, and he urged the pilot to do what he could to gain the harbor. The pilot said there was very little hope of making the harbor, as he had nothing to guide him as to how he should steer the ship. They tried all they could to get her in. She rode on the top of the waves and then into the trough of the sea, and at last they found themselves stranded on the beach, where the vessel was dashed to pieces. Someone had neglected the lower lights, and they had gone out.

Let us take warning. God keeps the upper lights burning as brightly as ever, but He has left us down here to keep the lower lights burning. We are to represent Him here, as Christ represents us up yonder. I sometimes think if we had as poor a representative in the courts above as God has down here on earth, we would have a pretty poor chance of getting to heaven. Let us have our loins girded and our lights brightly burning so that others may see the way and not walk in darkness.

Speaking of a lighthouse reminds me of what I heard about a man in the state of Minnesota who, some years ago, was caught in a fearful storm. That state is cursed with storms that come sweeping down so suddenly in winter that escape is difficult. The snow will fall and the wind will beat it into the face of the traveler so that he cannot see two feet ahead. Many a man has been lost on the prairies when he has been caught in one of those storms.

This man was caught and was almost on the point of giving up, when he saw a little light in a log house. He managed to get there and found a shelter from the fury of the tempest. He is now a wealthy man. As soon as he was able, he bought the farm and built a beautiful house on the spot where the log building stood. On the top of a tower he put a revolving light, and every night when there comes a storm he lights it up in hope that it may be the means of saving someone else. That is true gratitude, and that is what God wants us to show. If He has rescued us and brought us up out of the horrible pit, let us be always looking to see if there is not someone else whom we can help to be saved.

I remember hearing of two men who had charge of a revolving light in a lighthouse on a rock-bound and stormy coast. Somehow the machinery went wrong, and the light did not revolve. They were so afraid that those at sea would mistake it for some other light that they worked all the night through to keep the light moving round. Let us keep our lights in the proper place, so that the world may see that the religion of Christ is not a sham, but a reality. It is said that in the Grecian sports they had a game where the men ran with lights. They lit a torch at the altar and ran a certain distance; sometimes they were on horseback.

If a man came in with his light still burning, he received a prize; if his light had gone out, he lost the prize. How many there are who, in their old age, have lost their light and their joy! They were once burning and shining lights in the family, in the Sunday school, and in the church. But something has come in between them and God—the world or self—and their light has gone out. Reader, if you are one who has had this experience, may God help you to come back to the altar of the Savior's love and light up your torch anew, so that you can go out into the lanes and alleys and let the light of the gospel shine in these dark homes.

As I have already said, if we only lead one soul to Jesus Christ we may set a stream in motion that will flow on when we are dead and gone. Away up on the mountainside there is a little spring; it seems so small that an ox might drink it up at a draught. Before long it becomes a rivulet and other rivulets run into it. Soon it is a large brook, and then it becomes a broad river sweeping onward to the sea. On its banks are cities, towns, and villages where many thousands live. Vegetation flourishes on every side, and commerce is carried down its stately bosom to distant lands. So if you turn one to Christ, that one may turn a hundred; they may turn a thousand, and so the stream, small at first, goes on broadening and deepening as it rolls on toward eternity.

In the book of Revelation we read, "I heard a voice from heaven saying unto me, Write, Blessed are the dead which die in the Lord from henceforth. Yea, saith the Spirit, that they may rest from their labors; and their works do follow them." There are many mentioned in the Scriptures of whom we read that they lived so many years and then they died. The cradle and the grave are brought close together; they lived and they died, and that is all we know about them. So in these days you could write on the tombstone of a great many professing Christians that they were born on such a day and they died on such a day; there is nothing whatever between.

But there is one thing you cannot bury with a good man; his influence still lives. They have not buried Daniel yet. His influence is as great today as ever. Do you tell me that Joseph is dead? His influence still lives and will continue to live on and on. You may bury the frail tenement of clay that a good man lives in, but you cannot get rid of his influence and example. Paul was never more powerful than he is today.

Do you tell me that John Howard, who went into so many of the dark prisons in Europe, is dead? Is Henry Martyn, or Wilberforce, or John Bunyan dead? Go into the Southern states, and there you will find millions of men and women who once were slaves. Mention to any of them the name of Wilberforce and see how quickly the eye will light up. He lived for something else besides himself, and his memory will never die out of the hearts of those for whom he lived and labored.

Is Wesley or Whitefield dead? The names of those great evangelists were never more honored than they are now. Is John Knox dead? You can go to any part of Scotland today and feel the power of his influence.

I will tell you who are dead, the enemies of these servants of God—those who persecuted them and lied about them. But the men themselves have outlived all the lies that were uttered concerning them. Yet this is not the end. They will shine in another world. How true are the words of the old Book, "They that be wise shall shine as the brightness of the firmament; and they that turn many to righteousness as the stars forever and ever" (Daniel 12:3).

Let us go on turning as many as we can to righteousness. Let us be dead to the world, to its lies, its pleasures, and its ambitions. Let us live for God, continually going forth to win souls for Him.

Let me quote a few words by Dr. Chalmers:

"Thousands of men breathe, move and live, pass off the stages of life, and are heard no more. Why? They do not partake of good in the world, and none were therefore blessed. None could point to them as the means of their redemption. Not a line they wrote, not a word they spoke could be recalled; and so they perished. Their light went out in darkness, and they were not remembered more than insects of yesterday.

"Will you thus live and die, O man immortal? Live for something. Do well, and leave behind you a monument of virtue that the storms of time ever destroy. Write your name in kindness, love and mercy on the hearts of the thousands you come in contact with year by year; you will never be forgotten. No, your name, your deeds will be as legible on the hearts you leave behind as the stars on the brow of evening. Good deeds will shine as the stars of heaven."

Chapter 6

"COME THOU AND ALL THY HOUSE INTO THE ARK"

I want to call your attention to a text that you will find in the seventh chapter of Genesis, first verse. When God speaks, you and I can afford to listen. It is not man speaking now, but it is God.

"The Lord said unto Noah, Come thou and all thy house into the ark."

Perhaps some skeptic is reading this, and perhaps some church member will join with him and say, "I hope Mr. Moody is not going to preach about the ark. I thought that was given up by all intelligent people." But I want to say that I haven't given it up. When I do, I am going to give up the whole Bible.

There is hardly any portion of the Old Testament Scripture that the Son of God has not set His seal to it when He was down here in the world. Men say, "I don't believe in the story of the Flood." Christ connected His own return to this world with that flood, "And as it was in the days of Noah, so shall it be also in the days of the Son of Man. They did eat, they drank, they married wives, they were given in marriage, until the day that Noah entered into the ark, and the flood came, and destroyed them all."

I believe the story of the Flood just as much as I do the third chapter of John. I pity any man that is picking the old Book to pieces. The moment that we give up anyone of these things, we touch the deity of the Son of God. I have noticed that when a man does begin to pick apart the Bible, it doesn't take him long to tear it all to pieces. What is the use of being five years about what you can do in five minutes?

A Solemn Message

One hundred twenty years before God spoke the words of this text, Noah had received the most awful communication that ever came from heaven to earth. No man up to that time, and I think no man since, has ever received such a communication. God said that on account of the wickedness of the world He was going to destroy the world by water.

We can have no idea of the extent and character of that antediluvian wickedness. The Bible piles one expression on another in its effort to emphasize it. "God saw that the wickedness of man was great in the earth, and that every imagination of the thoughts of his heart was only evil continually. And it repented the Lord that He had made man on the earth, and it grieved Him at His heart. ... The earth also was corrupt before God, and the earth was filled with violence. And God looked upon the earth, and, behold, it was corrupt; for all flesh had corrupted his way upon the earth." Men lived five hundred years and more back then, and they had time to mature in their sins.

How the Message Was Received

For one hundred twenty years God strove with those antediluvians. He never smites without warning, and they had their warning. Every time Noah drove a nail into the ark it was a warning to them. Every sound of the hammer echoed, "I believe in God." If they had repented and cried as they would at Nineveh, I believe God would have heard their cry and they would have been spared. But there was no cry for mercy.

I have no doubt that they ridiculed the idea that God was going to destroy the world. I have no doubt that there were atheists who said there was not a God anyway. I got hold of one of them some time ago. I said, "How do you account for the formation of the world?" "Oh! Force and matter work together, and by chance the world was created." I said, "It is a singular thing that your tongue isn't on the top of your head if force and matter just threw it together in that manner."

If I should take out my watch and say that force and matter worked together and out came the watch, you would say I was a lunatic of the first order. Wouldn't you? And yet they say that this old world was made by chance! "It threw itself together!"

I met a man in Scotland, and he took the position that there was no God. I asked him, "How do you account for creation, for all these rocks?" (They have a great many rocks in Scotland.)

"Why, any schoolboy could account for that," he said.

"Well, how was the first rock made?"

"Out of sand."

"How was the first sand made?"

"Out of rock."

You see; he had it all arranged so nicely. Sand and rock; rock and sand. I have no doubt that Noah had these men to contend with. Then there was a class called agnostics, and there are a good many of their grandchildren alive today. Then there was another class who said they believed there was a God—they couldn't make themselves believe that the world happened by chance—but God was too merciful to punish sin. He was so full of compassion and love that He couldn't punish sin. The drunkard, the harlot, the gambler, the murderer, the thief, and the libertine would all share alike with the saints at the end.

Supposing the governor of your state was so tenderhearted that he could not bear to have a man suffer, could not bear to see a man put in jail, and he should go and set all the prisoners free. How long would he be governor? You would have him out of office before the sun set. These very men that talk about God's mercy would be the first to raise a cry against a governor who would not have a man put in prison when he had done wrong.

Then another class took the ground that God could not destroy the world anyway. They might have a great flood that would rise up to the meadowlands and lowlands, but all it would be necessary to do would be to go up on the hills and mountains. That would be a hundred times better than Noah's Ark. Or if it should come to that, they could build rafts that would be a good deal better than that ark. They had never seen such an ugly looking thing. It was about five hundred feet long, about eighty feet wide, and fifty feet high. It had three stories and only one window.

And then, I suppose there was a large class who took the ground that Noah must be wrong because he was in such a minority. That is a great argument now, you know. Noah was greatly in the minority. But he went on working. If they had saloons then—and I don't doubt but that they had, for we read that there was "violence in the land," and whenever you have alcohol you have violence. We read also that Noah planted a vineyard and fell into the sin of intemperance. He was a righteous man, and if he did that, what must the others have done? Well, if they had saloons, no doubt they sang ribald songs about Noah and his ark; and if they had theaters, they likely acted it out, and mothers took their children to see it. And if they had the press in those days, every now and then there would appear a skit about "Noah and his folly." Reporters would come and interview him, and if they had an Associated Press, every few days a dispatch would be sent out telling how the work on the ark was progressing. And perhaps they had excursions and offered as an inducement that people could go through the ark. And if Noah happened to be around they would nudge each other and say, "That's Noah. Don't you think there is a strange look in his eye?"

As a Scotchman would say, they thought him a little daft. ... A drunkard does not call himself mad when he is drinking up all his means. Those men who stand and deal out death and damnation to men are not called mad, but a man is called mad when he gets into the ark and is saved for time and eternity. And I expect if the word *crank* was in use, they called Noah "an old crank."

And so all manner of sport was made of Noah and his ark. And the businessmen went on buying and selling, while Noah went on preaching and toiling. They perhaps had some astronomers, and they were gazing up at the stars and saying, "Don't you be concerned. There is no sign of a coming storm in the heavens. We are very wise men, and if there was a storm coming, we should read it in the heavens." And they had geologists digging away, and they said, "There is no sign in the earth." Even the carpenters who helped build the ark might have made fun of him, but they were like lots of people at the present day that will help build a church, and perhaps give money for its support, but will never enter it themselves.

Well, things went on as usual. Little lambs skipped on the hillsides each spring. Men sought after wealth, and if they had leases I expect they ran for longer periods than ours do. We think ninety-nine years a long time, but I don't doubt but that theirs ran for nine hundred and ninety-nine years. And when they came to sign a lease they would say with a twinkle in their eyes, "Why, this old Noah says the world is coming to an end in one hundred and twenty years, and it's twenty years since he started the story. But I guess I will sign the lease and risk it."

Someone has said that Noah must have been deaf, or he could not have stood the jeers and sneers of his countrymen. But if he was deaf to the voice of men, he heard the voice of God when He told him to build the ark. I can imagine one hundred years have rolled away, and the work on the ark ceases. Men say, "What has he stopped the work for?" He has gone on a preaching tour to tell the people of the coming storm—that God is going to sweep every man from the face of the earth unless he is in the ark.

But he cannot get a man to believe him except his own family. Some of the old men have passed away, and they died saying, "Noah is wrong." Poor Noah! He must have had a hard time of it. I don't think I should have had the grace to work for one hundred twenty years without a convert. But he just toiled on, believing the word of God. And now the hundred and twenty years are up. In the spring of the year Noah did not plant anything, for he knew the flood was coming, and the people say, "Every year before he has planted, but this year he thinks the world is going to be destroyed, and he hasn't planted anything."

Moving In

But I can imagine one beautiful morning, not a cloud to be seen, Noah has got his communication. He has heard the voice that he heard one hundred twenty years before—the same old voice. Perhaps there had been silence for one hundred twenty years. But the voice rang through his soul once again, "Noah, come thou and all thy house into the ark."

The word *come* occurs about nineteen hundred times in the Bible, it is said, and this is the first time. It meant salvation. You can see Noah and all his family moving into the ark. They are bringing the household furniture.

Some of his neighbors say, "Noah, what is your hurry? You will have plenty of time to get into that old ark. What is your hurry?" ... But he heard the voice and obeyed.

Some of his relatives might have said, "What are you going to do with the old homestead?" Noah says, "I don't want it. The storm is coming." He tells them the day of grace is dosing, that worldly wealth is of no value, and that the ark is the only place of safety. We must bear in mind that these railroads that we think so much of will soon go down. They only run for a time, not for eternity. The heavens will be on fire, and then what will property, honor, and position in society be worth?

131

The first thing that alarms them is when they rise one morning and lo! the heavens are filled with the fowls of the air. They are flying into the ark, two by two. They come from the desert; come from the mountain; they come from all parts of the world. They are going into the ark. It must have been a strange sight. I can hear the people cry," ... "What is the meaning of this?" And they look down on the earth; and with great alarm and surprise, they see little insects creeping up two by two, coming from all parts of the world. Then behold! There come cattle and beasts two by two.

The neighbors cry out, "What does it mean?" They run to their statesmen and wise men who have told them that there was no sign of a coming storm, and ask them why it is that those birds, animals, and creeping things go toward the ark, as if guided by some unseen hand.

"Well," the statesmen and wise men say, "we cannot explain it, but give yourselves no trouble. God is not going to destroy the world. Business was never better than it is now. Do you think if God was going to destroy the world, He would let us go on so prosperously as He has? There is no sign of a coming storm.

"What has made these creeping insects and these wild beasts of the forest go into the ark, we do not know. We cannot understand it; it is very strange. But there is no sign of anything going to happen. The stars are bright, and the sun shines as bright as ever it did. Everything moves on, as it has been moving for all time past. You can hear the children playing in the street. You can hear the voice of the bride and bridegroom in the land, and all is merry as ever."

I imagine the alarm passed away, and they fell into their regular courses. Noah came out and said: "The door is going to be shut. Come in. God is going to destroy the world. See the animals, how they have come up. The communication has come to them direct from heaven." But the people only mocked on.

Do you know, when the hundred and twenty years were up, God gave the world seven days' grace? Did you ever notice that? If there had been a cry during these seven days, I believe it would have been heard. But there was none. At length the last day had come, the last hour, the last minute, and the last second! God Almighty came down and shut the door of that ark. No angel, no man, but God Himself shut that door.

When once the master of the house has risen and shut the door, the doom of the world is sealed, and the doom of that old world was forever sealed. The sun had gone down upon the glory of that old world for the last time. You can hear way off in the distance the mutterings of the storm. You can hear the thunder rolling. The lightning begins to flash, and the old world reels. The storm bursts upon them, and that old ark of Noah's would have been worth more than the whole world to them.

I want to say to any scoffer who reads this that you can laugh at the Bible, you can scoff at your mother's God, you can laugh at ministers and Christians, but the hour is coming when one promise in that old Book will be worth more to you than ten thousand worlds like this. The windows of heaven are opened and the fountains of the great deep are broken up. The waters come bubbling up, and the sea bursts its bounds and leaps over its walls. The rivers begin to swell. The people living in the lowlands flee to the mountains and highlands. They flee up the hillsides.

And there is a wail going up; "Noah, Noah, Noah! Let us in." They leave their homes and come to the ark now. They pound on the ark. Hear them cry, "Noah! Let us in. Noah! Have mercy on us." "I am your nephew." "I am your niece." "I am your uncle."

Ah, there is a voice inside saying, "I would like to let you in, but God has shut the door. I cannot open it!" God shut that door! When the door is shut, there is no hope. Their cry for mercy was too late. Their day of grace was closed. Their last hour had come. God pleaded with them. God had invited them to come in, but they had mocked at the invitation. They scoffed and ridiculed the idea of a deluge. Now it is too late.

God did not permit anyone to survive to tell us how they perished. When Job lost his family, there came a messenger to him, but there came no messenger from the antediluvians. Not even Noah himself could see the world perish. If he could, he would have seen men and women and children dashing against that ark, and the waves rising higher and higher, while those outside were perishing, dying in unbelief.

Some think they could escape by climbing the trees, and think the storm will soon go down; but it rains on, day and night, for forty days and forty nights. They are swept away as the waves dash against them. The statesmen and astronomers and great men call for mercy, but it is too late. They had disobeyed the God of mercy. He had called and they refused. He had pled with them, but they had laughed and mocked. But now the time is come for judgment instead of mercy.

Judgment

The time is coming again when God will deal in judgment with the world. It may be just a little while. We do not know when, but it is sure to come. God's word has gone forth that this world shall be rolled together like a scroll and shall be on fire. What then will become of your soul? It is a loving call, "Now come, thou and all thy house, into the ark." Twenty-four hours before the rain began to fall, Noah's ark, if it had been sold at auction, would not have brought as much as it would be worth for kindling wood. But twenty-four hours after the rain began to fall, Noah's ark was worth more than all the world. There was not then a man living but would have given all he was worth for a seat in the ark.

You may turn away and laugh. "I believe in Christ!" you say. "I would rather be without Him than have Him." But keep in mind; the time is coming when Christ will be worth more to you than ten thousand worlds like this. Bear in mind that He is offered to you now.

This is a day of grace. It is a day of mercy. You will find, if you read your Bible carefully, that God always precedes judgment with grace. Grace is a forerunner of judgment. He called these men in the days of Noah in love. They would have been saved if they had repented in those one hundred twenty years. When Christ came to plead with the people in Jerusalem, it was their day of grace; but they mocked and laughed at Him. He said. "O Jerusalem, Jerusalem, thou that killest the prophets, and stonest them which are sent unto thee, how often would I have gathered thy children together, even as a hen gathereth her chicks under her wings, and ye would not!" (Matthew 23:37). Forty years afterward, thousands of people begged that their lives might be spared, and eleven hundred thousand perished in that city.

In 1857 a revival swept over this country in the east and on to the western cities, clear over to the Pacific coast. It was God calling the nation to Himself. Half a million people united with the church at that time. Then the war broke out. We were baptized with the Holy Spirit in 1857, and in 1861 we were baptized in blood. It was a call of mercy, preceding judgment.

Are Your Children Safe?

The text that I selected has a special application to Christian people and to parents. This command of the Scripture was given to Noah not only for his own safety, but that of his household. And the question that I put to each father and mother is this: "Are your children in the ark of God?" You may scoff at it, but it is a very important question. Are all your children in? Are all your grand children in? Don't rest day or night until you get your children in. I believe my children have fifty temptations where I had one. I am one of those who believe that in the great cities there is a snare set upon the corner of every street for our sons and daughters. I don't believe it is our business to spend our time in accumulating bonds and stocks. Have I done all I can to get my children in? That is it.

Now, let me ask another question: "What would have been Noah's feelings if, when God called him into the ark, his children would not have gone with him? If he had lived such a false life that his children had no faith in his word, what would have been his feelings? He would have said, "There is my poor boy on the mountain. Would to God I had died in his place! I would rather have perished than had him perish." David cried over his son; "Oh, my son Absalom, my son, my son Absalom, would God I had died for thee." Noah loved his children, and they had confidence in him.

Someone sent me a paper a number of years ago containing an article that was marked. Its title was, "Are all the children in?" An old wife lay dying who was nearly one hundred years of age. The husband, who had taken the journey with her, sat by her side.

She was just breathing faintly, but suddenly she revived, opened her eyes, and said, "Why, it is dark."

"Yes, Janet, it is dark."

"Is it night?"

"Oh, yes! It is midnight."

"Are all the children in?"

There was that old mother living life over again. Her youngest child had been in the grave twenty years, but she was traveling back into the old days and she fell asleep in Christ asking, "Are all the children in?" Dear friend, are they all in? Put the question to yourself now. Is John in? Is James in? Or is he immersed in business and pleasure? Is he living a double and dishonest life? Say! Where is your boy, mother? Where is your son, your daughter? Is it well with your children? Can you say it is?

After being superintendent of a Sunday school in Chicago for a number of years, a school of over a thousand members—children that came from godless homes, having mothers and fathers working against me, taking the children off on excursions on Sunday and doing all they could to break up the work I was trying to do—I used to think that if I should ever stand before an audience I would speak to no one but parents. That would be my chief business.

It is an old saying, "Get the lamb, and you will get the sheep." I gave that up years ago. Give me the sheep, and then I will have someone to nurse the lamb. But get a lamb and convert him, and if he has a godless father and mother, you will have little chance with that child. What we want is godly homes. The home was established long before the church.

I have to say I have no sympathy with the idea that our children have to grow up before they are converted. Once I saw a lady with three daughters at her side, and I stepped up to her and asked if she was a Christian. "Yes, sir," she replied. Then I asked the oldest daughter if she was a Christian. The chin began to quiver, and the tears came into her eyes, and she said, "I wish I was."

The mother looked very angrily at me and said, "I don't want you to speak to my children on that subject. They don't understand." And in great rage she took them all away from me. One daughter was fourteen years old, one was twelve, and the other ten, but they were not old enough to be talked to about religion! Let them drift into the world and plunge into worldly amusements, and then see how hard it is to reach them.

Many a mother is mourning today because her boy has gone beyond her reach and will not allow her to pray with him. She may pray for him, but he will not let her pray or talk with him. In those early days when his mind was tender and young, she might have led him to Christ. Bring them in. "Suffer the little children to come unto me, and forbid them not: for of such is the kingdom of God" (Mark 10:14). Is there a prayerless father reading this? May God let the arrow go down into your soul! Make up your mind that (God helping you) you will reach the children. God's order is to the father first, but if he isn't true to his duty then the mother should be true and save the children from the wreck. Now is the time to do it while you have them under your roof. Exert your parental influence over them.

I speak to many parents, but I think of two fathers in particular; one who lived on the banks of the Mississippi, the other in New York. The first one devoted all his time to amassing wealth. He had a son to whom he was much attached, and one day the boy was brought home badly injured. The father was informed that the boy could live only a short time, and he broke the news to his son as gently as possible.

"You say I cannot live, Father? Oh, then pray for my soul," said the boy. In all those years that father had never said a prayer for that boy, and he told him he couldn't. Shortly after, the boy died. That father has said since that he would give all that he possessed if he could call that boy back only to offer one short prayer for him.

The other father had a boy who had been ill for some time, and he came home one day and found his wife weeping. She said, "I believe that this is going to prove fatal."

The man started and said, "If you think so, then I think we should tell him." But the mother could not tell her boy. The father went to the sickroom, and he saw that death was feeling for the cords of life, and he said, "My son, do you know you are not going to live?"

The little fellow looked up and said, "No; is this death that I feel stealing over me? Will I die today?"

"Yes, my son, you cannot live out the day."

And the little fellow smiled and said, "Well, Father, I shall be with Jesus tonight, shan't I?"

"Yes, you will spend the night with the Lord." And the father broke down and wept.

The little fellow saw the tears and said, "Don't weep for me. I will go to Jesus and tell Him that ever since I can remember you have prayed for me."

I have three children, and if God should take them from me, I would rather have them take such a message home to Him than to have the wealth of the whole world. Oh! What else could I say to you fathers and mothers, to stir you to get your children into the ark!

Chapter 7

HUMILITY

"Learn of me: for I am meek and lowly in heart"
(Matthew 11:29).

There is no harder lesson to learn than the lesson of humility. It is not taught in the schools of men, only in the schools of Christ. It is the rarest of all the gifts. Very rarely do we find a man or woman who is following closely the footsteps of the Master in meekness and humility. I believe that it is the hardest lesson that Jesus Christ had to teach His disciples while He was here upon earth.

It almost looked at first as though He had failed to teach it to the twelve men who had been with Him almost constantly for three years. I believe that if we were humble we would be sure to receive a great blessing. After all, I think that more depends upon us than upon the Lord, because He is always ready to give a blessing and give it freely, but we are not always in a position to receive it. He always blesses the humble, and if we can bow down in the dust before Him, no one will go away disappointed. It was Mary at the feet of Jesus, who had chosen the "better part."

Did you ever notice the reason Christ gave for learning of Him? He might have said, "Learn of Me, because I am the most advanced thinker of the age. I have performed miracles that no one else has performed. I have shown My supernatural power in a thousand ways." But no, the reason He gave was that He was "meek and lowly in heart."

We read of the three men in Scripture whose faces shined, and all three were noted for their meekness and humility. We are told that the face of Christ shined at His transfiguration; Moses, after he had been on the mount for forty days, came down from his communion with God with a shining face; and when Stephen stood before the Sanhedrin on the day of his death, his face was lit up with glory. If our faces are to shine we must get into the valley of humility. We must go down in the dust before God.

Bunyan says that it is hard to get down into the valley of humiliation—the descent into it is steep and rugged—but that it is very fruitful and fertile and beautiful when we finally get there. I think that no one will dispute that. Almost every man, even the ungodly, admires meekness.

Someone asked Augustine what was the first of the religious graces, and he said, "Humility." They asked him what was the second, and he replied, "Humility." They asked him the third, and he said, "Humility." I think that if we are humble, we have all the graces.

Some years ago I saw what is called a sensitive plant. I happened to breathe on it, and suddenly it dropped its head. I touched it, and it withered away. Humility is as sensitive as that. It cannot safely be brought out on exhibition. A man who flatters himself because he believes he is humble and is walking close to the Master is self-deceived. It consists not in thinking meanly of ourselves, but in not thinking of ourselves at all. Moses knew not that his face was shining. If humility speaks of itself, it is gone.

Someone has said that the grass is an illustration of this lowly grace. It was created for the lowliest service. Cut it, and it springs up again. The cattle feed upon it, and yet how beautiful it is.

The showers fall upon the mountain peaks and very often leave them barren because they rush down into the meadows and valleys and make the lowly places fertile. If a man is proud and lifted up, rivers of grace may flow over him and yet leave him barren and unfruitful, while they bring blessing to the man who has been brought low by the grace of God.

A man can counterfeit love, he can counterfeit faith, he can counterfeit hope and all the other graces, but it is very difficult to counterfeit humility. You soon detect false humility. They have a saying in the East among the Arabs that as the tares and the wheat grow they show which God has blessed. The ears that God has blessed bow their heads and acknowledge every grain, and the more fruitful they are the lower their heads are bowed. The tares, which God has sent as a curse, lift up their heads erect, high above the wheat, but they only bear forth evil.

I have a pear tree on my farm that is very beautiful. It appears to be one of the most beautiful trees on my land. Every branch seems to be reaching up to the light and stands almost like a wax candle, but I never get any fruit from it. I have another tree, which was so full of fruit last year that the branches almost touched the ground. If we only get down low enough, my friends, God will use every one of us to His glory.

"As the lark that soars the highest builds her nest the lowest; as the nightingale that sings so sweetly sings in the shade when all things rest; as the branches that are most laden with fruit bend lowest; as the ship most laden sinks deepest in the water; so the holiest Christians are the humblest."

The *London Times* some years ago told the story of a petition that was being circulated for signatures. It was a time of great excitement, and this petition was intended to have great influence in the House of Lords. But there was one word left out. Instead of reading, "We humbly beseech thee," it read, "We beseech thee." So it was ruled out. My friends, if we want to make an appeal to the God of heaven, we must humble ourselves; and if we do humble ourselves before the Lord, we shall not be disappointed.

As I have been studying some Bible characters that illustrate humility, I have been ashamed of myself. If you have any regard for me, pray that I may have some humility. When I put my life beside the life of some of these men, I say, "Shame on the Christianity of the present day." If you want to get a good idea of yourself, look at some of the Bible characters that have been clothed with meekness and humility; and see what a contrast is your position before God and man.

One of the meekest characters in history was John the Baptist. You remember when the Pharisees sent a deputation to him and asked if he was Elias, or this prophet, or that prophet, and he said, "No." Now he might have said some very flattering things of himself. He might have said, "I am the son of the old priest Zacharias. Haven't you heard of my fame as a preacher? I have baptized more people, probably, than any man living. The world has never seen a preacher like myself."

I honestly believe that in the present day most men standing in his position would do that. On the railroad train some time ago, I heard a man talking so loud that all the people in the car could hear him. He said that he had baptized more people than any man in his denomination. He told how many thousand miles he had traveled, how many sermons he had preached, how many open-air services he had held, and this and that; until I was so ashamed that I had to hide my head. This is the age of boasting. It is the day of the great "I."

My attention was recently called to the fact that in all the Psalms you cannot find any place where David refers to his victory over the giant Goliath. If it had been in the present day, there would have been a volume written about it at once. I don't know how many poems there would be telling of the great things that this man had done. He would have been in demand as a lecturer, and would have added a title to his name: G.G.K.—Great Giant Killer. That is how it is today; great evangelists, great preachers, great theologians, great bishops.

"John," they asked, "who are you?"

"I am nobody. I am to be heard, not to be seen. I am only a voice."

He hadn't a word to say about himself. I once heard a little bird faintly singing close by. At last it got clear out of sight, and then its notes were still sweeter. The higher it flew, the sweeter its notes sounded. If we can only get self out of sight and learn of Him who was meek and lowly in heart, we shall be lifted up into heavenly places.

Mark tells us, in the first chapter and seventh verse, that John came and preached saying, "There cometh one mightier than I after me, the latchet of whose shoes I am not worthy to stoop down and unloose." Think of that; and bear in mind that Christ was looked upon as a deceiver, a village carpenter, and yet here is John, the son of the old priest, who had a much higher position in the sight of men than that of Jesus. Great crowds were coming to hear him, and even Herod attended his meetings.

When his disciples came and told John that Christ was beginning to draw crowds, he nobly answered: "A man can receive nothing, except it be given him from heaven. Ye yourselves bear me witness that I said; I am not the Christ, but that I am sent before Him. He that hath the bride is the bridegroom; but the friend of the bridegroom, which standeth and heareth him, rejoiceth greatly because of the bridegroom's voice; thus my joy therefore is fulfilled. He must increase, but I must decrease" (John 3:27-30).

It is easy to read that, but it is hard for us to live in the power of it. It is very hard for us to be ready to decrease, to grow smaller and smaller, that Christ may increase. The morning star fades away when the sun rises. "He that cometh from above is above all; he that is of the earth is earthly, and speaketh of the earth: he that cometh from heaven is above all, and what he hath seen and heard, that he testifieth; and no man receiveth his testimony. He that hath received his testimony hath set to his seal that God is true. For he whom God hath sent speaketh the words of God: for God giveth not the Spirit by measure unto him" (John 3:31-34).

Let us now turn the light upon ourselves. Have we been decreasing of late? Do we think less of ourselves and of our position than we did a year ago? Are we seeking to obtain some position of dignity? Do we want to hold onto some title, and are we offended because we are not treated with the courtesy that we think is due us?

Some time ago I heard a man in the pulpit say that he should take offense if he was not addressed by his title. My dear friend, are you going to take that position that you must have a title, and that you must have every letter addressed with that title or you would be offended? John did not want any title, and when we are right with God, we shall not be caring about titles. In one of his early epistles Paul calls himself the least of all of the apostles. Later on he claims to be "less than the least of all saints," and again, just before his death, humbly declares that he is the "chief of sinners." Notice how he seems to have grown smaller and smaller in his own estimation. So it was with John. And I do hope and pray that as the days go by we may feel like hiding ourselves and letting God have all the honor and glory.

"When I look back upon my own religious experience," says Andrew Murray, "or round upon the church of Christ in the world, I stand amazed at the thought of how little humility is sought after as the distinguishing feature of the discipleship of Jesus. In preaching and living, in the daily intercourse of the home and social life, in the more special fellowship with Christians, in the direction and performance of work for Christ—alas! How much proof there is that humility is not esteemed the cardinal virtue, the only root from which the graces can grow, the one indispensable condition of true fellowship with Jesus."

Notice what Christ says about John. "He was a burning and a shining light" (John 5:35). Christ gave him the honor that belonged to him. If you take a humble position, Christ will see it. If you want God to help you, then take a low position. I am afraid that if we had been in John's place, many of us would have said, "What did Christ say? I am a burning and shining light?" Then we would have had that recommendation put in the newspapers and would have sent them to our friends, with that part marked in blue pencil. Sometimes I get a letter just full of clippings from the newspapers, stating that this man is more eloquent than Gough, etc. And the man wants me to get him some church.

Do you think that a man who has such eloquence would be looking for a church? No, they would all be looking for him. My dear friends, isn't it humiliating? Sometimes I think it is a wonder that any man is converted these days. Let another praise you. Don't be going around praising yourself. If we want God to lift us up, let us get down. The lower we get, the higher God will lift us. It is Christ's eulogy of John, "Greater than any man born of woman."

There is a story told of William Carey, the great missionary, that he was invited by the governor-general of India to go to a dinner party where there were some military officers belonging to the aristocracy. These men looked down upon missionaries with scorn and contempt. One of these officers said at the table, "I believe that Carey was a shoemaker, wasn't he, before he took up the profession of a missionary?"

Mr. Carey spoke up and said, "Oh no, I was only a cobbler. I could mend shoes, and wasn't ashamed of it." The one prominent virtue of Christ, next to His obedience, is His humility. Even His obedience grew out of His humility. "Who, being in the form of God, thought it not robbery to be equal with God, but He emptied Himself, taking the form of a bond-servant, and was made in the likeness of men.

And being found in form of a man, He humbled Himself, and became obedient unto death, yea, even the death of the Cross" (Philippians 2:6-8). In His lowly birth, His submission to His earthly parents, His seclusion for thirty years, His consorting with the poor and despised, His entire submission and dependence upon His Father, this virtue that was consummated in His death on the cross shines out.

One day Jesus was on His way to Capernaum and was talking about His coming death and suffering, and about His resurrection, and He heard quite a heated discussion going on behind Him. When he came into the house at Capernaum, He turned to His disciples and said, "What was all that discussion about?"

I see John look at James, and Peter at Andrew and they all look ashamed. "Who shall be the greater?" That discussion has wrecked party after party, one society after another—"Who shall be the greatest?"

The way Christ took to teach them humility was by putting a little child in their midst and taught them that if he who would be great must become like a little child, for example, and he who wants to be the greatest, let him be the servant of all.

To me, one of the saddest things in the life of Jesus Christ was the fact that just before His crucifixion, His disciples should have been striving to see who should be the greatest, that night He instituted the Supper, and they ate the Passover together.

It was His last night on earth, and they never saw Him so sorrowful before. He knew Judas was going to sell Him for thirty pieces of silver. He knew that Peter would deny

Him. And yet, in addition to this, when going into the very shadow of the Cross, there arose this strife as to who should be the greatest. He took a towel and girded Himself like a slave, and He took a basin of water and stooped and washed their feet. That was another object lesson of humility. He said, "Ye call me Master and Lord, and ye say well; for so I am" (John 13:13). If you want to be great in My kingdom, be servant of all. If you serve, you shall be great.

When the Holy Spirit came and those men were filled (see Acts 2), from that time there was a great change. Matthew took up his pen to write, and He kept Matthew out of sight. He told what Peter and Andrew did, but He called himself "Matthew the publican." He tells how they left all to follow Christ but does not mention the feast He gave. Jerome says that Mark's gospel is to be regarded as memoirs of Peter's discourses and to have been published by his authority. Yet here we constantly find that damaging things are mentioned about Peter, and things to his credit are not referred to. Mark's gospel omits all allusion to Peter's faith in venturing on the sea but goes into detail about the story of his fall and denial of our Lord. Peter put himself down, and lifted others up.

If the gospel of Luke was written today, the great Dr. Luke would sign it, and you would have his photograph as a frontispiece. But you can't find Luke's name; it is because he purposely keeps out of sight. He wrote two books, and his name is not to be found in either. John covers himself always under the expression "the disciple whom Jesus loved." None of the four men whom history and tradition assert to be the authors of the gospels lays claim to the authorship in his writings. Dear man of God, I would that I had the same spirit, that I could just set out of sight and hide myself.

My dear friends, I believe our only hope is to be filled with the Spirit of Christ. May God fill us, so that we shall be filled with meekness and humility. Let us take the hymn "O, to Be Nothing, Nothing" and make it the language of our hearts. It breathes the spirit of Him who said, "The Son can do nothing of himself!" (John 5:19)

O, to be nothing, nothing!
Only to lie at His feet,
A broken and emptied vessel,
For the Master's use made meek.
Emptied, that He might fill me
As forth to His service I go;
Broken, that so unhindered,
His life through me might flow.

Chapter 8

REST

Some years ago a gentleman came to me and asked what I thought was the most precious promise of all those that Christ left. I took some time to think them over, but I soon gave up. I found that I could not answer the question. It is like a man with a large family of children—he cannot tell which he likes best; he loves them all. But if not the best, this is one of the sweetest promises of all:

> *"Come unto me, all ye that labor and are heavy laden, and I will give you rest. Take my yoke upon you, and learn of me; for I am meek and lowly in heart; and ye shall find rest unto your souls. For my yoke is easy: and my burden is light"* (Matthew 11:28-30).

There are a good many people who think the promises are not going to be fulfilled. There are some that we do see fulfilled, and we cannot help but believe they are true. Now remember that some promises are given with, and others without, conditions attached to them. For instance, it says, "If I regard iniquity in my heart, the Lord will not hear me" (Psalm 66:18). Now, I need not pray as long as I am cherishing some known sin. He will not hear me, much less answer me. The Lord says in the eighty-fourth Psalm, "No good thing will be withheld from them that walk uprightly." If I am not walking uprightly I have no claims under the promise.

Again, some of the promises were made to certain individuals or nations. For instance, God said that He would make Abraham's seed multiply as the stars of heaven, but that is not a promise for you or me. Some promises were made to the Jews and do not apply to the Gentiles.

Then there are promises without conditions. He promised Adam and Eve that the world would have a Savior, and there was no power in earth or perdition that could keep Christ from coming at the appointed time. When Christ left the world, He said He would send us the Holy Spirit. He had only been gone ten days when the Holy Spirit came.

And so you can run right though the Scriptures, and you will find that some of the promises are with conditions, and some without. If we don't comply with the conditions we cannot expect them to be fulfilled.

I believe it will be the experience of every man and woman on the face of the earth, I believe that everyone will be obliged to testify in the evening of life, that if they have complied with the condition, the Lord has fulfilled His word to the letter. Joshua, the old Hebrew hero, was an illustration. After having tested God forty years in Egypt, forty years in the desert, and thirty years in the Promised Land, his dying testimony was: "Not one thing hath failed of all the good things which the Lord your God spake" (1 Kings 23:14).

I believe you could lift the ocean easier than break one of God's promises. So when we come to a promise like the one we have before us now, I want you to bear in mind that there is no discount upon it. "Come unto me, all ye that labor and are heavy laden, and I will give you rest."

Perhaps you say, "I hope Mr. Moody is not going to preach on this old text." Yes, I am. When I take up an album, it does not interest me if all the photographs are unfamiliar; but if I know any of the faces I stop at once. So it is with these old, well-known texts. They have quenched our thirst before, but the water is still bubbling up—we cannot drink it dry.

If you probe the human heart, you will find a want, and that want is rest. The cry of the world today is, "Where can rest be found?" Why are theaters and places of amusement crowded at night? What is the secret of Sunday driving, of the saloons and brothels? So many people think they are going to find rest in pleasure, others think they are going to get it in wealth, and others in literature. Yet, they are seeking and finding no rest.

Where Can Rest Be Found?

If I wanted to find a person who had found rest I would not go among the very wealthy. The man that we read of in the twelfth chapter of Luke thought he was going to find rest by multiplying his possessions, but he was disappointed. "Soul, take thine ease." I venture to say that there is not a person in this whole wide world who has tried to find rest in that way and found it. Money cannot buy it. Many a millionaire would gladly give millions if he could purchase rest as he does his stocks and shares. God has made the soul a little too large for this world. Roll the whole world in, and still there is room. There is care in getting wealth and more care in keeping it. Nor would I go among the pleasure seekers. They have a few hours of enjoyment, but the next day there is enough sorrow to counterbalance it. They may drink a cup of pleasure today, but the cup of pain comes on tomorrow.

To find rest I would never go among the politicians, or among the so-called great. Congress is the last place on earth that I would go. In the Lower House they want to go to the Senate; in the Senate they want to go to the Cabinet; and then they want to go to the White House; and rest has never been found there. Nor would I go among the halls of learning. "Much study is a weariness to the flesh." I would not go among the upper ten, the "bon ton," for they are constantly chasing after fashion. Have you not noticed their troubled faces on our streets? And the face is an indication of the soul. They have no hopeful look. Their worship of pleasure is slavery. Solomon tried pleasure and found bitter disappointment, and down the ages has come the bitter cry "All is vanity."

Now there is no rest in sin. The wicked know nothing about it. The Scriptures tell us the wicked "are like the troubled sea, when it cannot rest" (Isaiah 57:20). You have, perhaps, been on the sea when there is a calm, when the water is as clear as crystal, and it seemed as if the sea were at rest. But if you looked you would see that the waves came in and that the calm was only on the surface. Man, like the sea, has no rest. He has had no rest since Adam fell, and there is none for him until he returns to God again and the light of Christ shines into his heart.

Rest cannot be found in the world, and thank God the world cannot take it from the believing heart! Sin is the cause of all this unrest. It brought toil and labor and misery into the world.

Now if I would go to find true rest, I would go to someone who has heard the sweet voice of Jesus and has laid his burden down at the cross. There is rest, sweet rest. Thousands could testify to this blessed fact. They could truthfully say, I heard the voice of Jesus say:

"Come unto me and rest.
Lay down, thou weary one, lay down,
Thy head upon my breast."
I came to Jesus as I was,
Weary and worn and sad.
I found in Him a resting place,
And He hath made me glad."

Among all his writings, St. Augustine has said nothing sweeter than this:

"Thou hast made us for Thyself, O God, and our heart is restless till it rests in Thee."

Do you know that for four thousand years no prophet or priest or patriarch ever stood up and uttered a text like this? It would be blasphemy for Moses to have uttered a text like it. Do you think he had rest when he was teasing the Lord to let him go into the Promised Land? Do you think Elijah could have uttered such a text as this when, under the juniper tree, he prayed that he might die? And this is one of the strongest proofs that Jesus Christ was not only man, but He is God. He was God's Son, and this is heaven's proclamation, "Come unto me, and I will give you rest." He brought it down from heaven with Him.

Now, if this text was not true, don't you think it would have been found out by this time? I believe it as much as I believe in my own existence. Why? Because I not only find it in the Book, but in my own experience. The "I wills" of Christ have never been broken and never can be. I thank God for the word "give" in that passage. He doesn't sell it. Some of us are so poor that we could not buy it if it was for sale. Thank God, we can get it for nothing. I like to have text like this, because it takes us all in. "Come unto me all ye that labor." That doesn't mean a select few—refined ladies and cultured men. It doesn't mean good people only. It applies to saint and sinner. Hospitals are for the sick, not for healthy people. Do you think that Christ would shut the door in anyone's face and say, "I did not mean *all*. I only meant certain ones?" If you cannot come as a saint, come as a sinner. Only come!

A lady told me once that she was so hardhearted she couldn't come. "Well," I said, "my good woman, it doesn't say, 'All ye soft-hearted people come.' Blackhearts, vile hearts, hard hearts, soft hearts, all hearts come. Who can soften your hard heart but Jesus?" The harder the heart, the more need you have to come. If my watch stops I don't take it to a drugstore or to a blacksmith's shop, but to the watchmaker's to have it repaired. So if the heart gets out of order take it to its keeper, Christ, to have it set right. If you can prove that you are a sinner, you are entitled to the promise. Get all the benefit you can out of it.

Now, there are a good many believers who think this text applies only to sinners. No, it is just the thing for them too. What do we see today? The Church, Christian people, all loaded down with cares and troubles. "Come unto me, all ye that labor." All! I believe that includes the Christian whose heart is burdened with some great sorrow. The Lord wants you to come. Christ the Burden-Bearer, it says in another place, "Casting all your care upon him, for he careth for you" (1 Peter 5:7). We would have a victorious church if we

158

could get Christian people to realize that, but they have never made the discovery. They agree that Christ is the sin-bearer, but they do not realize that He is also the burden-bearer.

"Surely he hath borne our griefs, and carried our sorrows" (Isaiah 53:4). It is the privilege of every child of God to walk in unclouded sunlight. Some people go back into the past and rake up all the troubles they ever had, and then they look into the future and anticipate that they will have still more trouble, and they go reeling and staggering all through life. They give you the cold chills every time they meet you. They put on a whining voice and tell you what "a hard time they have had." I believe they embalm [their troubles] and bring out the mummy on every opportunity. The Lord says He wants us to cast all our cares upon Him. He wants to carry our burdens and our troubles. What we want is a joyful church, and we are not going to convert the world until we have it. We want to get this long-faced Christianity off the face of the earth.

Take these people that have some great burden, and let them come into a meeting. If you can get their attention upon the singing or preaching, they will say, "Oh, wasn't it grand! I forgot all my cares." And they just drop their bundle at the end of the pew. But the moment the benediction is pronounced they grab the bundle again and take it with them. You laugh, but you do it yourself. Cast your care on Him.

Sometimes they go into the closet and close the door, and they get so carried away and lifted up they forget their trouble; but they just take it up again the moment they get off their knees. Leave your sorrow now! Cast all your care upon Him. If you cannot come to Christ as a saint, come as a sinner. But if you are a saint with some trouble or care, bring it to Him. Saint and sinner, come! He wants you all.

Don't let Satan deceive you into believing that you cannot come if you will. Christ says, "Ye will not come unto me." With the command comes the power.

A man in one of our meetings in Europe said he would like to come, but he was chained and couldn't come. A [Scotsman] said to him, "Aye, man, why don't you come chain and all" He said, "I never thought of that."

Are you cross and peevish, and do you make things unpleasant at home? My friend, come to Christ and ask Him to help you. Whatever the sin is, bring it to Him.

What Does It Mean to Come?

Perhaps you say, "Mr. Moody, I wish you would tell us what it is to come." I have given up trying to explain it. I always feel like the minister who said he was going to *confound,* instead of *expound,* the chapter.

The best definition is just come. The more you try to explain it, the more you are mystified. One of the first things a mother teaches her child is to look. She takes the baby to the window, and says, "Look, baby, Papa is coming!" Then she teaches the child to come. She props it up against a chair and says, "Come!" and by and by the little thing pushes the chair along to Mama. That's coming. You don't need go to college to learn how. You don't need a minister to tell you what it is. Now will you come to Christ? He said, "Him that cometh to me I will in no wise cast out" (John 6:37).

When we have such a promise as this, let us cling to it and never give it up. Christ is not mocking us. He wants us to come with all our sins and backsliding and throw ourselves upon His bosom. It is our sins God wants, not our tears only. They alone do no good. And we cannot come through resolutions. Action is necessary. How many times at church have we said, "I will turn over a new leaf," but the Monday leaf is worse than the Saturday leaf.

The way to heaven is as straight as a rule, but it is the way of the cross. Don't try to get around it. Shall I tell you what the "yoke" referred to in the text is? It is the cross that Christians must bear. The only way to find rest in this dark world is by taking up the yoke of Christ. I do not know what it may include in your case, beyond taking up our Christian duties, acknowledging Christ, and acting as becomes one of His disciples. Perhaps it may be to erect a family altar; or to tell a godless husband that you have made up your mind to serve God; or to tell your parents that you want to be a Christian. Follow the will of God, and happiness and peace and rest will come. The way of obedience is always the way of blessing.

I was preaching in Chicago to a hall full of women one Sunday afternoon, and after the meeting was over a lady came to me and said she wanted to talk to me. She said she would accept Christ and after some conversation she went home. I looked for her for a whole week but didn't see her until the following Sunday afternoon. She came and sat down right in front of me, and her face had such a sad expression. She seemed to have entered into the misery, instead of the joy, of the Lord.

After the meeting was over I went to her and asked her what the trouble was. She said, "Oh, Mr. Moody, this has been the most miserable week of my life." I asked her if there was anyone with whom she had trouble and whom she could not forgive. She said, "No, not that I know of."

"Well, did you tell your friends about having found the Savior?"

"Indeed I didn't. I have been all the week trying to keep it from them."

"Well, that is the reason why you have no peace," I said.

She wanted to take the crown but did not want the cross. My friends, you must go by the way of Calvary. If you ever get rest, you must get it at the foot of the cross.

"Why," she said, "if I should go home and tell my infidel husband that I had found Christ, I don't know what he would do. I think he would turn me out."

"Well, go out," I said.

She went away, promising that she would tell him, timid and pale, but she did not want another wretched week. She was bound to have peace. The next night I gave a lecture to men only, and in the hall there were eight thousand men and one solitary woman. When I got through and went into the inquiry meeting, I found this lady with her husband. She introduced him to me (he was a doctor and a very influential man) and he said, "I want to become a Christian."

I took my Bible and told him all about Christ and he accepted Him. I said to his wife after it was all over, "It turned out quite differently from what you expected, didn't it?"

"Yes," she replied, "I was never so scared in my life. I expected he would do something dreadful, but it has turned out so well." She took God's way and got rest.

I want to say to young ladies, perhaps you have a godless father or mother, a skeptical brother, who is going down through drink, and perhaps there is no one who can reach them but you. How many times a godly, pure young lady has taken the light into some darkened home! Many a home might be lit up with the gospel if the mothers and daughters would only speak the word.

The last time Mr. Sankey and I were in Edinburgh, there were a father, two sisters, and a brother, who used every morning to take the morning paper and pick my sermon to pieces. They were indignant to think that the Edinburgh people should be carried away with such preaching. One day one of the sisters was going by the hall, and she thought she would drop in and see what class of people went there. She happened to take a seat by a godly lady, who said to her, "I hope you are interested in this work."

She tossed her head and said, "Indeed I am not. I am disgusted with everything I have seen and heard."

"Well, perhaps you came prejudiced," said the lady.

"Yes, and the meeting has not removed any of it, but has rather increased it."

"I have received a great deal of good from them."

"There is nothing here for me. I don't see how an intellectual person can be interested."

To make a long story short, when the meeting broke up, just a little of the prejudice had worn away. She promised to come back again the next day, and then she attended three or four more meetings and became quite interested. She said nothing to her family until finally the burden became too heavy, and she told them. They laughed at her and made her the butt of their ridicule.

One day the two sisters were together, and the other said, "Now what did you get at those meetings that you didn't have in the first place?"

"I have a peace that I never knew before. I am at peace with God, myself, and all the world."

Did you ever have a little war of your own with your neighbors, in your own family? And she said, "I have self-control. You know, sister, if you had said half of the mean things before I was converted that you have said since, I would have been angry and answered back, but if you remember correctly, I haven't answered once since I have been converted."

The sister said, "You certainly have something that I have not." The other told her it was for her too, and she brought the sister to the meetings, where she found peace.

Like Martha and Mary they had a brother, but he was a member of the University of Edinburgh. He thought, "Me be converted? Me go to these meetings?" It might do for women, but not for him. One night they came home and told him that a friend of his, a member of the University, had stood up and confessed Christ, and when he sat down his brother got up and confessed; and so it was with the third one.

When the young man heard it, he said, "Do you mean to tell me that he has been converted?"

"Yes."

"Well, there must be something to it," he said. He put on his hat and coat and went to see his friend, Black. Black got him down to the meetings, and he was converted.

We went through to Glasgow and had not been there six weeks when news came that the young man had been stricken down and died. When he was dying he called his father to his bedside and said, "Wasn't it a good thing that my sisters went to those meetings? Won't you meet me in heaven, Father?"

"Yes, my son, I am so glad you are a Christian. That is the only comfort that I have in losing you. I will become a Christian and will meet you again."

I tell this to encourage some sister to go home and carry the message of salvation. It may be that your brother may be taken away in a few months. My dear friends, are we not living in solemn days? Isn't it time for us to get our friends into the kingdom of God? Come, wife, won't you tell your husband? Come, sister, won't you tell your brother? Won't you take up your cross now? The blessing of God will rest on your soul if you will.

Once I was in Wales, and a lady told me this little story. An English friend of hers, a mother, had a child that was sick. At first they considered there was no danger, until one day the doctor came in and said that the symptoms were very unfavorable.

He took the mother out of the room and told her that the child could not live. It came to her like a thunderbolt. After the doctor had gone the mother went into the room where the child lay and began to talk to the child and tried to divert its mind.

"Darling, do you know you will soon hear the music of heaven? You will hear a sweeter song than you have ever heard on earth. You will hear them sing the song of Moses and the Lamb. You are very fond of music. Won't it be sweet, darling?"

And the little tired, sick child turned its head away, and said, "Oh, Mama, I am so tired and so sick that I think it would make me worse to hear all that music."

"Well, you will soon see Jesus," said the mother. "You will see the seraphim and cherubim and the streets all paved with gold." And she went on picturing heaven as it is described in Revelation.

The little tired child again turned its head away, and said, "Oh, Mama, I am so tired that I think it would make me worse to see all those beautiful things!"

At last the mother took the child up in her arms, and pressed her to her loving heart. And the little sick one whispered, "Oh, Mama, that is what I want. If Jesus will only take me in His arms and let me rest!"

Dear friend, are you not tired and weary of sin? Are you not weary of the turmoil of life? You can find rest in the bosom of the Son of God.

THE SEVEN "I WILL'S" OF CHRIST

THE SEVEN "I WILL'S" OF CHRIST

When a man says, "I will," it may not mean much. We
very often say, "I will," even when we don't intend
to fulfill what we say. But when we come to the "I will" of
Christ, He means to fulfill it. Everything He promised to
do, He is able and willing to accomplish. I cannot find any
Scripture where He says, "I will" do this or "I will" do that,
and it does not come to pass.

1. THE "I WILL" OF SALVATION

"Him that cometh to me I will in no wise cast out"
(John 6:37).

I imagine someone will say, "If I were what I know I
ought to be, I would come. But when I think about my past
record, it is too dark. I am not fit to come."

You must bear in mind that Jesus Christ came to save
not good people, not the upright and just, but sinners like
you and me who have gone astray—those who have sinned
and come short of the glory of God.

Listen to this "I will," it goes right into the heart: "Him
that cometh to me I will in no wise cast out." Surely that is

broad enough, is it not? I don't care who the man or woman is nor what his or her trials, troubles, sorrows or sins are. If that one will only come straight to the Master, He will not cast him out.

Come then, poor sinner; come just as you are and take Him at His word.

So anxious is He to save sinners that He will take everyone who comes. He will take those who are so full of sin that all who know them despise them. He accepts those who have been rejected by their fathers and mothers, and who have been cast off by the wives of their bosoms. He will take those who have sunk so low that upon them no eye of pity is cast. His occupation is to hear and save. That is why He left Heaven and came into the world. That is why He left the throne of God—to save sinners. "The Son of man is come to seek and to save that which was lost" (Luke 19:10). He did not come to condemn the world, but that the world through Him might be saved.

A wild and prodigal young man running a career headlong to ruin came into one of our meetings in Chicago. The Spirit of God got hold of him. While I was conversing with him and endeavoring to bring him to Christ, I quoted Luke 19:10. Then I asked him, "Do you believe Christ said that?"

"I suppose He did."

"Suppose He did? Do you believe it?"

"I hope so."

"Hope so? Do you believe it? You do your work, and the Lord will do His. Just come as you are. Throw yourself upon His bosom, and He will not cast you out."

This man thought it was too simple and easy. At last, light seemed to break in upon him, and he seemed to find comfort from it. It was past midnight before he got down on his knees, but down he went and was converted.

I warned him though, "Now, don't think you are going to get out of the Devil's territory without trouble. The Devil will come to you tomorrow morning and say it was all feeling, that you only imagined you were accepted by God. When he does, don't fight him with your own opinions, but fight him with John 6:37: 'Him that cometh to me I will in no wise cast out.' Let that be the 'sword of the Spirit.'"

I don't believe any man ever starts to go to Christ without the Devil striving somehow to trip him up. Even after he has come to Christ, the Devil tries to assail him with doubts and make him believe there is something wrong in it.

The struggle came sooner than I thought in this man's case. While he was on his way home, the Devil assailed him. He used John 6:37, but the Devil put this thought into his mind: "How do you know Christ ever said that after all? Perhaps the translators made a mistake."

Into darkness he went again till about two in the morning. At last he came to this conclusion: "I will believe it anyway; and when I get to Heaven, if it isn't true, I will just tell the Lord I did not make the mistake—the translators did."

When kings and princes of this world issue invitations, they call round them the rich, the mighty, the powerful, the honorable and the wise; but the Lord, when He was on earth, called to Himself the vilest of the vile. That was the principal fault the people found with Him. Those self-righteous Pharisees were not going to associate with harlots and publicans. The principal charge against Christ was: "This man receiveth sinners, and eateth with them."

Who would have such a man around him as John Bunyan in his time? He, a Bedford tinker, couldn't get inside one of the princely castles.

I was very much amused when I was over in England. They had erected a monument to John Bunyan, and lords and dukes and great men unveiled it. While he was on earth, they would not have allowed him inside the walls of their castles, yet he was made one of the mightiest instruments in the spread of the Gospel.

No book that has ever been written comes so near to the Bible as John Bunyan's *Pilgrim's Progress*; and yet the author was a poor Bedford tinker.

Thus it is with God. He picks up some poor lost tramp and makes him an instrument to turn hundreds and thousands to Christ.

George Whitefield, standing in his tabernacle in London and with a multitude gathered about him, cried out, "The Lord Jesus will save the Devil's castaways!"

Two poor, abandoned wretches standing outside in the street heard his silvery voice ring out on the air. Looking into each other's faces, they said, "That must mean you and me." They wept and rejoiced. They drew near and looked in at the door at the face of the earnest messenger, the tears streaming from his eyes as he pled with the people to give their hearts to God. One of them wrote him a little note and sent it to him.

Later that day, as he sat at the table of Lady Huntington, his special friend, someone present said, "Mr. Whitefield, did you not go a little too far today when you said that the Lord would save the Devil's castaways?"

Taking the note from his pocket, he gave it to Lady Huntington. "Will you read that note aloud?"

She read: "Mr. Whitefield: Two poor lost women stood outside your tabernacle today and heard you say that the Lord would save the Devil's castaways. We seized upon that as our last hope. Now we write to tell you that we rejoice now in believing in Him, and from this good hour we shall endeavor to serve Him who has done so much for us."

2. THE "I WILL" OF CLEANSING

The next "I will" is found in Luke, chapter 5. We read of a leper who came to Christ and said, *"Lord, if thou wilt, thou canst make me clean."* The Lord touched him, saying, "I will; be thou clean," and immediately the leprosy left him.

Any man or woman full of the leprosy of sin who reads this, if you would only go to the Master and tell all your case to Him, He will speak to you as He did to that poor leper: "I will; be thou clean," and the leprosy of your sins will flee from you.

The Lord and the Lord alone can forgive sins. If you say to Him, "Lord, I am full of sin; Thou canst make me clean"; "Lord, I have a terrible temper; Thou canst make me clean"; "Lord, I have a deceitful heart. Cleanse me, O Lord; give me a new heart. O Lord, give me the power to overcome the flesh and the snares of the Devil!" "Lord, I am full of unclean habits"—if you come to Him with a sincere spirit, you will hear the voice, "I will; be thou clean." It will be done.

The God who created the world out of nothing, who by a breath put life into the world—do you think if He says, "Be thou clean," you will not be clean?

Now, you can make a wonderful exchange today. You can have spiritual health in the place of sin-sickness; you can get rid of everything that is vile and hateful in the sight of God. The Son of God comes down and says, "I will take away your leprosy and give you health in its stead. I will take away that terrible sin disease that is ruining your body and soul and give you My righteousness instead. I will clothe you with the garments of salvation."

Isn't it wonderful? That's what He means when He says, "I will." Oh, lay hold on this "I will!"

3. THE "I WILL" OF CONFESSION

"Whosoever therefore shall confess me before men, him will I confess also before my Father which is in heaven"
(Matthew 10:32).

Confession is the next thing that takes place after a man is saved. When we have been washed in the blood of the Lamb, our mouths are opened. We have to confess Christ here in this dark world and tell of His love to others. We are not to be ashamed of the Son of God.

A man thinks it a great honor when he has achieved a victory that causes his name to be mentioned in the English Parliament or in the presence of the queen and her court.

How excited we used to be during the war when some general did something extraordinary and someone got up in Congress to confess his exploits! How the papers used to talk about it!

In China the highest ambition of the successful soldier is to have his name written in the palace or temple of Confucius.

But just think of having your name mentioned in the kingdom of Heaven by the Prince of Glory, by the Son of God, because you confessed Him here on earth! Confess Him here and He will confess you yonder.

If you wish to be brought into the clear light of liberty, you must take your stand on Christ's side. Many Christians go groping about in darkness and never get into the clear light of the kingdom because they are ashamed to confess the Son of God. We are living in a day when men want a religion without the cross, the crown but not the cross. But if we are to be disciples of Jesus Christ, we have to take up our crosses daily—not once a year or on the Lord's Day, but daily. And if we take up our crosses and follow Him, we shall be blessed in the very act.

A newly converted man in New York came to pray with me. His burden was that he was afraid to confess Christ. It seemed that down at the bottom of his trunk he had a Bible. He wanted to get it out and read it to the companion with whom he lived, but he was ashamed to do it.

After he had carried the burden for a whole week and after a terrible struggle, he made up his mind, "I will take my Bible out tonight and read it." He did. Soon he heard the footsteps of his roommate coming upstairs. His first impulse was to put the Bible away, but then he decided he would face his companion with it in hand.

His roommate came in. Seeing John at his Bible, he said, "Are you interested in these things?"

"Yes," John replied.

"How long has this been?" asked his companion.

"Exactly a week," he answered. "For a whole week I have tried to get out my Bible to read to you, but I have not done so till now."

"Well," said his friend, "it is a strange thing. I was converted on the same night, and I too was ashamed to take my Bible out."

You are ashamed to show your Bible and say, "I have lived a godless life for all these years, but I will commence now to live a life of righteousness." You are ashamed to open your Bible and read that blessed Psalm, "The Lord is my shepherd; I shall not want." You are ashamed to be seen on your knees.

No man can be a disciple of Jesus Christ without bearing his cross. A great many want to know how it is Christ has so few disciples while Muhammad has so many. The reason is Muhammad gives no cross to bear.

There are so few who will come out to take their stand.

I was struck during the Civil War with the fact that there were so many who could go to the cannon's mouth without trembling but who had no courage to take up their Bibles to read them at night. They were ashamed of the Gospel of Jesus Christ, which is the power of God unto salvation.

"Whosoever therefore shall confess me before men, him will I confess also before my Father which is in heaven. But whosoever shall deny me before men, him will I also deny before my Father which is in heaven" (Matt. 10:32,33).

4. THE "I WILL" OF SERVICE

There are a good many Christians who have been quickened and aroused to say, "I want to do some service for Christ." Well, Christ says, "Follow me, and I will make you fishers of men."

There is no Christian who cannot help to bring someone to the Savior. Christ says, "And I, if I be lifted up... will draw all men unto me"; and our business is just to lift up Christ.

Our Lord said, "Follow me, Peter, and I will make you a fisher of men"; and Peter simply obeyed. On that day of Pentecost we see the result. I doubt if Peter ever caught so many fish in one day as he did men on that day. It would have broken every net they had on board if they had had to drag up three thousand fish.

I read some time ago of a man who took passage in a stagecoach. There were first-, second- and third-class passengers. But when he looked into the coach, he saw all the passengers sitting together without distinction. He could not understand it.

By and by they came to a hill. The coach stopped. The driver called out, "First-class passengers keep their seats. Second-class passengers get out and walk. Third-class passengers get behind and push."

In the church we have no room for first-class passengers— people who think salvation means an easy ride all the way to Heaven. We have no room for second-class passengers— people who are carried most of the time, and who, when they should be showing their faith by their works, go trudging on never giving a thought to helping their fellows along. All church members ought to be third-class passengers—ready to dismount and push as needed.

John Wesley's definition of a church: "All at it and always at it." Every Christian is to be a worker. He need not be a preacher or an evangelist to be useful. He may be useful in business. See what power an employer has with his employees! Often a man can be as useful in one business sphere as in another.

There is one reason—and a great reason—why so many do not succeed at Christian service. I have been asked by a great many good men, "Why is it we don't have any results? We work hard, pray hard, and preach hard, yet the success does not come."

I tell them, "Because you spend all your time mending nets. No wonder you never catch anything."

The great matter is to give invitations and compel sinners to come and pull the net in and see if you caught anything. If you are always mending and setting the net, you won't catch many fish. Who ever heard of a man's going out to fish and setting his net, then letting it stop there and never pulling it in? Everybody would laugh at such a man's folly.

A minister in England came to me one day and said, "I wish you would tell me why we ministers don't succeed better than we do."

I brought before him this idea of pulling in the net: "You have to pull in your nets. There are many ministers in Manchester who can preach much better than I can, but I pull in the net."

Many people have objections to giving invitations, but I urge upon them the importance of offering people the chance to make a decision. The minister said, "I never did pull in my net; but I will try next Sunday." He did so, and eight anxious inquirers went into his study.

The next Sunday he came down to tell me he had never had such a Sunday in his life. He had met with marvelous blessing. The next time he drew in the net, there were forty! And when he came to see me later, he said to me joyfully, "Moody, I have had eight hundred conversions this last year! It is a great mistake I did not begin earlier to pull in the net."

My friends, if you want to catch men, just present the Gospel and pull in the net. If you only catch one, it will be something. It may be a little child, but I have known a little child to convert a whole family. You don't know what is in that little dull-headed boy in the inquiry room. He may become a Martin Luther, a reformer who shall make the world tremble.

God uses the weak things of this world to confound the mighty. God's promise is as good as a bank note. And here is one of Christ's promissory notes: "If you follow Me, I will make you fishers of men."

Will you not lay hold of the promise and trust it and follow Him now?

If a man preaches the Gospel faithfully, he ought to expect results then and there. It is the privilege of God's children to reap the fruit of their labor three hundred sixty-five days in the year.

"Well, but is there not a sowing time as well as a harvest?" you ask. Yes, there is; but then, you can sow with one hand and reap with the other. What would you think of a farmer who went on sowing all the year round and never thought of reaping? I repeat: we want to sow with one hand and reap with the other. And if we look for the fruit of our labors, we shall see it.

"I, if I be lifted up ... will draw all men unto me." We must lift Christ up, then seek men out and bring them to Him.

You must use the right kind of bait. A good many don't do this, then they wonder why they are not successful. You

180

see them using all kinds of entertainment with which to try to catch men. They go the wrong way to work.

This perishing world wants Christ and Him crucified. There's a void in every man's bosom that wants filling up, and if we only approach him with the right kind of bait, we shall catch him.

This poor world needs a Savior; and if we are going to be successful in catching men, we must preach Christ crucified—not His life only, but His death. And if we are only faithful in doing this, we shall succeed. Why? Because there is His promise: "If you follow Me, I will make you fishers of men."

That promise holds just as good to you and me as it did to His disciples and is as true now as it was in their time.

5. THE "I WILL" OF COMFORT

"I will not leave you comfortless" (John 14:18).

It is a sweet thought that Christ has not left us alone in this dark wilderness here below. Although He has gone up on high and taken His seat by the Father's throne, He has not left us comfortless.

In other words, He said, "I will not leave you orphans." He did not leave Joseph. When they cast him into prison, "God was with him." When Daniel was cast into the den of lions, they had to put the Almighty in with him. They were so bound together that they could not be separated.

181

If we have Christ with us, we can do all things. Let us not be thinking how weak we are. Let us lift up our eyes to Him and think of Him as our Elder Brother who has all power given to Him in Heaven and on earth. He says, "Lo, I am with you alway, even unto the end of the world."

Some of our children and friends leave us, and it is a very sad hour. But the believer and Christ shall never be separated! He is with us here, and we shall be with Him in person by and by. We shall see Him in His beauty. But not only is He with us, but He has sent us the Holy Ghost. Let us honor the Holy Spirit by acknowledging that He is here in our midst. He has power to give sight to the blind, liberty to the captive, and to open the ears of the deaf that they may hear the glorious words of the Gospel.

6. THE "I WILL" OF RESURRECTION

"I will raise him up at the last day" (John 6:40).

I rejoice to think that I have a Savior who has power over death. My blessed Master holds the keys of Death and Hell. I pity the poor unbeliever and infidel who do not have hope in the resurrection. But every child of God can open that chapter and read the promise, and his heart leaps within him for joy.

The tradesman generally puts the best specimens of his wares in the window to show us the quality of his stock. When Christ was down here, He gave us a specimen of what He could do. He raised three from the dead, that we might know what power He had—(1) Jairus' daughter, (2) the widow's son, and (3) Lazarus of Bethany. He raised all three so every doubt might be swept away from our hearts.

How dark and gloomy this world would be if we had no hope in the resurrection. But when we Christians lay our little children down in the grave, it is not without hope. We have seen them in the terrible struggle with death; but there has been one star to illumine the darkness and gloom–the thought that though the happy circle has been broken on earth, it shall be completed again in the next world of heavenly light.

If you have lost a loved one, rejoice as you read this "I will!" Those who have died in Christ shall come forth again by and by. The darkness shall flee away, and the morning light of the resurrection shall dawn upon us. It is only a little while, and the voice of Him who has said it shall come, shall be heard in the grave—"I will raise him up at the last day."

Precious promise! Precious "I will!"

I had an unsaved brother for whom I was very anxious. For fourteen long years I tried to lead that brother to "the Lamb of God, which taketh away the sin of the world." He was the Benjamin of the family, born a few weeks after my father's death. When he was seventeen, he had a long run of typhoid fever, and he never fully recovered from it.

I did everything I could to bring him to Christ. He was a young man of considerable promise. I know no one who could sit down and discuss against the divinity of Christ like that man. I was not any match for him in argument. But day-by-day I preached to him as best I knew how.

I think I never loved a man on earth as I loved that brother. (I never knew what it was to love a father, because he died before I remember.) Because he was sickly, that drew my love and sympathy toward him; and oh, how my heart yearned for his salvation!

After preaching one night, I said, "Now if any of this audience would like to take up his cross and follow Christ, I would like him to rise." I cannot tell you what a thrill of joy filled my soul when that brother of mine arose! It seemed the happiest night of my life. I was full of joy and thankfulness.

Afterwards my brother and I worked together for a time. We talked of the Gospel. And in the summer we sat upon the hillside and talked of the old home.

After a year had passed, I went to Chicago. He was to go with me. He bid me good-bye, and I said, "Samuel, I will see you in a few days, so I will only say good-bye till then."

A few days after, a telegram came, saying, "Samuel is dead." I traveled a thousand miles to bury him. I got more comfort out of that promise, "I will raise him up at the last day," than anything else in the Bible. How it cheered me! How it lighted up my path! As I went into the room and looked upon the lovely face of that brother, how that passage ran through my soul: "Thy brother shall rise again." Thank God for that promise! It is worth more than the world to me.

When we laid him in the grave, it seemed as if I could hear the voice of Jesus Christ saying, "Thy brother shall rise again." Blessed promise of the resurrection! Blessed "I will!" "I will raise him up at the last day."

7. THE "I WILL" OF GLORY

Father, I will that they also, whom thou hast given me, be with me where I am" (John 17:24).

This was in His last prayer in the guest chamber on the last night before He was crucified on Calvary. Many a believer's countenance begins to light up at the thought that he shall one day see the King in His beauty.

Yes, there is a glorious day before us in the future. Some think that on the first day we are converted we have everything. To be sure, we get salvation for the past and peace for the present, but there is the glory for the future in store. That's what kept Paul rejoicing. He said, 'These light afflictions, these few stripes, these few brickbats and stones that they throw at me—why, the glory that is beyond excels them so much that I count them as nothing, nothing at all, so that I may win Christ.

And so, when things go against us, cheer up! Remember that the night will soon pass away, and the morning will dawn upon us. Death never comes there. It is banished from that heavenly land. Sickness, pain and sorrow come not there to mar that grand and glorious Home where we shall be by and by with the Master. God's family will be all together there.

Glorious future, my friends! Yes, glorious day! And it may be a great deal nearer than many of us think. During these few days we are here, let us stand steadfast and firm, and by and by we shall be in the unbroken circle in yon world of light and have the King in our midst.

THE WAY TO GOD
AND HOW TO FIND IT

THE WAY TO GOD
AND HOW TO FIND IT

TO THE READER

In this small volume I have endeavored to show men the *Way to God*. I have embodied in this little book a considerable portion of several addresses that have been delivered in different cities, both in Great Britain and my own country. God has graciously owned them when spoken from the pulpit, and I trust will nonetheless add his blessing now they have been put into the printed page.

I have called attention first to the Love of God, the source of all Gifts of Grace. I have then endeavored to present truths to meet the special needs of representative classes, answering the question, "How can man be just with God?" and to lead souls to Him who is "the Way, the Truth, and the Life" (John 14:6).

The last chapter is specially addressed to backsliders—a class far too numerous among us. "I will love them freely: for Mine anger is turned away" (Hosea 14:4).

With the earnest prayer and hope that by the blessing of God on these pages the reader may be strengthened, established, and settled in the faith of Jesus Christ,

I am, yours in His service,

D. L. Moody

Chapter 1

"LOVE THAT PASSETH KNOWLEDGE"

"And to know the love of Christ, which passeth knowledge"—Ephesians 3:19.

If I could only make men understand the real meaning of the words of the apostle John—*"God is Love"* (1 John 4:8), I would take that single text, and would go up and down the world proclaiming this glorious truth. If you can convince a man that you love him you have won his heart. If we could really make people believe that God loves them, how we should find them crowding into the kingdom of heaven! The trouble is that men think God hates them; and so they are all the time running away from Him.

We built a church in Chicago some years ago, and we were very anxious to teach the people the love of God. We thought if we could not preach it into their hearts we would try and burn it in, so we put right over the pulpit in gas jets these words—God Is Love. A man going along the streets one night glanced through the door, and saw the text. He was a poor prodigal. As he passed on he thought to himself, "'God is Love!' No! He does not love me, for I am a poor miserable sinner." He tried to get rid of the text, but it seemed to stand out right before him in letters of fire. He went on a little further; then turned round, went back, and went into the meeting. He did not hear the sermon, but the words of that short text had got deeply lodged in his heart, and that was enough. It is of little account what men say if the Word of God only gets an entrance into the sinner's heart. He stayed after the first meeting was over and I found him there weeping like a child. As I unfolded the Scriptures and told him how God had loved him all the time, although he had wandered so far a way, and how God was waiting to receive him and forgive him, the light of the Gospel broke into his mind, and he went away rejoicing.

There is nothing in this world that men prize so much as they do love. Show me a person who has no one to care for or love him, and I will show you one of the most wretched beings on the face of the earth. Why do people commit suicide? Very often it is because this thought steals in upon them—that no one loves them; and they would rather die than live.

I know of no truth in the whole Bible that ought to come home to us with such power and tenderness as that of the Love of God; and there is no truth in the Bible that Satan would so much like to blot out. For more than six thousand years he has been trying to persuade men that God does not love them. He succeeded in making our first parents believe this lie, and he too often succeeds with their children.

The idea that God does not love us often comes from false teaching. Mothers make a mistake in teaching children that God does not love them when they do wrong, but only when they do right. This is not taught in Scripture. You never teach your child that you hate them when they do wrong. Their wrongdoing does not change your love for them to hate. God forbid! If your child has committed some act of disobedience, you do not cast him out as though he did not belong to you! No, he is still your child, and you love him. And if believers have gone astray from God it does not mean that He hates them. It is the sin that He hates.

I believe the reason why a great many people think God does not love them is because they are measuring God by their limited understanding. We love people as long as we consider them worthy of our love. When we believe they are not, we cast them off. But it is not so with God. "He loves us with an everlasting love."

The Power of God's Love

In Ephesians 3:18, we are told of "the breadth, and length, and depth, and height," of God's love. Many of us think we know something of God's love, but centuries hence we shall admit we have never found out much about it. Columbus discovered America, but what did he know about its great lakes, rivers, forests, and the Mississippi valley? He died, without knowing much about what he had discovered. So many of us have discovered something of God's love; but there are heights, depths, and lengths of it we do not know. His love is like a great ocean, and we must plunge into it before we can really understand and experience it.

When we wish to know the love of God we should go to Calvary. Can we look upon that scene, and say God did not love us? That cross speaks of the love of God. Greater love never has been taught than that which the cross teaches. What prompted God to give up Christ? What prompted Christ to die? Was it not love?

"Greater love hath no man than this, that a man lay down his life for his friends" (John 15:13).

Christ laid down His life for His enemies. Christ laid down His life for His murderers. Christ laid down His life for them that hated Him; and the spirit of the cross, the spirit of Calvary, is love. When they were mocking Him and deriding Him, what did he say? "Father, forgive them; for they know not what they do" (Luke 23:34).

That is love. He did not call down fire from heaven to consume them. There was nothing but love in His heart.

The Unchangeable Love of God

If you study the Bible you will find that the love of God is *unchangeable*. Many who loved you at one time have perhaps grown cold in their affection, and turned away from you. It may be that their love is changed to hatred. It is not so with God. It is recorded of Jesus Christ, just when He was about to be parted from His disciples and led away from Calvary, that, "having loved His own which were in the world, He loved them unto the end" (John 13:1).

He knew that one of His disciples would betray Him, yet He loved Judas. He knew that another disciple would deny Him, and swear that he never knew Him, and yet He loved Peter. It was the love that Christ had for Peter that broke his heart, and brought him back in penance to the feet of his Lord. For three years Jesus had been with the disciples trying to teach them His love, not only by His life and words, but also by His works. And, on the night of His betrayal, He takes a basin of water, girds Himself with a towel, and taking the place of a servant, washes their feet: He wanted to convince them of His unchanging love.

There is no portion of Scripture I read so often as John 14. And there is none that is sweeter to me. I never tire of reading it. Hear what our Lord says, as He pours out His heart to His disciples:

> "At that day ye shall know that I am in My Father, and ye in Me, and I in you. He that hath My commandments, and keepeth them, he it is that loveth Me: and **he that loveth Me shall be loved of My Father**" (John 14:20,21).

Think of the great God who created heaven and earth loving you and me ...

> "If a man love Me, he will keep My words: and My Father will love him; and We will come unto him, and make Our abode with him" (John 14:23).

Would to God that our puny minds could grasp this great truth that the Father and the Son so love us that they desire to come and abide with us. Not to tarry for a night, but to come and abide in our hearts. We have another passage more wonderful still in John 17:23:

> "I in them, and Thou in Me, that they may be made perfect in one; and that the world may know that Thou hast sent Me, **and hast loved them, as Thou hast loved Me.**"

I think that is one of the most remarkable sayings that ever fell from the lips of Jesus Christ. There was no reason why the Father should not love Him. He was obedient unto death. He never transgressed the Father's law, or turned aside from the path of perfect obedience by one hair's breadth. It is very different with us; and yet, notwithstanding all our rebellion and foolishness, He says that if we are trusting in Christ, the Father loves us as He loves the Son. Marvelous love! Wonderful love! That God can possibly love us as He loves His own Son seems too good to be true. Yet that is the teaching of Jesus Christ.

It is hard to make a sinner believe in this unchangeable love of God. When a man has wandered away from God he thinks that God hates him. We must make a distinction between sin and the sinner. God loves the sinner, but He hates the sin. He hates sin because it mars human life. It is just because God loves the sinner that He hates sin.

The Unfailing Love of God

God's love is not only unchangeable, but it is *unfailing.* In Isaiah 49:15,16 we read: "Can a woman forget her sucking child, that she should not have compassion on the son of her womb? Yea, they may forget; yet will I not forget thee. Behold, I have graven thee upon the palms of my hands; thy walls are continually before me."

Now the strongest human love that we know of is a *mother's love.* Many things will separate a man from his wife. A father may turn his back on his child; brothers and sisters may become inveterate enemies; husbands may desert their wives; wives, their husbands. But a mother's love endures through all. In good repute, in bad repute, in the face of the world's condemnation, a mother loves on, and hopes that her child may turn from his evil ways and repent. She remembers the infant smiles, the merry laugh of childhood, and the promise of youth. Death cannot quench a mother's love; it is stronger than death.

You have seen a mother watching over her sick child. How willingly she would take the disease into her own body if she could thus relieve her child! Week after week she will keep watch and she will let no one else take care of that sick child.

A friend of mine, some time ago, was visiting in a beautiful home where he met a number of friends. After everyone had all gone home, he realized he had left something behind, so he went back to get it. There he found the lady of the house, a wealthy lady, sitting behind a poor fellow who looked like a tramp. *He was her son.* Like the prodigal, he had wandered far away—yet the mother said, "This is my boy; I love him still." Take a mother with nine or ten children; if one goes astray, she seems to love that one more than any of the rest.

A Mother's Love

A leading minister in the state of New York once shared with me the story of a father who was a very bad character. The mother did all she could to prevent the contamination of her boy, but the influence of the father was strong. He led his son into all kinds of sin until the lad became one of the worst criminals. He committed murder and was put on trial. All through the trial the widowed mother (for the father had since died) sat in the court. When the witnesses testified against the boy it seemed to hurt the mother much more than the son. When he was found guilty and sentenced to die, everyone else feeling the justice of the verdict, seemed satisfied at the result. But the mother's love never faltered. She begged for a reprieve, but it was denied. After the execution she begged for his body, but that too was refused. He was buried in the prison yard. A little while afterwards the mother herself died. Before she left this world she expressed a desire to be buried by the side of her son, which was granted. A mother's love is so strong that she was not ashamed of being buried next to a murderer.

The story is told of a young woman in Scotland who left her home and became an outcast in Glasgow. Her mother sought her far and wide, but in vain. At last, she caused her picture to be hung upon the walls of the Midnight Mission rooms, where abandoned women resorted. Many gave the picture a passing glance. One lingered by the picture. It is the same dear face that looked down upon her in her childhood. She has not forgotten her, nor cast off her sinning child; or her picture would never have been hung upon those walls. The lips seemed to open, and whisper, "Come home: I forgive you, and love you still." The poor girl sank down overwhelmed with her feelings. She was the prodigal daughter. The sight of her mother's face had broken her heart. She became truly penitent for her sins, and with a heart full of sorrow and shame, returned to her forsaken home; and mother and daughter were once more united.

The Love of God Surpasses Even a Mother's Love

But let me tell you that no mother's love is to be compared with the love of God; it does not measure the height or the depth of God's love. No mother in this world ever loved her child as God loves you and me. Think of the love that God must have had when He gave His Son to die for the world. I used to think a good deal more of Christ than I did of the Father. Somehow or other I had the idea that God was a stern judge; that Christ came between God and me, and appeased the anger of God. But after I became a father, and for years had an only son, as I looked at my boy I thought of the Father giving His Son to die; and it seemed to me as if it required more love for the Father to give His Son, than for the Son to die. Oh, the love that God must have had for the world when He gave His Son to die for it!

> *"God so loved the world, that he gave his only-begotten Son, that whosoever believes in him should not perish, but have everlasting life"* (John 3:16).

I have never been able to preach from that text. I have often thought I would, but it is so high that I can never climb to its height. I have just quoted it and passed on. Who can fathom the depth of those words, *"God so* loved the world?"* We can never scale the heights of His love or fathom its depths. Paul prayed that he might know the height, the depth, the length, and the breadth, of the love of God; but it was past his finding out. It *"passeth knowledge"* (Ephesians 3:19).

The Love of God shown at the Cross of Christ

Nothing speaks to us of the love of God, like the Cross of Christ. Come with me to Calvary, and look upon the Son of God as He hangs there. Can you hear that piercing cry from His dying lips: "Father, forgive them; for they know not what they do!" (Luke 23:34) and say that He does not love you?

> *"Greater love hath no man than this, that; a man lay down his life for his friends"* (John 15:13).

Jesus Christ laid down His life *for His enemies.*

Another thought is this: He loved us long before we ever thought of Him. The idea that He does not love us until we first love Him is not to be found in Scripture. In 1 John 4:10 it is written:

> *"Herein is love, not that we loved God, but that He loved us, and sent His Son to be the propitiation for our sins."*

He loved us before we ever thought of loving Him. You loved your children before they knew anything about your love. And so, long before we ever thought of God, we were in His thoughts.

What brought the prodigal home? It was the thought that his father loved him. Suppose the news had reached him that he was cast off, and that his father did not care for him any more, would he have gone back? Never! But the thought dawned upon him that his father loved him still: so he rose up, and went back to his home. Dear reader, the love of the Father ought to bring us back to Him. It was Adam's calamity and sin that revealed God's love. When Adam fell God came down and dealt in mercy with him. If anyone is lost it will not be because God does not love him, it will be because he has resisted the love of God.

The Beauty of Heaven

Is it the pearly gates or the golden streets? No. Heaven will be attractive, because there we shall behold Him who loved us so much as to give His only begotten Son to die for us. What makes home attractive? Is it the beautiful furniture and stately rooms? No; some homes with all these are like white sepulchres.

In Brooklyn a mother was dying and it was necessary to take her child from her, because the little child could not understand the nature of the sickness and disturbed her mother. Every night the child sobbed herself to sleep in a neighbor's house, because she wanted to go back to her mother. But the mother grew worse, and they could not take the child home. At last the mother died, and after her death they thought it best not to let the child see her dead mother in her coffin. After the burial the child ran into one room crying "Mamma! Mamma!" and then into another crying "Mamma! Mamma" and so went over the whole house, and when the little creature failed to find that loved one she cried to be taken back to the neighbors. So what makes heaven attractive is the thought that we shall see Christ who has loved us and given Himself for us.

If you ask me why God should love us, I cannot tell. I suppose it is because He is a true Father. It is His nature to love, just as it is the nature of the sun to shine. He wants you to share in that love. Do not let unbelief keep you away from Him. Do not think that, because you are a sinner, God does not love you, or care for you. He does! He wants to save you and bless you.

> "*When we were yet without strength, in due time Christ died for the ungodly*" (Romans 5:6).

Is that not enough to convince you that He loves you? He would not have died for you if He had not loved you. Is your heart so hard that you can brace yourself up against His love, and spurn and despise it? You *can* do it, but it will be at your peril.

I can imagine some are saying to themselves, "Yes, we believe that God loves us, if we love Him. We believe that God loves the pure and the holy." Let me say, my friends, not only does God love the pure and the holy, He also loves the ungodly.

> "*God commendeth his love toward us, in that, **while we were yet sinners**, Christ died for us*" (Romans 5:8).

God sent Him to die for the sins of the whole world. If you belong to the world, then you have part and lot in this love that has been exhibited in the Cross of Christ.

The Kidnapping of Charlie Ross

There is a passage in Revelation (1:5) that I think a great deal of—"Unto Him that loved us, and washed us."

It might be thought that God would first wash us, and then love us. But no, He first loved us. About eight years ago there was intense excitement in America about Charlie Ross, a child of four years old, who was stolen. Two men in a carriage asked him and an older brother if they wanted some candy. They then drove away with the younger boy, leaving the older one. For many years a search has been made in every state and territory. Men have been over to Great Britain, France, and Germany, and have hunted in vain for the child. The mother still lives in the hope that she will see her long lost Charlie. I never remember the whole country to have been so much agitated about any event except the assassination of President Garfield. Well, suppose the mother of Charlie Ross was in a meeting and that while the preacher was speaking, she happened to look down among the audience and see her long lost son. Suppose that he was poor, dirty and ragged, shoeless and coatless, what would she do? Would she wait till he was washed and decently clothed before she would acknowledge him? No, she would get off the platform at once, rush towards him and take him in her arms. After that she would cleanse and clothe him. So it is with God. He loved us, and washed us. I can imagine one saying, "If God loves me, why does He not make me good?" God wants sons and daughters in heaven. He does not want machines or slaves. He could break our stubborn hearts, but He wants to draw us towards Himself by the cords of love.

He wants you to sit down with Him at the marriage supper of the Lamb, to wash you, and make you whiter than snow. He wants you to walk with Him the crystal pavement of yonder blissful world. He wants to adopt you into His family and to make you a son or a daughter of heaven. Will you trample His love under your feet? Or will you, this hour, give yourself to Him?

A Determined Mother's Touch

When our terrible civil war was going on, a mother received the news that her boy had been wounded in the battle of the Wilderness. She took the first train, and started her journey to reach her boy; although an order had gone forth from the War Department that no more women should be admitted within the lines. But a mother's love knows nothing about orders, and she managed by tears and entreaties to get through the lines to the Wilderness. At last she found the hospital where her boy was. Then she went to the doctor and she said, "Will you let me go to the ward and nurse my boy?" The doctor said, "I have just got your boy to sleep. He is in a very critical state, and I am afraid if you wake him up the excitement will be so great that it will kill him. You had better wait awhile, and remain without until I tell him that you have come and break the news gradually to him." The mother looked into the doctor's face and said, "Doctor, supposing my boy does not wake up, and I should never see him alive! Let me go and sit down by his side; I won't speak to him." "If you will not speak to him you may do so," said the doctor.

She crept to the cot and looked into the face of her boy. How she had longed to look at him! How her eyes seemed to be feasting as she gazed upon his countenance! When she got near enough she could not keep her hands off; she laid that tender, loving hand upon his brow. The moment the hand touched the forehead of her boy, without opening his eyes, he cried out: "Mother, you have come!" He knew the touch of that loving hand. There was love and sympathy in it.

The Tenderness of Jesus

Ah, sinner, if you feel the loving touch of Jesus you will recognize it; it is so full of tenderness. The world may treat you unkindly, but Christ never will. You will never have a better Friend in this world. What you need is to come to Him, today. Let His loving arm be underneath you. Let His loving hand be about you, and He will hold you with mighty power. He will keep you and fill that heart of yours with His tenderness and love.

I can imagine some of you saying, "How shall I go to Him?" Why, just as you would go to your mother. Have you done your mother a great injury and a great wrong? If so, you go to her and you say, "Mother, I want you to forgive me." Treat Christ in the same way. Go to Him today and tell Him that you have not loved Him, that you have not treated Him right. Confess your sins, and see how quickly He will bless you.

A Little Girl Pleads With President Lincoln

I am reminded of another incident—that of a boy who had been tried by court-martial and ordered to be shot. The hearts of the father and mother were broken when they heard the news. In that home was a little girl. She had read the life of Abraham Lincoln, and she said, "Now, if Abraham Lincoln knew how my father and mother loved their boy, he would not let my brother be shot." She wanted her father to go to Washington to plead for his boy. But the father said, "No; there is no use: the law must take its course. They have refused to pardon one or two who have been sentenced by that court-martial, and an order has gone forth that the President is not going to interfere again; if a man has been sentenced by court-martial he must suffer the consequences."

That father and mother had not faith to believe that their boy might be pardoned. But the little girl was strong in hope.

She got on the train away up in Vermont, and started off to Washington. When she reached the White House the soldiers refused to let her in, but she told her pitiful story and they allowed her to pass. When she got to the Secretary's room, where the President's private secretary was, he refused to allow her to enter the private office of the President. But the little girl told her story, and it touched the heart of the private secretary, so he passed her in. As she went into Abraham Lincoln's room, there were United States senators, generals, governors, and leading politicians, who were there about important business about the war; but the President happened to see that child standing at his door. He wanted to know what she wanted, and she went right to him and told her story in her own language. He was a father, and the great tears trickled down Abraham Lincoln's cheeks. He wrote a dispatch and sent it to the army to have that boy sent to Washington at once. When he arrived, the President pardoned him, gave him thirty days furlough, and sent him home with the little girl to cheer the hearts of the father and mother.

Do you want to know how to go to Christ? Go just as that little girl went to Abraham Lincoln. It may be possible that you have a dark story to tell. Tell it all out; keep nothing back. If Abraham Lincoln had compassion on that little girl, heard her petition, and answered it— do you think the Lord Jesus will not hear your prayer? Do you think that Abraham Lincoln, or any man that ever lived on earth, had as much compassion as Christ? No! He will be touched when no one else will. He will have mercy when no one else will. He will have pity when no one else will. If you will go right to Him, confessing your sin and your need, He will save you.

Chapter 2

THE GATEWAY
INTO THE KINGDOM

*"Except a man be born again he cannot enter
the Kingdom of God"*—John 3:3

There is no portion of the Word of God, perhaps, with
which we are more familiar than this passage. I suppose
if I were to ask those in any audience if they believed that
Jesus Christ taught the doctrine of the New Birth, nine-tenths
of them would say, "Yes, I believe He did."

Now if the words of this text are true they embody one of
the most solemn questions that can come before us. We can
afford to be deceived about many things rather than about
this one thing. Christ makes it very plain. He says, "Except a
man be born again, he cannot see the Kingdom of God" much
less inherit it. This doctrine of the New Birth is therefore the
foundation of all our hopes for the world to come. It is really
the "A B C" of the Christian religion. My experience has been
that if a man is unsound on this doctrine he will be unsound
on almost every other fundamental doctrine in the Bible. A
true understanding of this subject will help a man to solve a
thousand difficulties that he may meet with in the Word of
God. Things that before seemed very dark and mysterious
will become very plain.

The doctrine of the New Birth upsets all false religion—all false views about the Bible and about God. A friend of mine once told me that in one of his after-meetings a man came to him with a long list of questions written out for him to answer. He said, "If you can answer these questions satisfactorily, I have made up my mind to become a Christian." "Do you not think," said my friend, "that you had better come to Christ first? Then you can look into these questions." The man thought that perhaps he had better do so. After he had received Christ, he looked again at his list of questions, but it seemed to him as if they had all been answered. Nicodemus came with his troubled mind and Christ said to him, "Ye must be born again." He was treated altogether differently from what he expected, but I venture to say that was the most blessed night in all his life. To be "born again" is the greatest blessing that will ever come to us in this world.

Notice how the Scripture puts it. "Except a man be born again" (John 3:3), "born from above" (John 3:3; marginal reading), "born of the Spirit" (John 3:6). From amongst a number of other passages where we find this word "except" I would just name three:

1. "Except ye repent, ye shall all likewise perish" (Luke 13:3,5).
2. "Except ye be converted, and become as little children, ye shall not enter into the kingdom of heaven" (Matthew 18:3).
3. "Except your righteousness shall exceed the righteousness of the Scribes and Pharisees, ye shall in no case enter into the kingdom of heaven" (Matthew 5:20).

They all really mean the same thing.

I am so thankful that our Lord spoke of the New Birth to this ruler of the Jews, this doctor of the law, rather than to the woman at the well of Samaria, or to Matthew the publican, or to Zaccheus. If he had reserved His teaching on this great matter for these three, or such as these, people would have said: "Oh yes, these publicans and harlots need to be converted: but I am an upright man; I do not need to be converted." I suppose Nicodemus was one of the best specimens of the people of Jerusalem: there was nothing on record against him.

I think it is scarcely necessary for me to prove that we need to be born again before we are meet for heaven. I venture to say that there is no candid man but would say he is not fit for the kingdom of God, until he is born of another Spirit. The Bible teaches us that man is lost and guilty, and our experience confirms this. We know also that the best and holiest man, when he turns away from God, falls into sin.

What Regeneration Is Not

Now, let me say what regeneration is not. It is not going to church. Very often I see people, and ask them if they are Christians. "Yes, of course I am; at least, I think I am. I go to church every Sunday." Ah, but this is not regeneration. Others say, "I am trying to do what is right—am I not a Christian? Is not that a new birth?" No. What has that to do with being born again? There is yet another group of people—those who have "turned over a new leaf," and think they are regenerated. No, forming a new resolution is not being born again.

Nor will being baptized do you any good. Yet you hear people say, "Why, I have been baptized, and I was born again when I was baptized." They believe that because they were baptized into the church, they were baptized into the

Kingdom of God. I tell you that it is utterly impossible. You may be baptized into the visible church, and yet not be baptized into the Son of God. Baptism is all right in its place. God forbid that I should say anything against it. But if you put that in the place of Regeneration—in the place of the New Birth—it is a terrible mistake. You cannot be baptized into the Kingdom of God. "Except a man be *born again*, he cannot see the Kingdom of God." If anyone reading this rests his hopes on anything else—on any other foundation—I pray that God may sweep it away.

Others say, "I go to the Lord's Supper; I partake uniformly of the Sacrament." Blessed ordinance! Jesus hath said that as often as ye do it, ye commemorate His death. Yet, that is not being "born again." That is not passing from death unto life. Jesus says plainly—and so plainly that there need not be any mistake about it—"Except a man be born of... the Spirit, he cannot enter into the Kingdom of God." What has a sacrament to do with that? What has going to church to do with being born again?

Another man comes up and says, "I say my prayers regularly." Still I say that is not being born of the Spirit. It is a very solemn question, then, that comes up before us; and oh that every reader would ask himself earnestly and. faithfully, "Have I been born again? Have I been born of the Spirit? Have I passed from death unto life?"

Some say, "We Do Not Need to Be Converted"

There is a class of men who say that special religious meetings are very good for a certain class of people. They would be very good if you could get the drunkard there, or get the gambler there, or get other vicious people there—that would do a great deal of good. But "we do not need to be converted." To whom did Christ utter these words of wisdom?

To Nicodemus. Who was Nicodemus? Was he a drunkard, a gambler, or a thief? No! No doubt he was one of the very best men in Jerusalem. He was an honorable Councilor. He belonged to the Sanhedrin. He held a very high position. He was an orthodox man and was one of the very soundest men. And yet what did Christ say to him? "Except a man be born again, he cannot see the Kingdom of God."

But I can imagine someone saying, "What am I to do? I cannot create life. I certainly cannot save myself." You certainly cannot, and we do not claim that you can. We tell you it is utterly impossible to make a man better without Christ, but that is what so many men are trying to do. There must be new creation! Regeneration is a new creation, and if it is a new creation it must be the work of God. In the first chapter of Genesis man does not appear. There is no one there but God. Man is not there to take part. When God created the earth He was alone. When Christ redeemed the world He was alone.

"That which is born of the flesh is flesh; and that which is born of the Spirit is spirit" ^

The Ethiopian cannot change his skin, and the leopard cannot change his spots. You might as well try to make yourselves pure and holy without the help of God. It would be just as easy for you to do that as for the black man to wash himself white. A man might just as well try to leap over the moon as to serve God in the flesh. Therefore, "that which is born of the flesh is flesh; and that which is born of the Spirit is spirit."

Entering the Kingdom of God

Now God tells us in this chapter how we are to get into His kingdom. We are not to work our way in—not but that salvation is worth working for. We admit all that. If there were rivers and mountains in the way, it would be well worthwhile to swim those rivers, and climb those mountains. There is no doubt that salvation is worth all that effort, but we do not obtain it by our works. It is "to him that worketh not, but believeth" (Romans 4:5).

We work because we are saved, we do not work to be saved. We work from the Cross, but not toward it. It is written, "Work out your own salvation with fear and trembling" (Philippians 2:12).

Why, you must have your salvation before you can work it out. Suppose I say to my little boy, "I want you to spend that hundred dollars carefully." "Well," he says, "let me have the hundred dollars; and I will be careful how I spend it."

I remember when I first left home and went to Boston; I had spent all my money, and I went to the post office three times a day. I knew there was only one mail a day from home, but I thought by some possibility there might be a letter for me. At last I received a letter from my little sister; and oh, how glad I was to get it. She had heard that there were a great many pickpockets in Boston, and a large part of that letter was to urge me to be very careful not to let anybody pick my pocket. Now it is necessary for me to have something in my pocket before I could have it picked. So you must have salvation before you can work it out.

When Christ cried out on Calvary, "It is finished!" (John 19:30), He meant what He said. All that men have to do now is just accept the work of Jesus Christ. There is no hope for a man or woman so long as they are trying to work out salvation for themselves. I can imagine there are some people who will say, as Nicodemus possibly did, "This is a very mysterious thing." I see the scowl on that Pharisee's brow as he says, "How can these things be?" It sounds very strange to his ear. "Born again; born of the Spirit! How can these things be?" A great many people say, "You must reason it out; but if you do not reason it out, do not ask us to believe it." I can imagine a great many people saying that. When you ask me to reason it out, I tell you frankly I cannot do it.

"The wind bloweth where it listeth, and thou hearest the sound thereof, but canst not tell whence it cometh and whither it goeth—so is every one that is born of the Spirit" (John 3:8).

I do not understand everything about the wind. You ask me to reason it out. I cannot. It may blow due north here, and a hundred miles away due south. I may go up a few hundred feet, and find it blowing in an entirely opposite direction from what it is down here. You ask me to explain these currents of wind; but suppose that, because I cannot explain them, and do not understand them, I were to take my stand and assert, "Oh, there is no such thing as wind." I can imagine some little girl saying, "I know more about it than that man does; often have I heard the wind, and felt it blowing against my face"; and she might say, "Did not the wind blow my umbrella out of my hands the other day? And did I not see it blow a man's hat off in the street? Have I not seen it blow the trees in the forest, and the growing corn in the country?"

You might just as well tell me that there is no such thing as wind, as tell me there is no such thing as a man being born of the Spirit. I have felt the Spirit of God working in my heart, just as really and as truly as I have felt the wind blowing in my face. I cannot reason it out. There are a great

213

many things I cannot reason out, but which I believe I never could reason out the creation. I can see the world, but I cannot tell how God made it out of nothing. But almost every man will admit there was a creative power.

There are a great many things that I cannot explain and cannot reason out, and yet that I believe. I heard a commercial traveler say that he had heard that the ministry and religion of Jesus Christ were matters of revelation and not of investigation. "When it pleased God ... to reveal his Son in me," says Paul (Galatians 1:15-16).

There was a party of young men together, going up the country; and on their journey they made up their minds not to believe anything they could not reason out. An old man heard them and presently he said, "I heard you say you would not believe anything you could not reason out."

"Yes," they said, "that is so."

"Well," he said, "coming down on the train today, I noticed some geese, some sheep, some swine, and some cattle, all eating grass. Can you tell me by what process that same grass was turned into hair, feathers, bristles, and wool? Do you believe it is a fact?"

"Oh yes," they said, "We cannot help believing that, though we fail to understand it."

"Well," said the old man, "I cannot help believing in Jesus Christ."

And I cannot help believing in the regeneration of man, when I see men who have been reclaimed, when I see men who have been reformed. Have not some of the very worst men been regenerated- been picked up out of the pit, and had their feet set upon the Rock, and a new song put in their mouths? Their tongues were cursing and blaspheming; and, now are occupied in praising God. Old things have passed away, and all things have become new. They are not reformed only, but *regenerated*—new men in Christ Jesus.

Pictures of Regeneration

Down there in the dark alleys of one of our great cities is a poor drunkard. I think if you want to get near hell, you should go to a poor drunkard's home. Go to the house of that poor miserable drunkard. Is there anything more like hell on earth? See the want and distress that reign there. But hark! A footstep is heard at the door, and the children run and hide themselves. The patient wife waits to meet the man. He has been her torment. Many a time she has borne about the marks of his blows for weeks. Many a time that strong right hand has been brought down on her defenseless head. And now she waits expecting to hear his oaths and suffer his brutal treatment. He comes in and says to her: "I have been to the Meeting; and I heard there that if I will I can be converted. I believe that God is able to save me." Go down to that house again in a few weeks and what a change! As you approach you hear someone singing. It is not the song of a reveler, but the strains of that good old hymn, "Rock of Ages." The children are no longer afraid of the man, but cluster around his knee. His wife is near him, her face lit up with a happy glow. Is not that a picture of Regeneration? I can take you to many such homes, made happy by the regenerating power of the religion of Christ. What men want is the power to overcome temptation, the power to lead a right life.

The only way to get into the kingdom of God is to be "born" into it. The law in this country requires that the President should be born in this country. When foreigners come to our shores they have no right to complain against such a law, which forbids them from ever becoming Presidents. Now, has not God a right to make a law that all those who become heirs of eternal life must be "born" into His kingdom?

An unregenerate man would rather be in hell than in heaven. Take a man whose heart is full of corruption and wickedness and place him in heaven among the pure, the holy, and the redeemed; and he would not want to stay there. Certainly, if we are to be happy in heaven we must begin to make a heaven here on earth. Heaven is a prepared place for a prepared people. If a gambler or a blasphemer were taken out of the streets of New York and placed on the crystal pavement of Heaven and under the shadow of the tree of life he would say, "I do not want to stay here." If men were taken to heaven just as they are by nature, without having their hearts regenerated, there would be another rebellion in heaven. Heaven is filled with a company of those who have been *twice born.*

In verses 14 and 15 of this third chapter of John chapter we read: "As Moses lifted up the serpent in the wilderness, even so must the Son of Man be lifted up; that whosoever believeth in Him should not perish, but Have eternal life."

"Whosoever"

Mark that! Let me tell you who are unsaved what God has done for you. He has done everything that He could do toward your salvation. You need not wait for God to do anything more. In one place He asks the question, what more could He have done.

"What could have been done more to My vineyard, that I have not done in it?" (Isaiah 5:4).

He sent His prophets, and they killed them; then He sent His beloved Son, and they murdered Him. Now He has sent the Holy Spirit to convince us of sin and to show how we are to be saved.

In this chapter we are told how men are to be saved, namely, by Him who was lifted up on the Cross. Just as Moses lifted up the brazen serpent in the wilderness, so must the Son of Man be lifted up, "that whosoever believeth in Him should not perish, but have eternal life" (John 3:15). If you are lost, it will not be on account of Adam's sin.

Let me illustrate this, and perhaps you will be better able to understand it. Suppose I am dying of consumption, which I inherited from my father or mother. I did not get the disease by any fault of my own, by any neglect of my health; I inherited it, let us suppose. A friend happens to come along he looks at me, and says, "Moody, you have consumption."

I reply, "I know it very well; I do not want anyone to tell me that."

"But," he says, "there is a remedy."

"But, sir, I do not believe it. I have tried the leading physicians in this country and in Europe; and they tell me there is no hope."

"But you know me, Moody; you have known me for years."

"Yes, sir."

"Do you think, then I would tell you a falsehood?"

"No."

"Well, ten years ago I was as far gone. I was given up by the physicians to die; but I took this medicine and it cured, me. I am perfectly well. Look at me."

I say that it is "a very strange case."

"Yes, it may be strange; but it is a fact. The medicine cured me: take this medicine, and it will cure you. Although it has cost me a great deal, it shall not cost you anything. Do not make light of it, I beg of you."

"Well," I say, "I should like to believe you; but this is contrary to my reason."

Hearing this, my friend goes away and returns with another friend, and that one testifies to the same thing. I am still disbelieving; so he goes away, and brings in another friend, and another, and another, and another; and they all testify to the same thing. They say they were as bad as myself that they took the same medicine that has been offered to me and that it has cured them. My friend then hands me the medicine. I dash it to the ground; I do not believe in its saving power; I die. The reason is then that I spurned the remedy. So, if you perish it will not be because Adam fell, but because you spurned the remedy offered to save you. You will choose darkness rather than light. How then shall we escape, if we neglect so great salvation? There is no hope for you if you neglect the remedy. It does no good to look at the wound.

If we had been in the Israelities camp and had been bitten by one of the fiery serpents, it would have done us no good to look at the wound. Looking at a wound will never save anyone. What you must do is to look at the Remedy—look away to Him who hath power to save you from your sin.

Behold the camp of the Israelites; look at the scene that is pictured to your eyes! Many are dying because they neglect the remedy that is offered. In that arid desert is many a short and tiny grave. The fiery serpents have bitten many children. Fathers and mothers are bearing away their children. Over yonder they are just burying a mother; a loved mother is about to be laid in the earth. All the weeping family gathers around the beloved form. You hear the mournful cries; you see the bitter tears. The father is being borne away to his last resting place. There is wailing going up all over the camp. Tears are pouring down for thousands who have passed away; thousands more are dying, and the plague is raging from one end of the camp to the other.

God's Remedy for Sin: Look to Christ and Live

I see in one tent an Israelite mother bending over the form of a beloved boy just coming into the bloom of life, just budding into manhood. She is wiping away the sweat of death that is gathering upon his brow. Yet a little while, and his eyes are fixed and glassy, for life is ebbing fast away. The mother's heartstrings are torn and bleeding. All at once she hears a noise in the camp. A great shout goes up. What does it mean? She goes to the door of the tent. "What is the noise in the camp?" she asks those passing by. And someone says: "Why, my good woman have you not heard the good news that has come into the camp?"

"No," says the woman, "Good news! What is it?"

"Why, have you not heard about it? God has provided a remedy."

"What! For the bitten Israelites? Oh, tell me what the remedy is!"

"Why, God has instructed Moses to make a brazen serpent, and to put in on a pole in the middle of the camp; and He has declared that whosoever looks upon it shall live. The shout that you hear is the shout, of the people when they see the serpent lifted up."

"And the LORD said unto Moses, Make thee a fiery serpent, and set it upon a pole: and it shall come to pass, that every one that is bitten, when he looketh upon it, shall live. And Moses made a serpent of brass, and put it upon a pole, and it came to pass, that if a serpent had bitten any man, when he beheld the serpent of brass, he lived" (Numbers 21:8,9).

The mother goes back into the tent, and she says, "My boy, I have good news to tell you. You need not die! My boy, my boy, I have come with good tidings; you can live!" He is already getting stupefied; he is so weak he cannot walk to the door of the tent. She puts her strong arms under him and lifts him up. "Look yonder; look right there under the hill!" But the boy does not see anything, he says. And she says: "Keep looking, and you will see it."

At last he catches a glimpse of the glistening serpent; and lo, he is well! And thus it is with many a young convert. Some men say, "Oh, we do not believe in sudden conversions." How long did it take to cure that boy? How long did it take to cure those serpent-bitten Israelites? It was just a look; and they were well.

That Hebrew boy is a young convert. I can fancy that, I see him now calling on all those who were with him to praise God. He sees another young man bitten as he was; and he runs up to him and tells him, "You need not die."

"Oh," the young man replies, "I cannot live; it is not possible. There is not a physician in Israel who can cure me." He does not know that he need not die.

"Why, have you not heard the news? God has provided a remedy."

"Why, God has told Moses to lift up a brazen serpent, and has said that none of those who look upon that serpent shall die."

I can just imagine the young man. He may be what you call an intellectual young man. He says to the young convert, "You do not think I am going to believe anything like that? If the physicians in Israel cannot cure me, how do you think that an old brass serpent on a pole is going to cure me?"

"Why, sir, I was as bad as yourself!"

"You do not say so!"

"Yes, I do."

"That is the most astonishing thing I ever heard," says the young man. "I wish you would explain the philosophy of it."

"I cannot. I only know that I looked at that serpent, and I was cured. That did it.

"My mother told me the reports that were being heard through the camp; and I just believed what my mother said, and I am perfectly well."

"Well, I do not believe you were bitten as badly as I have been."

The young man pulls up his sleeve. "Look there! That mark shows where I was bitten; and I tell you I was worse than you are."

"Well, if I understood the philosophy of it I would look and get well."

"Let your philosophy go: *look and live.*"

"But, sir, you ask me to do an unreasonable thing. If God had said, Take the brass and rub it into the wound, there might be something in the brass that would cure the bite. Young man, explain the philosophy of it."

I have often seen people before me who have talked in that way. But the young man calls in another, and takes him into the tent, and says: "Just tell him how the Lord saved you"; and he tells just the same story; and he calls in others, and they all say the same thing.

The young man says it is a very strange thing. "If the Lord had told Moses to go and get some herbs, or roots, and stew them, and take the product as a medicine, there would be something in that. But it is so contrary to nature to do such a thing as look at the serpent, that I cannot do it."

At length his mother, who has been out in the camp, comes in, and she says, "My boy, I have just the best news in the world for you. I was in the camp, and I saw hundreds who were very far gone, and they are all perfectly well now."

The young man says: "I should like to get well; it is a very painful thought to die; I want to go into the promised land, and it is terrible to die here in this wilderness; but the fact is, I do not understand the remedy. It does not appeal to my reason. I cannot believe that I can get well in a moment." And the young man dies in consequence of his own unbelief.

God provided a remedy for this bitten Israelite: "Look and live!" And there is eternal life for every poor sinner. Look, and you can be saved, my reader, this very hour. God has provided a remedy; and it is offered to all. The trouble is, a great many people are looking at the pole. Do not look at the pole; that is the church. You need not look at the church; the church is all right, but the church cannot save you. Look beyond the pole. Look at the Crucified One. Look to Calvary. Keep in mind, sinner, Jesus died for us all. You need not look at ministers; they are just God's chosen instruments to hold up the Remedy—to hold up Christ. And so, my friend, take your eyes off from men. Take your eyes off from the church. Lift them up to Jesus who took away the sin of the world and there will be life for you from this hour.

Thank God, we do not require education to teach us how to look. That little girl, that little boy, only four years old, who cannot read, can look. When the father is coming home, the mother says to her little boy, "Look! Look! Look!" and the little child learns to look long before he is a year old. And that is the way to be saved. It is to look at "the Lamb of God, which taketh away the sin of the world" (John 1:29);

and there is life this moment for every one who is willing to look.

How to Be Saved

Some men say, "I wish I knew how to be saved." Just take God at His word and trust His Son this very day—this very hour—this very moment. He will save you if you will trust Him. I imagine I hear someone saying, "I do not feel the bite as much as I wish I did. I know I am a sinner, and all that; but I do not feel the bite enough." How much does God want you to feel it?

When I was in Belfast I knew a doctor who had a friend, a leading surgeon there; and he told me that the surgeon's custom was, before performing any operation, to say to the patient, "Take a good look at the wound, and then fix your eyes on me and do not take them off till I get through." I thought at the time that was a good illustration. Sinner, take a good look at your wound; and then fix your eyes on Christ, and do not take them off. It is better to look at the Remedy than at the wound. See what a poor wretched sinner you are; and then look at "the Lamb of God, which taketh away the sin of the world." He died for the ungodly and the sinner. Say, "I will take Him!" And may God help you to lift your eye to the Man on Calvary. And as the Israelites looked upon the serpent and were healed, so may you look and live.

The Dying Soldier's Conversion

After the battle of Pittsburgh Landing I was in a hospital at Murfreesboro. In the middle of the night I was aroused and told that a man in one of the wards wanted to see me. I went to him and he called me "chaplain"—I was not the chaplain—and said he wanted me to help him die.

And I said, "I would take you right up in my arms and carry you into the kingdom of God if I could, but I cannot do what you ask. I cannot help you die!"

And he said, "Who can?"

I said, "The Lord Jesus Christ can. He came for that purpose."

He shook his head, and said, "He cannot save me; I have sinned all my life."

And I said, "But He came to save sinners."

I thought of his mother in the north, and I was sure that she was anxious that he should die in peace, so I resolved I would stay with him. I prayed two or three times and repeated all the promises I could, for it was evident that in a few hours he would be gone.

I said I wanted to read him a conversation that Christ had with a man who was anxious about his soul. I turned to the third chapter of John. His eyes were riveted on me, and when I came to the fourteenth and fifteenth verses—the passage before us—he caught up the words, "As Moses lifted up the serpent in the wilderness, even so must the Son of Man be lifted up; that whosoever believeth in Him should not perish, but have eternal life."

He stopped me and said, "Is that there?"

I said, "Yes." He asked me to read it again; and I did so.

225

He leaned his elbows on the cot, and clasping his hands together, said, "That's good. Won't you read it again?"

I read it the third time, and then went on with the rest of the chapter. When I had finished, his eyes were closed, his hands were folded, and there was a smile on his face. Oh, how it was lit up! What a change had come over it! I saw his lips quivering, and leaning over him I heard in a faint whisper, "As Moses lifted up the serpent in the wilderness, even so must the Son of Man be lifted up; that whosoever believeth in Him should not perish, but have eternal life."

He opened his eyes and said, "That's enough, don't read any more." He lingered a few hours, pillowing his head on those two verses, and then went up in one of Christ's chariots to take his seat in the Kingdom of God.

Christ said to Nicodemus: "Except a man be born again, he cannot see the Kingdom of God."

You may see many countries, but there is one country—the land of Beulah, which John Bunyan saw in a vision—you should never behold, unless you are born again and regenerated by Christ. You can look abroad and see many beautiful trees, but the Tree of Life you shall never behold unless your eyes are made clear by faith in the Savior. You may see the beautiful rivers of the earth and you may ride upon their bosoms, but bear in mind that your eye will never rest upon the river which bursts out from the Throne of God and flows through the upper Kingdom, unless you are born again. God has said it. Not man. You will never see the kingdom of God except you are born again. You may see the kings and lords of the earth, but the King of kings and Lord of lords you will never see except you are born again. When you are in London you may go to the Tower and see the crown of

England, which is worth thousands of dollars and is guarded there by soldiers, but bear in mind that your eye will never rest upon the crown of life except you are born again.

You may hear the songs of Zion that are sung here, but one song—that of Moses and the Lamb—the uncircumcised ear shall never hear. Its melody will only gladden the ear of those who have been born again. You may look upon the beautiful mansions of earth, but bear in mind that the mansions that Christ has gone to prepare you shall never see unless you are born again. It is God who says it. You may see ten thousand beautiful things in this world, but the city that Abraham caught a glimpse of—and from that time became a pilgrim and sojourner—you shall never see unless you are born again (Hebrews 11:8, 10-16). You may often be invited to marriage feasts here, but you will never attend the marriage supper of the Lamb except you are born again. It is God who says it, dear friend. You may be looking on the face of your sainted mother tonight and feel that she is praying for you, but the time will come when you shall never see her anymore unless you are born again.

"I'll Meet You in Heaven"

The reader may be a young man or a young lady who has recently stood by the bedside of a dying mother; and she may have said, "Be sure and meet me in heaven," and you made the promise. Ah! You shall never see her anymore, except you are born again. I believe Jesus of Nazareth sooner than those infidels who say you do not need to be born again. Parents, if you hope to see your children who have gone before, you must be born of the Spirit. Possibly you are a father or a mother who has recently borne a loved one to the grave; and how dark your home seems! Never again will you see your child, unless you are born again. If you wish to be reunited to your loved one, you must be born again.

I may be addressing a father or a mother who has a loved one up yonder. If you could hear that loved one's voice, it would say, "Come this way." Have you a sainted friend up yonder? Young man or young lady, have you not a mother in the world of light? If you could hear her speak, would not she say, "Come this way, my son,"—"Come this way, my daughter"? If you would ever see her anymore you must be born again.

We all have an Elder Brother there. Over nineteen hundred years ago He crossed over, and from the heavenly shores He is calling you to heaven. Let us turn our backs upon the world. Let us give a deaf ear to the world. Let us look to Jesus on the Cross and be saved. Then we shall one day see the King in His beauty, and we shall go no more out.

Chapter 3

THE TWO CLASSES

"Two men went up into the temple to pray"
—Luke 18:10.

I now want to speak of two classes of people: First, those who do not feel their need of a Savior, who have not been convinced of sin by the Spirit; and Second, those who are convinced of sin and cry, "What must I do to be saved?" (Acts 16:30).

All inquirers can be ranged under two heads; they have either the spirit of the Pharisee, or the spirit of the publican. If a man having the spirit of the Pharisee comes into the after-meeting, I know of no better portion of Scripture to meet his case than Romans 3:10: "As it is written, there is none righteous, no, not one: there is none that, understandeth; there is none that seeketh after God."

Paul is here speaking of the natural man: "They are all gone out of the way, they are together become unprofitable; there is none that doeth good, no, not one."

And in verse 17 and those that follow, we have: "And the way of peace have they not known: there is no fear of God before their eyes. Now we know what things soever

229

the law saith, it saith to them who are under the law: that every mouth may be stopped, and all the world may become guilty before God."

All Have Sinned

Then observe the last clause of verse 22: "For there is no difference: for all have sinned, and come short of the glory of God." Not part of the human family—but *all*—"have sinned, and come short of the glory of God."

Another verse which has been very much used to convict men of their sin is 1 John 1:8: "If we say that we have no sin, we deceive ourselves, and the truth is not in us."

I remember that on one occasion we were holding meetings in an eastern city of forty thousand inhabitants. A lady came and asked us to pray for her husband whom she purposed bringing into the after-meeting. I have traveled a good deal and met many pharisaical men, but this man was so clad in self-righteousness that you could not get the point of the needle of conviction in anywhere. I said to his wife, "I am glad to see your faith, but we cannot get near him; he is the most self-righteous man I ever saw." She said: "You *must!* My heart will break if these meetings end without his conversion." She persisted in bringing him and I got so tired of the sight of him.

But towards the close of our meetings of thirty days, he came up to me and put his trembling hand on my shoulder. The place in which the meetings were held was rather cold and there was an adjoining room in which only the gas had been lighted; and he said to me, "Can't you come in here for a few minutes?" I thought that he was shaking from cold, and I did not particularly wish to go where it was colder. But he said, "I am the worst man in the State of Vermont. I want you to pray for me." I thought he had committed a murder, or some other awful crime; and I asked, "Is there any one sin that particularly troubles you?" And he said, "My whole life has been a sin. I have been a conceited, self-righteous Pharisee. I want you to pray for me." He was under deep conviction. Man could not have produced this result, but the Spirit had. About two o'clock in the morning light broke in upon his soul and he went up and down the business street of the city and told what God had done for him. He has been a most active Christian ever since.

There are four other passages in dealing with inquirers, which were used by Christ Himself.

In Luke 13:3 we read, *"Except ye repent, ye shall all likewise perish."*

In Matthew 18, when the disciples came to Jesus to know who was to be the greatest in the Kingdom of Heaven, we are told that He took a little child and set him in the midst and said, *"Verily I say unto you, Except ye be converted, and become as little children, ye shall not enter into the kingdom of heaven" (18:1-3).*

There is another important "Except" in Matthew 5:20, *"Except your righteousness shall exceed the righteousness of the Scribes and Pharisees, ye shall in no case enter into the kingdom of heaven."*

A man must be made meet before he will want to go into the kingdom of God. I would rather go into the kingdom with the younger brother than stay outside with the elder. Heaven would be hell to such a one. An elder brother who could not rejoice at his younger brother's return would not be "fit" for the kingdom of God. It is a solemn thing to contemplate; but the curtain drops and leaves him outside, and the younger brother within. To him the language of the Savior under other circumstances seems appropriate, *"Verily I say unto you, That the publicans and the harlots go into the kingdom of God before you" (Matthew 21:31).*

The Prodigal Son Dilemma

A lady once came to me and wanted a favor for her daughter. She said, "You must remember I do not sympathize with you in your doctrine."

I asked, "What is your trouble?"

She said: "I think your abuse of the elder brother is horrible. I think he is a noble character."

I said that I was willing to hear her defend him, but that it was a solemn thing to take up such a position, and that the elder brother needed to be converted as much as the younger. When people talk of being moral it is as well to get them to have a good look at the old man pleading with his boy who would not go in.

But we will pass on now to the other class with which we have to deal. It is composed of those who are convinced of sin and from whom the cry comes as from the Philippian jailer, "What must I do to be saved?" To those who utter this penitential cry there is no necessity to administer the law. It is well to bring them straight to the Scripture: "Believe on the Lord Jesus Christ, and thou shalt be saved" (Acts 16:31).

Many will meet you with a scowl and say, "I don't know what it is to believe." And though it is the law of heaven that they must believe, in order to be saved, yet they ask for something besides that. We are to tell them what, and where, and how, to believe.

In John 3:35 and 36 we read, "The Father loveth the Son, and hath given all things into his hand. He that believeth on the Son hath everlasting life: and he that believeth not the Son shall not see life; but the wrath of God abideth on him."

Now this looks reasonable. Man lost life by unbelief—by not believing God's word. We get life back again by believing—by taking God at His word. In other words we get up where Adam fell down. He stumbled and fell over the stone of unbelief, but we are lifted up and stand upright by believing. When people say they cannot believe, show them chapter and verse and hold them right to this one thing, "Has God ever broken His promise for these six thousand years?" The devil and men have been trying all the time and have not succeeded in showing that He has broken a single promise, and there would be a jubilee in hell today if one word that He has spoken could be broken. If a man says that he cannot believe it is well to press him on that one thing.

I can believe God better today than I can my own heart. "The heart is deceitful above all things, and desperately wicked: who can know it?" (Jeremiah 17:9).

I can believe God better than I can myself. If you want to know the way of life, believe that Jesus Christ is a personal Savior; cut away from all doctrines and creeds, and come right to the heart of the Son of God. If you have been feeding on dry doctrine there is not much growth on that kind of food. Doctrines are to the soul what the streets that lead to the house of a friend who has invited me to dinner are to the body. They will lead me there if I take the right one, but

233

if I remain in the streets my hunger will never be satisfied. Feeding on doctrines is like trying to live on dry husks; and lean indeed must the soul remain which partakes not of the Bread sent down from heaven.

Some ask: "How am I to get my heart warmed?" It is by believing. You do not get power to love and serve God until you believe.

The apostle John says: "If we receive the witness of men, the witness of God is greater: for this is the witness of God which He hath testified of His Son. He that believeth on the Son of God hath the witness in himself: he that believeth not God hath made Him a liar; because he believeth not the record that God gave of His Son. And this is the record that God hath given to us eternal life, and this life is in His Son. He that hath the Son hath life; and he that hath not the Son of God hath not life" (1 John 5:9-12).

The Testimony of Men

Human affairs would come to a standstill if we did not take the testimony of men. How should we get on in the ordinary intercourse of life and how would commerce get on, if we disregarded men's testimony? Things social and commercial would come to a deadlock within forty-eight hours! This is the drift of the apostle's argument here. "If we receive the witness of men the witness of God is greater." God has borne witness to Jesus Christ, and if man can believe his fellow men who are frequently telling untruths and whom we are constantly finding unfaithful, why should we not take God at His word and believe His testimony?

Faith is a belief in testimony. It is not a leap in the dark, as some tell us. That would be no faith at all. God does not ask any man to believe without giving him something to believe. You might as well ask a man to see without eyes; to hear without ears; and to walk without feet as to bid him believe without giving him something to believe.

When I started for California I procured a guidebook. This told me, that after leaving the State of Illinois, I should cross the Mississippi, and then the Missouri; get into Nebraska; then go over the Rocky Mountains to the Mormon settlement at Salt Lake City, and proceed by the way of the Sierra Nevada into San Francisco. I found the guidebook all right as I went along; and I would have been a miserable skeptic if, having proved it to be correct three-fourths of the way, I had said that I would not believe it for the remainder of the journey.

Suppose a man, in directing me to the post office, gives me ten landmarks; and that, in my progress there, I find nine of them to be as he told me; I would have good reason to believe that I was coming to the post office.

And if, by believing, I get a new life, and a hope, a peace, a joy, and a rest to my soul, that I never had before; if I get self-control, and find that I have a power to resist evil and to do good, I have pretty good proof that I am in the right road to the "city which hath foundations, whose builder and maker is God" (Hebrews 11:10). And if things have taken place and are now taking place, as recorded in God's Word, I have good reason to conclude that what yet remains will be fulfilled. And yet people talk of doubting. There can be no true faith where there is fear. Faith is to take God at His word, unconditionally. There cannot be true peace where there is fear. "Perfect love casteth out fear" (1 John 4:18). How wretched a wife would be if she doubted her husband! How miserable a mother would feel if after her boy had gone away from home she had reason, from his neglect, to question that son's devotion! True love never has a doubt.

Essential Elements of Faith

There are three things indispensable to faith: knowledge, assent, and appropriation.

We must know God. "And this is life eternal, that they might know thee the only true God, and Jesus Christ whom thou hast sent" (John 17:3).

Then we must not only give our assent to what we know, but we must lay hold of the truth. If a man simply gives his assent to the plan of salvation, it will not save him. He must accept Christ as his Savior. He must receive and appropriate Him.

Some say they cannot tell how a man's life can be affected by his belief. But let someone cry out that some building in which we happen to be sitting, is on fire; and see how soon we should act on our belief and get out. We are all the time influenced by what we believe. We cannot help it. And let a man believe the record that God has given of Christ, and it will very quickly affect his whole life.

Take John 5:24. There is enough truth in that one verse for every soul to rest upon for salvation. It does not admit the shadow of a doubt.

"Verily, verily"—which means truly, truly—"I say unto you, He that heareth my word, and believeth on Him that sent me, hath—*hath*—everlasting life, and shall not come into condemnation; but is passed from death unto life."

Now if a person really hears the word of Jesus and believes with the heart on God who sent the Son to be the Savior of the world, and lays hold of and appropriates this great salvation, there is no fear of judgment. He will not be looking forward with dread to the Great White Throne, for we read in 1 John 4:17, "Herein is our love made perfect, that we may have boldness in the day of judgment: because as he is, so are we in this world."

If we believe, then there is for us no condemnation—no judgment. That is behind us, and passed; and we shall have boldness in the Day of Judgment.

The Ultimate Pardon

I remember reading of a man who was on trial for his life. He had friends with influence; and they procured a pardon for him from the king on condition that he was to go through the trial, and be condemned. He went into court with the pardon in his pocket. The feeling ran very high against him, and the judge said that the court was shocked that he was so much unconcerned. But, when the sentence was pronounced, he pulled out the pardon, presented it, and walked out a free man. He had been pardoned; and so have we. Then let death come, we have nothing to fear. All the gravediggers in the world cannot dig a grave large enough and deep enough to hold eternal life; all the coffin-makers in the world cannot make a coffin large enough and tight enough to hold eternal life. Death has had his hand on Christ once, but never again.

Jesus said, "I am the Resurrection, and the Life, he that believeth in me, though he were dead, yet shall he live: and whosoever liveth and believeth in me shall never die" (John 11:25-26).

And in the Apocalypse we read that the risen Savior said to John, "I am he that liveth, and was dead; and, behold, I am alive forevermore" (Revelation 1:18).

Death Cannot Touch Him again.

We get life by believing. In fact we get more than Adam lost, for the redeemed child of God is heir to a richer and more glorious inheritance than Adam in Paradise could ever have conceived. Yea, and that inheritance endures forever—it is inalienable.

I would much rather have my life hid with Christ in God than have lived in Paradise, for Adam might have sinned and fallen after being there ten thousand years. But the believer is safer, if these things become real to him. Let us make them a fact, and not a fiction. God has said it and that is enough. Let us trust Him even where we cannot trace Him. Let the same confidence animate us that was in little Maggie as related in the following simple but touching incident which I read in the *Bible Treasury:*

The Story of Little Maggie

I had been absent from home for some days, and was wondering, as I again drew near the homestead, if my little Maggie, just able to sit alone, would remember me. To test her memory, I stationed myself where I could not be seen by her, and called her name in the familiar tone, "Maggie!" She dropped her playthings, glanced around the room, and then looked down upon her toys. Again I repeated her name, 'Maggie' when she once more surveyed the room, but not seeing her father's face, she looked very sad, and slowly resumed her employment. Once more I called, 'Maggie!' when, dropping her playthings, and bursting into tears, she stretched out her arms in the direction whence the sound proceeded, knowing that, though she could not see him, her father *must be there* for she knew his voice."

Now, we have power to see and to hear, and we have power to believe. It is all folly for the inquirers to take the ground that they cannot believe. They can, if they will. But the trouble with most people is that they have connected *feeling* with *believing*. Now *feeling* has nothing whatever to do with *believing*. The Bible does not say, He that feeleth, or he that feeleth and believeth, hath everlasting life. Nothing of the kind. I cannot control my feelings. If I could, I would never feel ill, or have a headache or toothache. I should be well all the while. But I can believe God, and if we get our feet on that rock, let doubts and fears come and the waves surge around us, the anchor will hold.

Genuine Faith, Not Sensationalism

Some people are all the time looking at their faith. Faith is the hand that takes the blessing. I heard this illustration of a beggar. Suppose you were to meet a man in the street that you had known for years as being accustomed to beg, and you offered him some money, and he was to say to you: "I thank you; I don't want your money. I am not a beggar."

"How is that?"

"Last night a man put a thousand dollars into my hands."

"He did! How did you know it was good money?"

"I took it to the bank and deposited it and have got a bank-book."

"How did you get this gift?"

"I asked for alms, and after the gentleman talked with me he took out a thousand dollars in money and put it in my hand."

"How do you know that he put it in the right hand?"

"What do I care about which hand; just so I have got the money."

Many people are always thinking whether the faith by which they lay hold of Christ is the right kind, but what is far more essential is to see that we have the right kind of Christ.

Faith is the eye of the soul, and who would ever think of taking out an eye to see if it were the right kind so long as the sight was perfect? It is not my taste, but is what I taste, that satisfies my appetite. So, dear friends, it is taking God at His Word that is the means of our salvation. The truth cannot be made too simple.

There is a man living in the city of New York who has a home on the Hudson River. His daughter and her family went to spend the winter with him, and in the course of the season the scarlet fever broke out. One little girl was put in quarantine, to be kept separate from the rest. Every morning the old grandfather used to go and bid his grandchild "Good bye," before going to his business. On one of these occasions the little thing took the old man by the hand, and, leading him to a corner of the room, without saying a word she pointed to the floor where she had arranged some small crackers so they would spell out, "Grandpa, I want a box of paints." He said nothing. On his return home he hung up his overcoat and went to the room as usual. When his little grandchild, without looking to see if her wish had been compiled with, took him into the same corner, where he saw spelled out in the same way, "Grandpa, I thank you for the box of paints." The old man would not have missed gratifying the child for anything. That was faith.

Faith is taking God at His word, and those people who want some token are always getting into trouble. We want to come to this; God says it, so let us believe it.

But some say faith is the gift of God. So is the air, but you have to breathe it. So is the bread, but you have to eat it. So is water, but you have to drink it. Some are searching for a miraculous kind of feeling. That is not faith.

"Faith cometh by hearing; and hearing by the Word of God" (Romans 10:17).

That is when faith comes. It is not for me to sit down and wait for faith to come stealing over me with a strange sensation. It is for me to take God at His word. And you cannot believe, unless you have something to believe. So take the Word as it is written, and appropriate it, and lay hold of it.

In John 6:47-48 we read: "Verily, verily, I say unto you, He that believeth on me hath everlasting life. I am that bread of life."

There is the bread right at hand. Partake of it. I might have thousands of loaves within my home, and as many hungry men in waiting. They might assent to the fact that the bread was there, but unless they each took a loaf and commenced eating, their hunger would not be satisfied. So

Christ is the Bread of heaven, and as the body feeds on natural food, so the soul must feed on Christ.

Faith Illustrated

If a drowning man sees a rope thrown out to rescue him he must lay hold of it. In order to do so he must let go of everything else. If a man is sick he must take the medicine; for simply looking at it will not cure him. Knowledge of Christ will not help the inquirer, unless he believes in Him, and takes hold of Him as his only hope. The bitten Israelites might have believed that the serpent was lifted up, but unless they had looked they would not have lived.

> *"And the LORD sent fiery serpents among the people, and they bit the people; and much people of Israel died. Therefore the people came to Moses, and said, We have sinned, for we have spoken against the LORD, and against thee; pray unto the LORD, that he take away the serpents from us. And Moses prayed for the people. And the LORD said unto Moses, Make thee a fiery serpent, and set it upon a pole: and it shall come to pass, that every one that is bitten, when he looketh upon it, shall live. And Moses made a serpent of brass, and put it upon a pole, and it came to pass, that if a serpent had bitten any man, **when he beheld the serpent of brass, he lived**"* (Numbers 21:6-9).

I believe that a certain line of steamers will convey me across the ocean, because I have tried it; but this will not help another man who may want to go, unless he acts upon my knowledge. So knowledge of Christ does not help us unless we act upon it. That is what it is to believe on the Lord Jesus Christ. It is to act on what we believe. As a man steps on board a steamer to cross the Atlantic, so we must take

Christ and make a commitment of our souls to Him. He has promised to keep all who put their trust in Him. To believe on the Lord Jesus Christ is simply to take Him at His word.

Chapter 4

WORDS OF COUNSEL

"A bruised reed shall he not break"
—Isaiah 42:3; Matthew 12:20

It is dangerous for those who are seeking salvation to lean upon the experience of other people. Many are waiting for a repetition of the experience of their grandfather or grandmother. I had a friend who was converted in a field; and he thinks the whole town ought to go down into that meadow and be converted. Another was converted under a bridge; and he thinks that if any inquirer were to go there he would find the Lord. The best thing for the anxious is to go right to the Word of God. If there are any persons in the world to whom the Word ought to be very precious it is those who are asking how to be saved.

For instance a man may say, "I have no strength." Let him turn to Romans 5:6. "For when we were yet without strength, in due time Christ died for the ungodly." It is because we have no strength that we need Christ. He has come to give strength to the weak.

Another may say, "I cannot see." Christ says, "I am the light of the world" (John 8:12). He came, not only to give light, but "to open the blind eyes" (Isaiah 42:7).

Another may say, "I do not think a man can be saved all at once." A person holding that view was in the inquiry-room one night, and I drew his attention to Romans 6:23: "The wages of sin is death; but the *gift* of God is eternal life, through Jesus Christ our Lord."

How long does it take to accept a gift? There must be a moment when you have it not, and another when you have it—a moment when it is another's, and the next when it is yours. It does not take six months to get eternal life. It may however in some cases be like the mustard seed, very small at the commencement. Some people are converted so gradually that, like the morning light, it is impossible to tell when the dawn began. While with others, it is like the flashing of a meteor and the truth bursts upon them suddenly.

I would not go across the street to prove when I was converted, but what is important is for me to know that I really have been. It may be that a child has been so carefully trained that it is impossible to tell when the new birth began, but there must have been a moment when the change took place—when he became a partaker of the Divine nature.

Sudden Conversions

Some people do not believe in sudden conversion. But I will challenge anyone to show a conversion in the New Testament that was not instantaneous.

> "As Jesus passed by He saw Levi, the son of Alpheus, sitting at the receipt of custom, and saith unto him, follow Me: and he arose and followed Him" (Matthew 9:9).

Nothing could be more sudden than that.

Zacchaeus, the publican, sought to see Jesus, and because he was little of stature he climbed up a tree. When Jesus came to the place He looked up and saw him, and said, "Zacchaeus, make haste, and come down" (Luke 19:5).

His conversion must have taken place somewhere between the branch and the ground. We are told that he received Jesus joyfully, and said, "Behold, Lord, the half of my goods I give to the poor; and if I have taken anything from any man by false accusation, I restore him fourfold" (Luke 19:8). Very few in these days could say that in proof of their conversion.

The whole house of Cornelius was converted suddenly; for as Peter preached Christ to him and his company the Holy Ghost fell on them, and they were baptized (Acts 10). On the day of Pentecost three thousand gladly received the Word. They were not only converted, but they were baptized the same day (Acts 2). And when Philip talked to the eunuch, as they went on their way, the eunuch said to Philip, "See, here is water: what doth hinder me to be baptized?" Nothing hindered. And Philip said, "If thou believest with all thine heart, thou mayest. And they both went down into the water; and the man of great authority under Candace, the queen of the Ethiopians, was baptized, and went on his way rejoicing" (Acts 8:26-38). You will find all through Scripture that conversions were sudden and instantaneous.

A man has been in the habit of stealing money from his employer. Suppose he has taken $1,000 in twelve months; should we tell him to take $500 the next year, and less the next year, and the next, until in five years the sum taken would be only $50? That would be upon the same principle as gradual conversion. If such a person were brought before the court and pardoned, because he could not change his mode of life all at once, it would be considered a very strange proceeding. But the Bible says, "Let him that stole steal no more" (Ephesians 4:28).

It is "right about face!" Suppose a person is in the habit of cursing one hundred times a day: should we advise him not to utter more than ninety oaths the following day, and eighty the next day; so that in the course of time he would get rid of the habit? God's Word commands that we do not curse.

"But the tongue can no man tame; it is an unruly evil, full of deadly poison. Therewith bless we God, even the Father; and therewith curse we men, which are made after the similitude of God. Out of the same mouth proceedeth blessing and cursing. My brethren, these things ought not so to be" (James 3:8-10).

Suppose another man is in the habit of getting drunk and beating his wife twice a month; if he only did so once a month, and then only once in six months, that would be, upon the same ground, as reasonable as gradual conversion. Suppose Ananias had been sent to Paul, when he was on his way to Damascus breathing out threats and slaughter against the disciples, and casting them into prison, to tell him not to kill so many as he intended; and to let enmity die out of his heart, gradually, but not all at once. Suppose he had been told that it would not do to stop breathing out threats and slaughter, and to commence preaching Christ all at once, because the philosophers would say that the change was so sudden it would not hold out. This would be the same kind of reasoning as is used by those who do not believe in instantaneous conversion.

Then another class of people say that they are afraid that they will not hold out. This is a numerous and a very hopeful class. I like to see a man distrust himself. It is a good thing to get such to look to God, and to remember that it is not he who holds God, but that it is God who holds him. Some want to lay hold of Christ, but the thing is to get Christ to lay hold of you in answer to prayer. Let such read Psalm 121, "I will lift up mine eyes unto the hills, from whence cometh my help. My help cometh from the Lord, which made heaven and earth. He will not suffer thy foot to be moved: He that keepeth thee will not slumber. Behold, He that keepeth Israel shall neither slumber nor sleep. The Lord is thy keeper. The Lord is thy shade upon thy right hand. The sun shall not smite thee by day, or the moon by night. The Lord shall preserve thee from all evil. He shall preserve thy soul. The Lord shall preserve thy going out and thy coming in, from this time forth, and even for evermore."

Someone calls that the traveler's psalm. It is a beautiful psalm for those of us who are pilgrims through this world, and one with which we should be well acquainted. God can do what He has done before. He kept Joseph in Egypt; Moses before Pharaoh; Daniel in Babylon; and enabled Elijah to stand before Ahab in that dark day. And I am thankful that these I have mentioned were men of like passions with ourselves. It was God who made them so great. What man wants is to look to God. Real true faith is man's weakness leaning on God's strength. When man has no strength, if he leans on God he becomes powerful. The trouble is that we have too much strength and confidence in ourselves.

Again in Hebrews 6:17-20 we read, "Wherein God, willing more abundantly to show unto the heirs of promise the immutability of His counsel, confirmed, it by an oath: that by two immutable things, in which it was impossible for God to lie, we might have a strong consolation, who have fled for refuge to lay hold upon the hope set before us which hope we have as an anchor of the soul, both sure and steadfast, and which entereth into that within the veil; whither the Forerunner is for us entered, even Jesus, made an high priest for ever after the order of Melchisedec."

Rest in the Shepherd

Now these are precious verses to those who are afraid of falling, which fear that they will not hold out. It is God's work to hold. It is the Shepherd's business to keep the sheep. Who ever heard of the sheep going to bring back the shepherd? People have an idea that they have to keep themselves and Christ too. It is a false idea. It is the work of the Shepherd to look after them, and to take care of those who trust Him. And He has promised to do it. I once heard that when a sea captain was dying he said, "Glory to God; the anchor holds." He trusted in Christ. His anchor had taken hold of the solid rock. An Irishman said, on one occasion, "he trembled; but the Rock never did." We want to get sure footing.

In 2 Timothy 1:12 Paul says: "I know whom I have believed, and am persuaded that he is able to keep that which I have committed unto him against that day." That was Paul's persuasion.

During the late war of the rebellion, one of the chaplains, going through the hospitals, came to a man who was dying. Finding that he was a Christian, he asked to what persuasion he belonged, and was told "Paul's persuasion."

"Is he a Methodist?" he asked; for the Methodists all claim Paul.

"No."

"Is he a Presbyterian?" for the Presbyterians lay special claim to Paul.

"No," was the answer.

"Does he belong to the Episcopal Church?" for all the Episcopalian brethren contend that they have a claim to the Chief Apostle.

"No," he was not an Episcopalian.

"Then, to what persuasion does he belong?"

"I am persuaded that He is able to keep that which I have committed unto Him against that day." It is a grand persuasion, and it gave the dying soldier rest in a dying hour.

Let those who fear that they will not hold out turn to verse 24 of the Epistle of Jude: "Now unto Him that is able to keep you from falling, and to present you faultless before the presence of His glory with exceeding joy."

Then look at Isaiah 41:10, "Fear thou not; for I am with thee: be not dismayed; for I am thy God: I will strengthen thee; yea, I will help thee; yea, I will uphold thee with the right hand of my righteousness."

Then see verse 13, "For I the Lord thy God will hold thy right hand, saying unto thee, Fear not; I will help thee."

God Has the Power to Keep

Now if God has got hold of my right hand in His, cannot He hold me and keep me? Has not God the power to keep? The great God who made heaven and earth can keep a poor sinner like you and like me if we trust Him. To refrain from feeling confidence in God for fear of falling would be like a man who refused a pardon for fear that he would fall into prison again; or like a drowning man who refused to be rescued for fear of falling into the water again.

Many men look forth at the Christian life, and fear that they will not have sufficient strength to hold out to the end. They forget the promise that "as thy days, so shall thy strength be" (Deuteronomy 33:25).

It reminds me of the pendulum to the clock that grew disheartened at the thought of having to travel so many thousands of miles, but when it reflected that the distance was to be accomplished by "tick, tick, tick," it took fresh courage to go its daily journey. So it is the special privilege of the Christian to commit himself to the keeping of his heavenly Father and to trust Him day by day. It is a comforting thing to know that the Lord will not begin the good work without also finishing it.

Two Types of Skeptics

There are two kinds of skeptics—one class with honest difficulties; and another class who delight only in discussion. I used to think that this latter class would always be a thorn in my flesh, but they do not prick me now. I expect to find them right along the journey. Men of this kind used to hang around Christ to entangle Him in His talk. They come into our meetings to hold a discussion. To all such I would commend Paul's advice to Timothy, "But foolish and unlearned questions avoid, knowing that they do gender strifes" (2 Timothy 2:23).

Unlearned questions! Many young converts make a woeful mistake. They think they are to defend the whole

Bible. I knew very little of the Bible when I was first converted and I thought that I had to defend it from beginning to end against all comers, but a Boston infidel got hold of me, floored all my arguments at once and discouraged me. But I'm over that now. There are many things in the Word of God that I do not profess to understand.

When I am asked what I do with them, I say, "I don't do anything."

"How do you explain them?"

"I don't explain them."

"What do you do with them?"

"Why, I believe them."

And when I am told, "I would not believe anything that I do not understand," I simply reply that I do.

There are many things that were dark and mysterious five years ago, on which I have since had a flood of light. I expect to be finding out something fresh about God throughout eternity. I make a point of not discussing disputed passages of Scripture. An old divine has said that some people, if they want to eat fish, commence by picking the bones. I leave such things till I have light on them. I am not bound to explain what I do not comprehend.

"The secret things belong unto the Lord our God: but those things which are revealed belong unto us, and to our children forever" (Deuteronomy 29:29); and these I take, and eat and feed upon, in order to get spiritual strength.

Sound Advice

Then there is a little sound advice in Titus 3:9; "But avoid foolish questions and genealogies, and contentions, and strivings about the law; for they are unprofitable and vain."

But now here comes an honest skeptic. With him I would deal as tenderly as a mother with her sick child. I have no sympathy with those people who, because a man is skeptical, cast him off and will have nothing to do with him.

I was in an inquiry-meeting, some time ago, and I handed over to a Christian lady, whom I had known some time, one who was skeptical. On looking round soon after I noticed the inquirer marching out of the hall. I asked, "Why have you let her go?" "Oh, she is a skeptic!" was the reply. I ran to the door and got her to stop, and introduced her to another Christian worker who spent over an hour in conversation and prayer with her.

He visited her and her husband, and in the course of a week that intelligent lady cast off her skepticism and came out an active Christian. It took time, tact, and prayer; but if a person of this class is honest we ought to deal with such a one, as the Master would have us.

Here are a few passages for doubting inquirers: "If any man will do his will, he shall know of the doctrine, whether it be of God, or whether I speak of myself" (John 7:17).

If a man is not willing to do the will of God he will not know the doctrine. There is no class of skeptics who are ignorant of the fact that God desires them to give up sin. If a man is willing to turn from sin and take the light and thank Him for what He does give, and not expect to have light on the whole Bible all at once, he will get more light day by day; make progress step by step; and be led right out of darkness into the clear light of heaven.

In Daniel 12:10 we are told; "Many shall be purified, and made white, and tried but the wicked shall do wickedly; and none of the wicked shall understand; but the wise shall understand."

Now God will never reveal His secrets to His enemies. Never! And if a man persists in living in sin he will not know the doctrines of God. "The secret of the Lord is with them that fear him; and he will show them his covenant" (Psalm 25:14).

And in John 15:15 we read, "Henceforth I call you not; servants; for the servant knoweth not what his Lord doeth but I have called you friends; for all things that I have heard of my Father I have made known unto you." When you become friends of Christ you will know His secrets. The Lord said, "Shall I hide from Abraham that thing which I do?" (Genesis 18:17)

Now those who resemble God are most likely to understand God. If a man is not willing to turn from sin he will not know God's will, nor will God reveal His secrets to him. But if a man is willing to turn from sin he will be surprised to see how the light will come in!

Where God Meets Every Soul

I remember one night when the Bible was the driest and darkest book in the universe to me. The next day it became entirely different. I thought I had the key to it. I had been born of the Spirit. But before I knew anything of the mind of God I had to give up my sin. I believe God meets every soul on the spot of self-surrender, when they are willing to let Him guide and lead. The trouble with many skeptics is their self-conceit. They know more than the Almighty! And they do not come in a teachable spirit. But the moment a man comes in a receptive spirit he is blessed, for "If any of you lack wisdom, let him ask of God, that giveth to all men liberally, and upbraideth not; and it shall be given him" (James 1:5).

Chapter 5

A DIVINE SAVIOR

"Thou art the CHRIST, the Son of the living God"
—Matthew 16:16; John 6:69.

We meet with a certain class of inquirers who do not believe in the Divinity of Christ. There are many passages that will give light on this subject.

In 1 Corinthians 15:47, we are told, "The first man is of the earth earthy: the second man is the Lord from heaven." In 1 John 5:20: "We know that the Son of God is come, and hath given us an understanding, that we may know him that is true; and we are in him that is true, even in his Son Jesus Christ ... This is the true God and eternal life." Again in John 17:3: "And this is life eternal, that they might know thee, the only true God; and Jesus Christ whom thou hast sent."

And then, in Mark 14:60: "The high priest stood up in the midst, and asked Jesus, saying, Answerest thou nothing? What is it which these witness against thee? But he held his peace, and answered nothing. Again the high priest asked him, and said unto him, Art thou the Christ, the Son of the Blessed? And Jesus said, I am: and ye shall see the Son of man sitting on the right hand of power, and coming in the clouds of heaven. Then the high priest rent his clothes, and saith, what need we any further witnesses? Ye have heard the blasphemy: what think ye? And they all condemned him to be guilty of death."

The Divinity of Christ

What brought me to believe in the Divinity of Christ was this: I did not know where to place Christ, or what to do with Him, if He were not divine. When I was a boy I thought that He was a good man like Moses, Joseph, or Abraham. I even thought that He was the best man who had ever lived on the earth. But I found that Christ had a higher claim. He claimed to be God-Man, to be divine and to have come from heaven. He said, "Before Abraham was I am" (John 8:58).

I could not understand this, and I was driven to the conclusion—and I challenge any candid man to deny the inference, or meet the argument—that Jesus Christ is either an impostor or deceiver, or He is the God-Man, God manifest in the flesh. And for these reasons: The first commandment is, "Thou shalt have no other gods before Me" (Exodus 20:3).

Look at the millions throughout Christendom who worship Jesus Christ as God. If Christ were not God this is idolatry. We are all guilty of breaking the first commandment, if Jesus Christ were mere man—if He were a created being, and not what He claims to be.

Some people, who do not admit His divinity, say that He was the best man who ever lived; but if He were not Divine, for that very reason He ought not to be reckoned a good man, for He laid claim to an honor and dignity to which these very people declare He had no right or title. That would rank Him as a deceiver.

Others say that He thought He was divine, but that He was deceived. As if Jesus Christ were carried away by a delusion and deception, and thought that He was more than He was! I could not conceive of a lower idea of Jesus Christ than that. This would not only make Him out an impostor; but that He was out of His mind, and that He did not know who He was, or where He came from. Now if Jesus Christ was not what He claimed to be—the Savior of the world, and if He did not come from heaven, He was a gross deceiver.

But how can anyone read the life of Jesus Christ and make Him out a deceiver? A man has generally some motive for being an impostor. What was Christ's motive? He knew that the course He was pursuing would conduct Him to the Cross; that His name would be cast out as vile; and that many of His followers would be called upon to lay down their lives for His sake. Nearly every one of the apostles was a martyr; and they were considered as off scouring and refuse in the midst of the people. If a man is an impostor, he has a motive at the back of his hypocrisy. But what was Christ's object? The record is that He "went about doing good" (Acts 10:38). This is not the work of an imposter. Do not let the enemy of your soul deceive you.

In John 5:21-23 we read: "For as the Father raiseth up the dead, and quickeneth them; even so the Son quickeneth whom He will. For the Father judgeth no man, but hath committed all judgment unto the Son: that all men should honor the Son, even as they honor the Father. He that honoureth not the Son honoureth not the Father which hath sent Him."

Now, notice that by the Jewish law if a man were a blasphemer he was to be put to death; and supposing Christ to be merely human, if this is not blasphemy I do not know where you will find it.

259

"He that honoureth not the Son honoureth not the Father" (John 5:23). That is downright blasphemy if Christ be not divine. If Moses, or Elijah, or Elisha, or any other mortal had said, "You must honor me as you honor God"; and had put himself on a level with God, it would have been downright blasphemy.

The Jews put Christ to death because they said that He was not what He claimed to be. It was on that testimony He was put under oath. The high priest said, "I adjure thee by the living God, that thou tell us whether thou be the Christ, the Son of God" (Matthew 26:63).

> *And when the Jews came round Him and said, "How long dost Thou make us to doubt? If Thou be the Christ tell us plainly." Jesus said, "I and My Father are one." Then the Jews took up stones again to stone Him (John 10:24-33). They said they did not want to hear more, for that was blasphemy. It was for declaring Himself to be the Son of God that He was condemned and put to death* (Matthew 26:63-66).

Now if Jesus Christ was mere man the Jews did right, according to their law, in putting Him to death. In Leviticus 24:16 we read, "And he that blasphemeth the name of the Lord, he shall surely be put to death, and all the congregation shall certainly stone him: as well the stranger, as he that is born in the land, when he blasphemeth the name of the Lord, shall be put to death."

This law obliged them to put to death everyone who blasphemed. It was making the statement that He was divine that cost Him His life; and by the Mosaic Law He ought to have suffered the death penalty. In John 16:15 Christ says,

260

"All things that the Father hath are mine: therefore said I, that he shall take of mine, and shall show it unto you."

How could He be merely a good man and use language as that? No doubt has ever entered my mind on the point since I was converted.

Divinity of Christ

A notorious sinner was once asked how he could prove the divinity of Christ. His answer was, "Why, He has saved me; and that is a pretty good proof, is it not?"

An infidel on one occasion said to me, "I have been studying the life of John the Baptist, Mr. Moody. Why don't you preach him? He was a greater character than Christ. You would do a greater work."

I said to him, "My friend, *you* preach John the Baptist; and I will follow you and preach Christ, and we will see who will do the most good."

"You will do the most good," he said, "because the people are so superstitious." Ah! John was beheaded, and his disciples begged for his body and buried it. But Christ has risen from the dead. "Thou hast ascended on high; Thou hast led captivity captive; Thou hast received gifts for men" (Psalm 68:18).

Our Christ Lives!

Our Christ LIVES. Many people have not found out that Christ has risen from the grave. They worship a dead Savior, like Mary, who said, "They have taken away my Lord; and I know not where they have laid him" (John 20:13). That is the trouble with those who doubt the divinity of our Lord.

Then look at Matthew 18:20. "Where two or three are gathered together in my name, there am I in the midst of them." "There am I." Well now, if He is a mere man, how can He be there? All these are strong passages.

Again in Matthew 28:18. "And Jesus came and spake unto them, saying, All power is given unto me in heaven and in earth." Could He be a mere man and talk in that way? "All power is given unto Me in heaven and in earth!"

Then again in Matthew 28:20, "Teaching them to observe all things whatsoever I have commanded you: and, lo I am with you alway, even unto the end of the world." If He were mere man how could He be with us? Yet He says, "I am with you alway, even unto the end of the world!"

Then again in Mark 2:7-9, "Why doth this man thus speak blasphemies? Who can forgive sins but God only? And immediately when Jesus perceived in his spirit that they so reasoned within themselves, he said unto them, Why reason ye these things in your hearts? Whether is it easier to say to the sick of the palsy, Thy sins be forgiven thee; or to say, Arise, and take up thy bed, and walk?"

Some men will meet you and say, "Did not Elisha also raise the dead?" Notice that in the rare instances in which men have raised the dead they did it by the power of God. They called on God to do it. But when Christ was on earth He did not call upon the Father to bring the dead to life. When He went to the house of Jairus He said, "Damsel, I say unto thee, Arise" (Mark 5:41).

He had power to impart life. When they were carrying the young man out of Nain, He had compassion on the widowed mother and came and touched the bier and said, "Young man, I say unto thee, Arise" (Luke 7:14).

He spoke, and the dead arose. And when He raised Lazarus He called with a loud voice, "Lazarus, come forth!" (John 11:43) And Lazarus heard, and came forth. Someone has said, it was a good thing that Lazarus was mentioned by name, or all the dead within the sound of Christ's voice would have immediately risen.

In John 5:25 Jesus says, "Verily, verily, I say unto you, The hour is coming, and now is, when the dead shall hear the voice of the Son of God: and they that hear shall live." What blasphemy would this have been, had He not been divine! The proof is overwhelming, if you would only examine the Word of God.

Christ Accepts Our Worship

No good man except Jesus Christ has ever allowed anybody to worship Him. When this was done He never rebuked the worshipper. In John 9:38 we read that when the blind man was found by Christ he said, "Lord, I believe. And he worshipped him." The Lord did not rebuke him.

Then again, Revelation 22:6-9 runs thus: "And he said unto me, these things are faithful and true; and the Lord God of the holy prophets sent his angel to show unto his servants the things which must shortly be done. Behold, I come quickly: blessed is he that keepeth the sayings of the prophecy of this book. And I John saw these things and heard them. And when I had heard and seen, I fell down to worship before the feet of the angel that showed me these things. Then saith he unto me, See thou do it not; for I am thy fellow-servant and of thy brethren the prophets, and of them which keep the sayings of this book: *worship God.*"

263

We see here, that even that angel would not allow John to worship him. Even an angel from heaven! And if Gabriel came down here from the presence of God it would be a sin to worship him or any seraph, or any cherub, or Michael, or any archangel. "WORSHIP GOD!" And if Jesus Christ were not God manifest in the flesh we are guilty of idolatry in worshipping Him.

In Matthew 14:33 we read: "Then they that were in the ship came and *worshipped* him, saying, Of a truth thou art the Son of God." He did not rebuke them.

And in Matthew 8:2 we also read, "And, behold, there came a leper and *worshipped* Him, saying, Lord, if thou wilt, thou canst make me clean."

In Matthew 15:25: "Then came she, and *worshipped* him, saying, Lord, help me!" There are many other passages, but I give these as sufficient in my opinion to prove beyond any doubt the Divinity of our Lord.

In Acts 14, we are told the heathen of Lystra came with garlands and would have done sacrifice to Paul and Barnabas because they had cured an impotent man. But the evangelists rent their clothes and told these Lystrans that they were but men, and not to be worshipped, as if it were a great sin. And if Jesus Christ is a mere man, we are all guilty of a great sin in worshipping Him.

But if He is, as we believe, the only-begotten and well-beloved Son of God, let us yield to His claims upon us. Let us rest on His all-atoning work, and go forth to serve Him all the days of our life.

Chapter 6

REPENTANCE AND RESTITUTION

"God commandeth all men everywhere to repent"
—Acts 17:30

Repentance is one of the fundamental doctrines of the Bible. Yet I believe it is one of those truths that many people little understand at the present day. There are more people today in the mist and the darkness about Repentance, Regeneration, the Atonement, and such-like fundamental truths, than perhaps on any other doctrines. Yet from our earliest years we have heard about them. If I were to ask for a definition of Repentance, a great many would give a very strange and false idea of it.

A man is not prepared to believe or to receive the Gospel unless he is ready to repent of his sins and turn from them. Until John the Baptist met Christ, he had only one text, "Repent ye; for the kingdom of heaven is at hand" (Matthew 3:2). But if he had continued to say this, and had stopped there without pointing the people to Christ the Lamb of God, he would not have accomplished much.

When Christ came, He took up the same wilderness cry, "Repent; for the kingdom of heaven is at hand" (Matthew

4:17). And when our Lord sent out His disciples, it was with the same message, "that men should repent" (Mark 6:12).

After He had been glorified, and when the Holy Ghost came down, we find Peter on the day of Pentecost raising the same cry, "Repent!" It was this preaching—Repent, and believe the Gospel—that wrought such marvelous results (Acts 2:38-47). And we find that, when Paul went to Athens, he uttered the same cry, *"God ... now commandeth all men, everywhere, to repent" (Acts 17:30).*

What Repentance Is Not

Before I speak of what repentance is, let me briefly say what it *is not*. Repentance is not *fear*. Many people have confounded the two. They think they have to be alarmed and terrified, and they are waiting for some kind of fear to come down upon them. But multitudes become alarmed who do not really repent. You have heard of men at sea during a terrible storm. Perhaps they had been very profane men; but when the danger came they suddenly grew quiet, and began to cry to God for mercy. Yet you would not say they repented. When the storm had passed away, they went on swearing the same as before. You might think that the king of Egypt repented when God sent the terrible plagues upon him and his land. But it was not repentance at all. The moment God's hand was removed Pharaoh's heart was harder than ever. He did not turn from a single sin. He was the same man. So there was no true repentance.

Often, when death comes into a family, it looks as if the event would be sanctified to the conversion of all who are in the house. Yet in six months' time all may be forgotten. Some who read this have passed through that experience. When God's hand was heavy upon them, it looked as if they were going to repent, but the trial has been removed the impression has all but gone.

Then again, repentance is not a *feeling*. I find a great many people are waiting for a certain kind of feeling to come. They would like to turn to God; but think they cannot do it until this feeling comes. When I was at Baltimore I used to preach every Sunday in the penitentiary to nine hundred convicts. There was hardly a man there who did not feel miserable enough—they had plenty of feeling. For the first week or ten days of their imprisonment many of them cried half the time. Yet, when they were released, most of them would go right back to their old ways. The truth was, that they felt very bad because they had got caught; that was all. So you have seen a man in the time of trial show a good deal of feeling, but very often it is only because he has got into trouble; not because he has committed sin, or because his conscience tells him he has done evil in the sight of God. It seems as if the trial were going to result in true repentance; but the feeling too often passes away.

Once again, repentance is not *fasting and afflicting the body*. A man may fast for weeks and months and years, and yet not repent of one sin. Neither is it *remorse*. Judas had terrible remorse—enough to make him go and hang himself; but that was not repentance. I believe if he had gone to his Lord, fallen on his face, and confessed his sin he would have been forgiven. Instead of this he went to the priests, and then put an end to his life. A man may do all sorts of penance, but there is no true repentance in that. Put that down in your mind. You cannot meet the claims of God by offering the fruit of your body for the sin of your soul. Away with such a delusion!

267

Repentance is not *conviction of sin*. That may sound strange to some. I have seen men under such deep conviction of sin that they could not sleep at night; they could not enjoy a single meal. They went on for months in this state and yet they were not converted; they did not truly repent. Do not confound conviction of sin with repentance.

That too, may sound strange. Many people, when they become anxious about their soul's salvation, say, "I will pray, and read the Bible"; and they think that will bring about the desired effect. But it will not do it. You may read the Bible and cry to God a great deal, and yet never repent. Many people cry loudly to God, and yet do not repent.

Another thing; repentance is not the *breaking off someone's sin*. A great many people make that mistake. A man who has been a drunkard signs a pledge and stops drinking. Breaking off one sin is not repentance. Forsaking one vice is like breaking off one limb of a tree, when the whole tree has to come down. When a profane man stops swearing that is good, but if he does not break off *from every sin* it is not repentance—it is not the work of God in the soul. When God works He hews down the whole tree. He wants to have a man turn from every sin. Supposing I am in a vessel out at sea and I find the ship leaks in three or four places. I may go and stop up one hole, yet down goes the vessel. Or suppose I am wounded in three or four places, and I get a remedy for one wound. But if the other two or three wounds are neglected, my life will soon be gone. True repentance is not merely breaking off this or that particular sin.

What *Is* Repentance?

Well then, you will ask, what is repentance? I will give you a good definition: it is "right about face!" In the Irish language the word "repentance" means even more than "right

268

about face!" It implies that a man who has been walking in one direction has not only faced about, but is actually walking in an exactly contrary direction. "Turn ye, turn ye from your evil ways; for why will ye die?" (Ezekiel 33:11).

A man may have little feeling or much feeling, but if he does not turn away from sin God will not have mercy on him. Repentance has also been described as "a change of mind." For instance, there is the parable told by Christ: "A certain man had two sons; and he came to the first, and said, Son, go work today in my vineyard. He answered and said, I will not" (Matthew 21:28, 29).

After he said, "I will not," he thought over it, and changed his mind. Perhaps he may have said to himself, "I did not speak very respectfully to my father. He asked me to go and work, and I told him I would not go. I think I was wrong." But suppose he had only said this, and still had not gone he would not have repented. He was not only convinced that he was wrong; but he went off into the fields, hoeing, or mowing, or whatever it was. That is Christ's definition of repentance. If a man says, "By the grace of God I will forsake my sin, and do His will," that is repentance—a turning right about.

Can a man at once repent? Certainly he can. It does not take a long while to turn around. It does not take a man six months to change his mind. There was a vessel that went down some time ago on the Newfoundland coast. As she was bearing towards the shore, there was a moment when the captain could have given orders to reverse the engines and turn back. If the engines had been reversed then, the ship would have been saved. But there was a moment when it was too late. So there is a moment, I believe, in every man's life when he can halt and say, "By the grace of God I will go no further towards death and ruin. I repent of my sins and turn from them." You may say you have not got feeling enough, but if you are convinced that you are on the wrong road, turn around and say, "I will no longer go on in the way of rebellion and sin as I have done." Just then, when you are willing to turn towards God, salvation may be yours.

I find that every case of conversion recorded in the Bible was instantaneous. Repentance and faith came very suddenly. The moment a man made up his mind, God gave him the power. God does not ask any man to do what he has not the power to do. He would not "command all men everywhere to repent" (Acts 17:30), if they were not able to do so. Man has no one to blame but himself if he does not repent and believe the Gospel.

A Story of Conversion

One of the leading ministers of the Gospel in Ohio wrote me a letter some time ago describing his conversion; it very forcibly illustrates this point of instantaneous decision, He says:

"I was nineteen years old, and was reading law with a Christian lawyer in Vermont. One afternoon when he was away from home, his good wife said to me as I came into the house, 'I want you to go to class-meeting with me tonight and become a Christian, so that you can conduct family worship while my husband is away.'

"'Well, I'll do it,' I said, without any thought. When I came into the house again she asked me if I was honest in what I had said. I replied, 'Yes, so far as going to meeting with you is concerned, that is only courteous.'

"I went with her to the class-meeting, as I had often done before. About a dozen persons were present in a little schoolhouse. The leader had spoken to all in the room except for two others and myself. He was speaking to the person next me, when the thought occurred to me, he will ask me if I have anything to say. I said to myself, I have decided to be a Christian sometime; why not begin now? In less time than a minute after these thoughts had passed through my mind he said, speaking to me familiarly— for he knew me very well—'Brother Charles, have you anything to say?'

"I replied, with perfect coolness, 'Yes, sir. I have just decided, within the last thirty seconds, that I will begin a Christian life, and would like to have you pray for me.'

"My coolness staggered him. I think he almost doubted my sincerity. He said very little, but passed on and spoke to the other two. After a few general remarks, he turned to me and said, 'Brother Charles, will you close the meeting with prayer?'

"He knew I had never prayed in public. Up to this moment I had no feeling. It was purely a business transaction. My first thought was I cannot pray, and I will ask him to excuse me. My second was. I have said I will begin a Christian life; and this is a part of it. So I said, 'Let us pray.' And somewhere between the times I started to kneel and the time my knees struck the floor the Lord converted my soul.

"The first words I said were, 'Glory to God!' What I said after that I do not know, and it does not matter, for my soul was too full to say much but 'Glory!' From that hour the devil has never dared to challenge my conversion. To Christ is all the praise."

Many people are waiting, they cannot exactly tell for what, but for some sort of miraculous feeling to come stealing over them—some mysterious kind of faith. I was speaking to a man some years ago, and he always had one answer to give me. For five years I tried to win him to Christ, and every year he said, "It has not 'struck me' yet."

"Man, what do you mean? What has not struck you?"

"Well," he said, "I am not going to become a Christian until it strikes me, and it has not struck me yet. I do not see it in the way you see it."

"But don't you know you are a sinner?"

"Yes, I know I am a sinner."

"Well, don't you know that God wants to have mercy on you—that there is forgiveness with God? He wants you to repent and come to Him."

"Yes, I know that; but it has not struck me yet." He always fell back on that. Poor man! He went down to his grave in a state of indecision. Sixty long years God gave him to repent; and all he had to say at the end of those years was that it "had not struck him yet!"

The Time to Believe is Now

Is any reader waiting for some strange feeling? Nowhere in the Bible is a man told to wait. God is commanding you *now* to repent.

Do you think God can forgive a man when he does not want to be forgiven? Would he be happy if God forgave him in this state of mind? Why, if a man went into the kingdom of God without repentance, heaven would be hell to him. Heaven is a prepared place for a prepared people. If your boy has done wrong, and will not repent, you cannot forgive him. You would be doing him an injustice. Suppose he goes to your desk, and steals $10, and squanders it. When you come home your servant tells you what your boy has done. You ask if it is true, and he denies it. But at last you have certain proof. Even when he finds he cannot deny it any longer, he will not confess the sin, but says he will do it again the first chance he gets. Would you say to him, "Well, I forgive you," and leave the matter there? No! Yet people say that God is going to save all men, whether they repent or not: drunkards, thieves, harlots, whoremongers, it makes no difference. "God is so merciful," they say. Dear friends, do not be deceived by the god of this world. Where there is true repentance and a turning from sin unto God, He will meet and bless you; but He never blesses until there is sincere repentance.

David's Mistake With Absalom

David made a woeful mistake in this respect with his rebellious son, Absalom. He could not have done his son a greater injustice than to forgive him when his heart was unchanged. There could be no true reconciliation between them when there was no repentance. But God does not make these mistakes. David got into trouble on account of his error of judgment. His son soon drove his father from the throne.

Speaking on repentance, Dr. Brooks, of St. Louis, well remarks:

"Repentance, strictly speaking, means a 'change of mind or purpose' consequently it is the judgment which the sinner pronounces upon himself, in view of the love of God displayed in the death of Christ, connected with the abandonment of all confidence in himself and with trust in the only Savior of sinners. Saving repentance and saving faith always go together; and you need not be worried about repentance if you will believe.

"Some people are not sure that they have 'repented enough.' If you mean by this that you must repent in order to incline God to be merciful to you, the sooner you give over such repentance the better. God is already merciful, as He has fully shown at the Cross of Calvary; and it is a grievous dishonor to His heart of love if you think that your tears and anguish will move Him, 'not knowing that the goodness of God leadeth thee to repentance' (Romans 2:4). It is not your badness, therefore, but His goodness that leads to repentance; hence the true way to repent is to believe on the Lord Jesus Christ, 'who was delivered for our offenses, and was raised again for our justification' (Romans 4:25)."

Genuine Repentance

Another thing. If there is true repentance it will bring forth fruit. If we have done wrong to anyone we should never ask God to forgive us, until we are willing to make restitution. If I have done any man a great injustice and can make it good, I need not ask God to forgive me until I am willing to make it good. Suppose I have taken something that

274

does not belong to me. I have no right to expect forgiveness until I make restitution.

I remember preaching in one of our large cities, when a fine-looking man came up to me at the close. He was in great distress of mind. "The fact is," he said, "I am a defaulter. I have taken money that belonged to my employers. How can I become a Christian without restoring it?"

"Have you got the money?"

He told me he had not got it all. He had taken about $1,500, and he still had about $900. He said, "Could I not take that money and go into business, and make enough to pay them back?"

I told him that was a delusion of Satan; that he could not expect to prosper on stolen money; that he should restore all he had, and go and ask his employers to have mercy upon him and forgive him.

"But they will put me in prison," he said. "Cannot you give me any help?"

"No, you must restore the money before you can expect to get any help from God."

"It is pretty hard," he said.

"Yes, it is hard, but the great mistake was in doing the wrong at first."

His burden became so heavy that it got to be insupportable. He handed me the money—$950 and some cents—and asked me to take it back to his employers. The next evening the two employers and myself met in a side room of the church. I laid the money down, and informed them it was from one of their *employees*. I told them the story, and said he wanted mercy from them, not justice. The tears trickled down the cheeks of these two men, and they said, "Forgive him? Yes, we will be glad to forgive him." I went downstairs and brought him up. After he had confessed his guilt and had been forgiven, we all got down on our knees and had a blessed prayer meeting. God met us and blessed us there.

There was a friend of mine, who some time ago, had come to Christ and wished to consecrate himself and his wealth to God. He had formerly had transactions with the government, and had taken advantage of it. This thing came up when he was converted, and his conscience troubled him. He said, "I want to consecrate my wealth; but it seems as if God will not take it." He had a terrible struggle; his conscience kept rising up and smiting him. At last he drew a check for $1,500 and sent it to the United States Treasury. He told me he received such a blessing when he had done it. That was bringing forth "fruits meet for repentance" (Matthew 3:8). I believe a great many men are crying to God for light; and they are not getting it because they are not honest.

I was once preaching, and a man came to me who was only thirty-two years old, but whose hair was very gray. He said, "I want you to notice that my hair is gray, and I am only thirty-two years old. For twelve years I have carried a great burden."

"Well," I said, "what is it?"

He looked around as if afraid someone would hear him. "Well," he answered, "my father died and left my mother with the county newspaper, and left her only that. That was all she had. After he died the paper began to waste away, and

I saw my mother was fast sinking into a state of need. The building and the paper were insured for a thousand dollars, and when I was twenty years old I set fire to the building, and obtained the thousand dollars, and gave it to my mother. For twelve years that sin has been haunting me. I have tried to drown it by indulgence in pleasure and sin. I have cursed God, I have gone into infidelity, I have tried to convince myself that the Bible is not true, I have done everything I could—but all these years I have been tormented."

I said, "There is a way out of that."

He inquired "How?"

I said, "Make restitution. Let us sit down and calculate the interest, and then you pay the Company the money."

It would have done you good to see that man's face light up when he found there was mercy for him. He said he would be glad to pay back the money and interest if he could only be forgiven.

There are men today who are in darkness and bondage because they are not willing to turn from their sins and confess them; and I do not know how a man can hope to be forgiven if he is not willing to confess his sin.

Bear in mind that *now* is the only day of mercy you will ever have. You can repent now, and have the awful record blotted out. God waits to forgive you; He is seeking to bring you to Himself. But I think the Bible teaches clearly that there is *no repentance after this life*. There are some who tell you of the possibility of repentance in the grave; but I do not find that in Scriptures. I have looked my Bible over very carefully, and I cannot find that a man will have another opportunity of being saved. *Why should he ask for any more time?* You have time enough to repent now. You can turn from your sins this moment if you will. God says, "I have no pleasure in the death of him that dieth; wherefore turn, and live ye" (Ezekiel 18:32).

Christ said He "came not to call the righteous, but sinners to repentance." (Mark 2:17). Are you a sinner? Then the call to repent is addressed to you. Take your place in the dust at the Savior's feet, and acknowledge your guilt. Say, like the publican of old, "God be merciful to me a sinner!" (Luke 18:13), and see how quickly He will pardon and bless you. He will even justify you and reckon you as righteous, by virtue of the righteousness of Him who bore your sins in His own body on the Cross.

There are some perhaps who think themselves righteous; and that, therefore, there is no need for them to repent and believe the Gospel. They are like the Pharisee in the parable, who thanked God that he was not as other men— "extortionists, unjust, adulterers, or even as this publican" (Luke 18:11); and who went on to say, "I fast twice a week; I give tithes of all I possess" (Luke 18:12). What is the judgment about such self-righteous persons?

"I tell you this man [the poor, contrite, repenting publican] went down to his house justified rather than the other" (Luke 18:11-14).

"There is none righteous; no, not one ... All have sinned, and come short of the glory of God" (Romans 3:10, 23).

Let no one say he does not need to repent. Let each one take his true place—that of a sinner; then God will lift him up to the place of forgiveness and justification.

"*Whosoever exalteth himself shall be abased; and he that humbleth himself shall be exalted*" (Luke 14:11).

Wherever God sees true repentance in the heart He meets that soul.

Chapter 7

ASSURANCE OF SALVATION

"These things have I written unto you that believe on the name of the Son of God; that ye may know that ye have eternal life. and that ye may believe on the name of the Son of God"—1 John 5:13

Someone will ask, "Have all God's people assurance?" No. I think a good many of God's dear people have no assurance. But it is the privilege of every child of God to have, beyond doubt, knowledge of his own salvation. No man who is fit for God's service is filled with doubts. If a man is not sure of his own salvation, how can he help anyone else into the kingdom of God? If I seem in danger of drowning and do not know whether I shall ever reach the shore, I cannot assist another. I must first get on the solid rock myself, and then I can lend my brother a helping hand. If I myself being blind were to tell another blind man how to get sight, he might reply, "First get healed yourself and then you can tell me."

There are two classes who ought not to have assurance. First, those who are in the Church, but who are not converted, having never been born of the Spirit. Second, those not willing to do God's will; who are not ready to take the place that God has mapped out for them, but want to fill some other place.

None will have time or heart to work for God, who are not assured as to their own salvation. They have as much as they can attend to; and being themselves burdened with doubts, they cannot help others to carry their burdens. There is no rest, joy, or peace—no liberty, nor power—where doubts and uncertainty exist.

Now it seems as if there are three wiles of Satan against which we ought to be on our guard. In the first place he moves his kingdom to keep us away from Christ, then he devotes himself to get us into "Doubting Castle." But if we have, in spite of him, a clear ringing witness for the Son of God, he will do all he can to blacken our characters and belie our testimony.

Do Not Doubt

Some seem to think that it is presumption not to have doubts: but doubt is very dishonoring to God. If anyone were to say that they had known a person for thirty years and yet doubted him, it would not be very creditable: and when we have known God for ten, twenty, or thirty years does it not reflect on His veracity to doubt Him?

Could Paul and the early Christians and martyrs have gone through what they did if they had been filled with doubts, and had not known whether they were going to heaven or to perdition after they had been burned at the stake? They must have had assurance.

C. H. Spurgeon says:

"I never heard of a stork that when it met with a fir tree demurred as to its right to build its nest there; and I never heard of a coney (a small rock badger) that ever questioned whether it had a permit to run into the rock. Why, these creatures would soon perish if they were always doubting and fearing as to whether they had a right to use providential provisions.

"The stork says to himself, 'Ah, here is a fir tree:' he consults with his mate, 'Will this do for the nest in which we may rear our young?' 'Aye,' she says; and they gather the materials, and arrange them. There is never any deliberation, 'May we build here?' but they bring their sticks and make their nest.

"The wild goat on the crag does not say, 'Have I a right to be here?' No, he must be somewhere; and there is a crag that exactly suits him, and he springs upon it.

"Yet, though these dumb creatures know the provision of their God, the sinner does not recognize the provision of his Savior. He quibbles and questions, 'May I?' and 'I am afraid it is not for me;' and 'I think it cannot be meant for me;' and 'I am afraid it is too good to be true.'

"And yet nobody ever said to the stork, 'Whosoever buildeth on this fir tree shall never have his nest pulled down.' No inspired word has ever said to the coney, 'Whosoever runs into this rock-cleft shall never be driven out of it.' If it had been so, it would make assurance doubly sure.

"And yet here is Christ provided for sinners, just the sort of a Savior sinners need; and the encouragement is added, 'Him that cometh to Me I will in no wise cast out' (John 6:37), 'Whosoever will, let him take the water of life freely' (Revelation 22:17)."

Christ Our Advocate

Now let us come to the Word. John tells us in his Gospel what Christ did for us on earth. In his Epistle he tells us what He is doing for us in heaven as our Advocate. In his Gospel there are only two chapters in which the word "believe" does not occur. With these two exceptions, every chapter in John is "Believe! Believe!! BELIEVE!!!" He tells us in 20:31, "But these are written, that ye might believe that Jesus is the Christ, the Son of God; and that, believing, ye might have life through his name."

That is the purpose for which he wrote the Gospel—"that we might believe that Jesus is the Christ, the Son of God; and that, believing, we might have life through his name" (John 20:31).

Turn to 1 John 5:13. There he tells us why he wrote this Epistle: "These things have I written unto you that believe on the name of the Son of God." Notice to whom he writes it. "You that believe on the name of the Son of God; that ye may know that ye have eternal life, and that ye may believe on the name of the Son of God."

There are only five short chapters in this first Epistle, and the word "know" occurs over forty times. It is "*Know!* KNOW!! KNOW!!!*" The key to it is KNOW! And all through the Epistle there rings out the refrain—"that we might know that we have eternal life."

I went twelve hundred miles down the Mississippi in the spring some years ago. Every evening, just as the sun went down, you might have seen men, and sometimes women, riding up to the banks of the river on either side on mules or horses. Sometimes they would be coming on foot for the purpose of lighting up the Government lights. All down that mighty river there were landmarks that guided the pilots in their dangerous navigation. Now God has given us lights or landmarks to tell us whether we are His children or not. What we need to do is to examine the tokens He has given us.

Five Things Worth Knowing

In the third chapter of John's first Epistle there are these five things worth knowing:

1. In the fifth verse we read; "And ye *know* that He was manifested to take away our sins; and in Him is no sin." Not what I have done, but what HE has done. Has He failed in His mission? Is He not able to do what He came for? Did ever any heaven-sent man fail yet? And could God's own Son fail? *He was manifested to take away our sins!*

2. In the nineteenth verse, the Lord tells us; "And hereby *we know* that we are of the truth, and shall *assure* our hearts before Him." We KNOW that we are of the TRUTH. And if the truth sets us free, we shall be free indeed. "If the Son therefore shall make you free, ye shall be free indeed" (John 8:36).

3. The third thing worth knowing is in the fourteenth verse. "We *know* that we have passed from death unto life, because we love the brethren." The natural man does not like godly people, nor does he care to be in their company. "He that loveth not his brother abideth in death." He has no spiritual life.

4. The fourth thing worth knowing we find in verse twenty-four. "And he that keepeth His commandments

dwelleth in Him, and He in him. And hereby we *know* that He abideth in us, by the Spirit which He hath given us." We can tell what kind of spirit we have if we possess the Spirit of Christ—a Christ-like spirit—not the same in degree, but the same in kind. If I am meek, gentle, and forgiving; if I have a spirit filled with peace and joy; if I am long-suffering and gentle, like the Son of God—that is a test—and in that way we are to tell whether we have eternal life or not.

5. The fifth thing worth knowing, and the best of all, is; "Beloved, *now.*" Notice the word "now." It does not say when you come to die. "Beloved, *now* are we the sons of God; and it doth not yet appear what we shall be: but we *know* that, when He shall appear, we shall be like Him; for we shall see Him as He is" (v. 2).

Can a Person Sin After Becoming a Christian?

But some will say, "Well, I believe all that, but I have sinned since I became a Christian." Is there a man or a woman on the face of the earth who has not sinned since becoming a Christian? Not one. There never has been, and never will be, a soul on this earth who has not sinned, or who will not sin, at some time of their Christian experience. But God has made provision for believers' sins. *We* are not to make provision for them; but God has. Bear that in mind.

Turn to 1 John 2:1: "My little children, these things write I unto you, that ye sin not. And if any man sin, we have an Advocate with the Father, Jesus Christ the righteous."

He is here writing to the righteous. "If any man sin, *we* (John put himself in) have an Advocate with the Father, Jesus Christ the righteous." What an Advocate! He attends to our interests at the very best place—the throne of God.

He said, "Nevertheless, I tell you the truth; it is expedient for you that I go away" (John 16:7). He went away to become our High Priest, and also our Advocate. He has had some hard cases to plead; but He has never lost one: and if you entrust your immortal interests to Him, He will "present you faultless before the presence of His glory with exceeding joy" (Jude 24).

Confession Brings Forgiveness

The past sins of Christians are all forgiven as soon as they are confessed, and they are never to be mentioned. That is a question not to be opened up again. If our sins have been put away, that is the end of them. They are not to be remembered, and God will not mention them anymore. This is very plain. Suppose I have a son who, while I am away from home, does wrong. When I go home he throws his arms around my neck and says, "Papa, I did what you told me not to do. I am sorry. Do forgive me?" I say, "Yes, my son," and kiss him. He wipes away his tears, and goes off rejoicing.

But the next day he says: "Papa, I wish you would forgive me for the wrong I did yesterday." I should say: "Why, my son, that thing is settled, and I don't want it mentioned again." "But I wish you would forgive me. It would help me to hear you say, 'I forgive you.'" Would that be honoring me? Would it not grieve me to have my boy doubt me? But to gratify him I say again, "I forgive you, my son."

And if, the next day, he were again to bring up that old sin, and ask forgiveness, would not that grieve me to the heart? And so, my dear readers, if God has forgiven us, never let us mention the past. Let us forget those things that are behind, and reach forth unto those which are before, and press toward the mark for the prize of the high calling of God in Christ Jesus. Let the sins of the past go; for "If we confess our sins, he is faithful and just to forgive us our sins, and to cleanse us from all unrighteousness" (1 John 1:9).

And let me say that this principle is recognized in courts of justice. A case came up in the courts of a country in which a man had trouble with his wife. He forgave her, and then afterwards brought her into court. And, when it was known that he had forgiven her, the judge said that the thing was settled. The judge recognized the soundness of the principle, that if a sin were once forgiven there was an end of it. And do you think the Judge of all the earth will forgive you and me, and open the question again? Our sins are gone for time and eternity, if God forgives. What we have to do is to confess and forsake our sins.

How to Know If You Are A Child of God
In 2 Corinthians 13:5 we read, "Examine yourselves whether ye be in the faith; prove your own selves. Know ye not your own selves, how that Jesus Christ is in you, except ye be reprobates?"

Now examine yourselves. Try your religion. Put it to the test. Can you forgive an enemy? That is a good way to know if you are a child of God. Can you forgive an injury, or take an affront, as Christ did? Can you be censured for doing well, and not murmur? Can you be misjudged and misrepresented, and yet keep a Christ-like spirit?

Another good test is to read Galatians 5, and notice the fruit of the Spirit; and see if you have them. "The fruit of the Spirit is love, joy, peace, long-suffering, gentleness, goodness, faith, meekness, temperance: against such there is no law."

If I have the fruit of the Spirit I must have the Spirit. I could not have the fruits without the Spirit any more than there could be an orange without the tree. And Christ says; "Ye shall know them by their fruit" (Matthew 7:16); "for the tree is known by his fruit" (Matthew 12:33).

Make the tree good, and the fruit will be good. The only way to get the fruit is to have the Spirit. That is the way to examine ourselves whether we are the children of God.

Then there is another very striking passage. In Romans 8:9, Paul says, "Now if any man have not the Spirit of Christ, he is none of his." That ought to settle the question, even though one may have gone through all the external forms that are considered necessary by some to constitute a church membership. Acceptance as a member of a church is not proof that you are born again—that you are a new creature in Christ Jesus.

Growing in Wisdom and Grace

But although you may be born again, it will require time to become a full-grown Christian. Justification is instantaneous, but sanctification is a life-long process. We are to grow in wisdom. Peter says, "Grow in grace, and in the knowledge of our Lord and Savior Jesus Christ" (2 Peter 3:18); and in the first chapter of his Second Epistle, "Add to your faith virtue; and to virtue knowledge; and to knowledge temperance; and to temperance patience; and to patience godliness; and to godliness brotherly kindness; and to brotherly kindness charity. For if these things be in you and abound they make you that ye shall neither be barren nor unfruitful in the knowledge of our Lord Jesus Christ."

So we are to add grace to grace. A tree may be perfect in its first year of growth, but it does not attain its maturity. So it is with the Christian. He may be a true child of God, but not a matured Christian. The eighth of Romans is very important, and we should be very familiar with it. In the fourteenth verse the apostle says, "For as many as are led by the Spirit of God they are the sons of God."

Just as the soldier is led by his captain, or the pupil by his teacher, or the traveler by his guide; so the Holy Spirit will be the guide of every true child of God.

Paul's Teaching On Assurance

Now let me call your attention to another fact. All Paul's teaching in nearly every Epistle rings out the doctrine of assurance, He says in 2 Corinthians 5:1, "For we *know* that if our earthly house of this tabernacle were dissolved, we have a building of God, a house not made with hands, eternal in the heavens."

He had a title to the mansions above, and he says, *"I know it."* He was not living in uncertainty. He said, "I have a desire to depart and to be with Christ" (Philippians 1:23); and if he had been uncertain he would not have said that. Then in Colossians 3:4, he says, "When Christ, who is our life, shall appear, then shall ye also appear with him in glory."

I am told that Dr. Watts' tombstone bears this same passage of Scripture. There is no doubt there.

Then we see in Colossians 1:12, "Giving thanks unto the Father, which hath made us meet to be partakers of the inheritance of the saints in light; who hath delivered us from the power of darkness, and hath translated us into the kingdom of his dear Son."

Here we have three "haths."
1. "HATH made us meet";
2. "HATH delivered us"; and

3. "HATH translated us."

It does not say that He is going to make us meet; that He is going to deliver; that He is going to translate.

Then again in verse fourteen: "In whom we have redemption through his blood, even the forgiveness of sins."

We are either forgiven or we are not. We should not give ourselves any rest until we get into the kingdom of God, nor until we can each look up and say, "I know that if my earthly house of this tabernacle were dissolved, I have a building of God, a house not made with hands, eternal in the heavens" (2 Corinthians 5:1).

Look at Romans 8:32: "He that spared not his own Son, but delivered him up for us all, how shall he not with him also freely give us all things?"

If He gave us His Son, will He not give us the certainty that He is ours. I have heard this illustration. There was a man who owed $10,000, and would have been made a bankrupt, but a friend came forward and paid the sum. It was found afterwards that he owed a few dollars more; but he did not for a moment entertain a doubt that, as his friend had paid the larger amount, he would also pay the smaller. And we have high warrant for saying that if God has given us His Son He will "with him also freely give us all things"; and if we want to realize our salvation beyond controversy He will not, leave us in darkness.

Again in the thirty-third verse: "Who shall lay anything to the charge of God's elect? It is God that justifieth. Who is he that condemneth? It is Christ that died, yea rather, that is risen again, who is even at the right hand of God, who also

291

maketh intercession for us. Who shall separate us from the love of Christ? Shall tribulation, or distress, or persecution, or famine, or nakedness, or peril, or sword? As it is written, "For thy sake we are killed all the day long; we are accounted as sheep for the slaughter. Nay, in all these things we are more than conquerors through him that loved us. For I am persuaded that neither death, nor life, nor angels, nor principalities, nor powers, nor things present, nor things to come, nor height, nor depth, nor any other creature, shall be able to separate us from the love of God, which is in Christ Jesus our Lord."

You Can Have Assurance

This has a beautiful ring to it. There is assurance for you! "I KNOW." Do you think that the God who has justified me will condemn me? That is quite an absurdity. God is going to save us so that neither men, angels, nor devils, can bring any charge against us. He will have the work complete.

Job lived in a darker day than we do, but we read in Job 19:25: "I *know* that my Redeemer liveth, and that he shall stand in the latter day upon the earth."

The same confidence breathes through Paul's last words to Timothy: "For the which cause I also suffer these things: nevertheless I am not ashamed; for I *know* whom I have believed: and am persuaded that he is able to keep that which I have committed unto him against that day" (2 Timothy 1:12).

It is not a matter of doubt, but of knowledge. "I know." "I am persuaded." The word "Hope," is not used in the Scripture to express doubt. It is used in regard to the second coming of Christ, or to the resurrection of the body. We do not say that we "hope" we are Christians. I do not say that

I "hope" I am an American, or that I "hope" I am a married man. These are settled things. I may say that I "hope" to go back to my home; or I "hope" to attend such a meeting. I do not say that I "hope" to come to this country, for I am here. And so, if we are born of God we know it; and He will not leave us in darkness if we search the Scriptures.

Christ taught this doctrine to His seventy disciples when they returned elated with their success, saying, "Lord, even the devils are subject unto us through Thy name." The Lord seemed to check them, and said that He would give them something to rejoice in: "Notwithstanding in this rejoice not, that the spirits are subject unto you; but rather rejoice because your names are written in heaven" (Luke 10:20).

Our Salvation Is Sure

It is the privilege of every one of us to know, beyond a doubt, that our salvation is sure. Then we can work for others. But if we are doubtful of our own salvation, we are not fit for the service of God.

Another passage is John 5:24: "Verily, verily I say unto you: He that heareth my word, and believeth on him that sent me, hath everlasting life, and shall not come into *'judgment'*" (the revised version has it so) "but is passed from death unto life."

Some people say that you never can tell till you are before the Great White throne of Judgment whether you are saved or not. Why, my dear friend, if your life is hid with Christ in God, you are not coming into judgment for your sins. We may come into judgment for reward. This is clearly taught where the lord reckoned with the servant to whom five talents had been given, and who brought other five talents saying, "Lord, thou deliveredst unto me five talents; behold, I have gained

293

beside them five talents more. His lord said unto him, Well done, thou good and faithful servant: thou hast been faithful over a few things; I will make thee ruler over many things: enter thou into the joy of thy lord" (Matthew 25:20, 21).

We shall be judged for our stewardship. That is one thing, but salvation—eternal life—is another. Will God demand payment twice of the debt that Christ has paid for us? If Christ bore my sins in His own body on the tree, am I to answer for them as well?

Isaiah tells us that, "He was wounded for our transgressions; He was bruised for our iniquities; the chastisement of our peace was upon Him: and with His stripes we are healed" (53:5).

In Romans 4:25 we read, "He was delivered for our offenses, and was raised again for our justification." Let us believe, and get the benefit of His finished work.

Then again in John 10:9: "I am the door: by me if any man enter in he shall be saved, and shall go in and out, and find pasture."

Then in the twenty-seventh verse, "My sheep hear my voice; and I know them, and they follow me. And I give unto them eternal life; and they shall never perish, neither shall any man pluck them out of my hand. My Father which gave them me is greater than all; and no man is able to pluck them out of my Father's hand."

Think of that! The Father, the Son, and the Holy Ghost, are pledged to keep us. You see that it is not only the Father, not only the Son, but the three persons of the Triune God.

Beware of Doubting

Now a great many people want some token outside of God's word. That habit always brings doubt. If I made a promise to meet a man at a certain hour and place tomorrow, and he were to ask me for my watch as a token of my sincerity, it would be a slur on my truthfulness. We must not question what God has said: He has made statement after statement, and multiplied figure upon figure. Christ says:

"I am the door; by me if any man enter in he shall be saved" (John 10:9).

"I am the good shepherd, and know my sheep, and am known of mine" (John 10:14).

"I am the light of the world; he that followeth me shall not walk in darkness, but shall have the light of life" (John 8:12).

"I am ... the Truth:" (John 14:6). Receive Him, and you will have the truth; for He is the embodiment of truth.

Do you want to know the way? "I am the Way" (John 14:6). Follow Him, and He will lead you into the kingdom.

Are you hungering after righteousness? "I am the Bread of Life:" (John 6:35). If you eat of Him you shall never hunger.

I am "the water of life:" if you drink of this water it shall be within you "a well of water springing up unto everlasting life" (Revelation 21:6; John 4:14).

"I am the resurrection and the life: he that believeth in me, though he were dead, yet shall he live; and whosoever liveth and believeth in me shall never die" (John 11:25, 26).

Let me remind you where our doubts come from. A good many of God's dear people never get beyond knowing themselves servants. He calls us "friends." "Ye are my friends, if ye do whatsoever I command you" (John 15:14).

If you go into a house you will soon see the difference between the servant and the son. The son walks at perfect liberty all over the house, because he is at home. But the servant takes a subordinate place. What we want is to get beyond servants. We ought to realize our standing with God as sons and daughters. He will not disinherit His children. God has not only adopted us, but we are His by birth. We have been born into His kingdom. My little boy was as much mine when he was a day old as now that he is fourteen. He was *my son;* although it did not appear what he would be when he attained manhood. He is mine, although he may have to undergo probation under tutors and governors.

Another origin of doubts is looking at ourselves. If you want to be wretched and miserable, filled with doubts from morning till night, look at yourself. "Thou wilt keep him in perfect peace whose mind is stayed on Thee" (Isaiah. 26:3). Many of God's dear children are robbed of joy because they keep looking at themselves.

Someone has said, "There are three ways to look. If you want to be wretched, look within; if you wish to be distracted, look around; but if you would have peace, look up."

"Peter looked away from Christ, and he immediately began to sink. The Master said to him: O thou of little faith! Wherefore didst thou doubt?" (Matthew 14:31).

He had God's eternal Word, which was sure footing, and better than any marble, granite, or iron. But the moment he took his eyes off Christ, down he went. Those who look around cannot see how unstable and dishonoring is their walk. We want to look straight at the "Author and Finisher of our faith" (Hebrews 12:2).

When I was a boy I could only make a straight track in the snow, by keeping my eyes fixed upon a tree or some object before me. The moment I took my eye off the mark set in front of me, I walked crooked. It is only when we look fixedly on Christ that we find perfect peace. After He rose from the dead He showed His disciples His hands and His feet. "Behold my hands and my feet, that it is I myself: handle me, and see; for a spirit hath not flesh and bones, as ye see me have" (Luke 24:39).

That was the ground of their peace. If you want to scatter your doubts, look at the blood, and if you want to increase your doubts, look at yourself. You will get doubts enough for years by being occupied with yourself for a few days.

Then again, look at what He is, and at what He has done; not at what you are, and what you have done. That is the way to find peace and rest.

Abraham Lincoln's Proclamation

Abraham Lincoln issued a proclamation declaring the emancipation of three millions of slaves. On a certain day their chains were to fall off, and they were to be free. That proclamation was put up on the trees and fences wherever the

Northern Army marched. A good many slaves could not read, but others read the proclamation, and most of them believed it. So on that day a glad shout went up, "We are free!" Some did not believe it, and stayed with their old masters, but it did not alter the fact that they were free. Christ, the Captain of our salvation, has proclaimed freedom to all who have faith in Him. Let us take Him at His word. Their feelings would not have made the slaves free. The power must come from the outside. Looking at ourselves will not make us free, but it is looking to Christ with the eye of faith.

Bishop J. C. Ryle has strikingly said:

"Faith is the root, and Assurance is the flower. Doubtless you can never have the flower without the root; but it is no less certain you may have the root and not the flower.

"Faith is that poor, trembling woman who came behind Jesus in the press, and touched the hem of His garment. (Mark 5:27) Assurance is Stephen standing calmly in the midst of his murderers, and saying, 'I see the heavens opened, and the Son of Man standing on the right hand of God' (Acts 7:56).

"Faith is the penitent thief, crying, 'Lord, remember me' (Luke 23:42). Assurance is Job sitting in the dust, covered with sores, and saying, 'I know that my Redeemer liveth.' 'Though He slay me, yet will I trust in Him' (Job 19:25; 13:15).

"Faith is Peter's drowning cry, as he began to sink, 'Lord, save me!' (Matthew 14:30). Assurance is that same Peter declaring before the Council, in after-times, 'This is the stone which was set at naught of you builders, which is become the head of the corner: neither is there salvation in any other; for there is none other name under heaven given among men whereby we must be saved' (Acts 4:11, 12).

"Faith is the anxious, trembling voice, 'Lord, I believe; help thou mine unbelief!' (Mark 9:24). Assurance is the confident challenge, 'Who shall lay anything to the charge of God's elect? Who is he that condemneth?' (Romans 8:33, 34).

"Faith is Saul praying in the house of Judas at Damascus, sorrowful, blind, and alone. 'And the Lord said unto him, Arise, and go into the street which is called Straight, and inquire in the house of Judas for one called Saul, of Tarsus: for, behold, he prayeth' (Acts 9:11). Assurance is Paul, the aged prisoner, looking calmly into the grave, and saying, 'I know whom I have believed.' 'There is a crown laid up for me' (2 Timothy 1:12; 4:8).

"Faith is Life! How great is the blessing! Who can tell of the gulf between life and death? And yet life may be weak, sickly, unhealthy, painful, trying, anxious, worn, burdensome, joyless, or smileless, to the very end.

"Assurance is more than life! It is health, strength, power, vigor, activity, energy, manliness, and beauty."

(Assurance. By Bishop J. C. Ryle, Pp. 15, 16).

A minister once pronounced the benediction in this way, "The heart of God to make us welcome; the blood of Christ to make us clean, and the Holy Spirit to make us certain."

299

The security of the believer is the result of the operation of the Holy Spirit.

Another writer says, "I have seen shrubs and trees grow out of the rocks, and overhang fearful precipices, roaring cataracts, and deep running waters; but they maintained their position, and threw out their foliage and branches as much as if they had been in the midst of a dense forest." It was their hold of the rock that made them secure and the influences of nature that sustained their life. So believers are oftentimes exposed to the most horrible dangers in their journey to heaven; but, so long as they are "rooted and grounded" (Ephesians 3:17) in the Rock of Ages, they are perfectly secure. Their hold of Him is their guarantee and the blessings of His grace give them life and sustain them in life. And as the tree must die, or the rock fall, before a dissolution can be effected between *them,* so either the believer must lose his spiritual life, or the rock must crumble, ere their union can be dissolved.

Chapter 8

CHRIST ALL AND IN ALL

"Where there is neither Greek nor Jew, circumcision nor uncircumcision, Barbarian, Scythian, bond nor free: but Christ is all, and in all"—Colossians 3:11

Christ is *all* to us that we make Him to be. I want to emphasize that word "ALL." Some men make Him to be, "a root of a dry ground ... without form or comeliness" (Isaiah 53:2). He is nothing to them. They do not want Him. Some Christians have a very small Savior, for they do not let Him do great and mighty things for them. Others have a mighty Savior, because they make Him to be great and mighty.

Our Savior from Sin

If we would know what Christ wants to be to us, we must first of all know Him as our Savior from sin. When the angel came down from heaven to proclaim that He was to be born into the world, you remember he gave His name, "He shall be called Jesus, (Savior) for He shall save His people from their sins" (Matthew 1:21). Have we been delivered from sin? He did not come to save us *in* our sins, but *from* our sins.

Now, there are three ways of knowing a man. Some men you know only by hearsay; others you merely know by having been once introduced to them—you know them very slightly; others again you know by having been acquainted with them for years—you know them intimately. So I believe there are three classes of people today in the Christian Church and out of it: those who know Christ only by reading or by hearsay—those who have a historical Christ; those who have a slight personal acquaintance with Him; and those who thirst, as Paul did, to "know Him and the power of His resurrection" (Philippians 3:10). The more we know of Christ the more we shall love Him, and the better we shall serve Him.

Let us look at Him as He hangs upon the Cross, and see how He has put away sin. He was manifested that He might take away our sins, and if we really know Him we must first of all see Him as our Savior from sin. You remember how the angels said to the shepherds on the plains of Bethlehem.

"Behold, I bring you good tidings of great joy, which shall be to all people: for unto you is born this day, in the city of David, a Savior, which is Christ the Lord" (Luke 2:10-11).

Then if you go clear back to Isaiah, seven hundred years before Christ's birth, you will find these words: "I, even I, am the Lord; and beside me there is no Savior" (43:11).

Again, in the First Epistle of John (4:14) we read: "We have seen, and do testify, that the Father sent the Son to be the Savior of the world."

All the heathen religions, we read, teach men to work their way up to God; but the religion of Jesus Christ is God coming down to men to save them, to lift them up out of the pit of sin. In Luke 19:10 we read that Christ Himself told the people what He had come for: "The Son of Man is come to seek and to save that which was lost."

So we start from the Cross, not from the cradle. Christ has opened up a new and living way to the Father. He has taken all the stumbling blocks out of the way, so that every man who accepts Christ as his Savior can have salvation.

Know Christ More Intimately

But Christ is not only a Savior. I might save a man from drowning and rescue him from an untimely grave; but I might probably not be able to do any more for him. Christ is something more than a Savior. When the children of Israel were placed behind the blood, that blood was their salvation; but they would still have heard the crack of the slave-driver's whip if they had not been delivered from the Egyptian yoke of bondage—then it was that God delivered them from the hand of the king of Egypt. I have little sympathy with the idea that God comes down to save us, and then leaves us in prison, the slaves of our besetting sins. No. He has come to deliver us, and to give us victory over our evil tempers, our passions, and our lusts. Are you a professed Christian, but one who is a slave to some besetting sin? If you want to get victory over that temper or that lust, go on to know Christ more intimately.

He brings deliverance for the past, the present, and the future. "Who delivered ... and doth deliver ... who will yet deliver" (2 Corinthians 1:10).

Christ Our Redeemer

How often, like the children of Israel when they came to the Red Sea, have we become discouraged because everything looked dark before us, behind us, and around us, and we knew not which way to turn. Like Peter we have said, "To whom shall we go?" (John 6:68). But God has appeared for our deliverance. He has brought us through the Red Sea right out into the wilderness, and opened up the way into the Promised Land. But Christ is not only our Deliverer; He is our Redeemer. That is something more than being our Savior. He has bought us back.

"Ye have sold yourselves for naught; and ye shall be redeemed without money" (Isaiah 52:3). We "were not redeemed with corruptible things, as silver and gold" (1 Peter 1:18). If gold could have redeemed us, could He not have created ten thousand worlds full of gold?

When God had redeemed the children of Israel from the bondage of Egypt, and brought them through the Red Sea, they struck out for the wilderness; and then God became to them their Way. I am so thankful the Lord has not left us in darkness as to the right way. There is no living man who has been groping in the darkness but may know the way. "I am the Way," says Christ. If we follow Christ we shall be in the right way, and have the right doctrine. Who could lead the children of Israel through the wilderness like the Almighty God Himself? He knew the pitfalls and dangers of the way, and guided the people through their wilderness journey right into the Promised Land. It is true that if it had not been for their accursed unbelief they might have crossed into the land at Kadesh-barnea, and taken possession of it. But they desired something besides God's word, so they were turned back and had to wander in the desert for forty years. I believe there are thousands of God's children wandering in the wilderness still. The Lord has delivered them from the hand of the Egyptian, and would at once take them through the wilderness right into the Promised Land, if they were only willing to follow Christ. Christ has been down here, and has made the rough places smooth, and the dark places light, and the crooked places straight. If we would only be led by Him, and follow Him, all will be peace, and joy, and rest.

"Blazing the Way"

In the frontier when a man goes out hunting he takes a hatchet with him, and cuts off pieces from the bark of the trees as he goes along through the forest: this is called "blazing the way." He does it that he may know the way back, as there is no pathway through these thick forests. Christ has come down to this earth. He has "blazed the way," and now that He has gone up on high. If we will just follow Him, we shall remain in the right path. I will tell you how you may know if you are following Christ or not. If someone has slandered you, or misjudged you, do you treat them, as your Master would have done? If you do not bear these things in a loving and forgiving spirit, all the churches and ministers in the world cannot make you right.

"If any man have not the Spirit of Christ, he is none of His" (Romans 8:9).

"If any man be in Christ he is a new creature—old things are passed away; behold, all things are become new" (2 Corinthians 5:17).

Christ is not only our way, but He is the Light upon the way. He says, "I am the light of the world" (John 8:12; 9:5; 12 46). He goes on to say, "He that followeth me shall not walk in darkness, but shall have the light of life." It is impossible for any man or woman who is following Christ to walk in darkness. If your soul is in the darkness, groping around in the fog and mist of earth, let me tell you it is because you have got away from the true light. There is nothing but light that will dispel darkness. So let those who are walking in spiritual darkness admit Christ into their hearts. He is the Light. I call to mind a picture I used to think about a good deal, but now I have come to look more closely. I would not hang it up in my house unless I turned the face to the wall. It represents Christ as standing at a door, knocking, and having a big lantern in His hand. Why, you might as well hang up a lantern to the sun as put one into Christ's hand. He is the Sun of Righteousness, and it is our privilege to walk in the light of an unclouded sun.

Lifted Out of Darkness

Many people are hunting after light, and peace, and joy. We are nowhere told to seek after these things. If we admit Christ into our hearts these will all come of themselves. I remember, when a boy, I used to try in vain to catch my shadow. One day I was walking with my face to the sun; as I happened to look round I saw that my shadow was following me. The faster I went the faster my shadow followed; I could not get away from it. So when our faces are directed to the Sun of Righteousness, the peace and the joy are sure to come.

A man said to me some time ago, "Moody, how do you feel?" It was so long since I had thought about my feelings I had to stop and consider awhile, in order to find out. Some Christians are all the time thinking about their feelings; and because they do not feel just right they think their joy is all gone. If we keep our faces towards Christ, and are occupied with Him, we shall be lifted out of the darkness and the trouble that may have gathered round our path.

I remember being in a meeting after the war of the rebellion (Civil War) broke out. The war had been going on for about six months. The army of the North had been defeated at Bull Run. In fact, we had nothing but defeat, and it looked as though the Republic was going to pieces. So we were much cast down and discouraged. At this meeting every speaker seemed as if he had hung his harp upon the willow, and it was one of the gloomiest meetings I ever attended. Finally an old man with beautiful white hair got up to speak, and his face literally shone. "Young men," he said, "you do not talk like sons of the King. Though it is dark just here, remember it is light somewhere else." Then he went on to say that if it were dark all over the world it was light up around the Throne.

He told us he had come from the East, where a friend had described to him how he had been up a mountain to spend the night and see the sun rise. As the party was climbing up the mountain, and before they had reached the summit, a storm came on. This friend said to the guide, "I will give this up; take me back." The guide smiled, and replied; "I think we shall get above the storm soon." On they went, and it was not long before they got up to where it was as calm as a summer evening. Down in the valley a terrible storm raged. They could hear the thunder rolling, and see the lightning's flash, but all was serene on the mountaintop. "And so, my young friends," continued the old man, "though all is dark around you, come a little higher, and the darkness will flee away." Often when I have been inclined to get discouraged, I have thought of what he said. Now if you are down in the valley amid the thick fog and the darkness, get a little higher; get nearer to Christ, and know more of Him.

You remember the Bible says, that when Christ expired on the Cross, the light of the world was put out. God sent His Son to be the light of the world, but men did not love the light because it reproved them of their sins. When they had tried to put out this light, what did Christ say to His disciples? "Ye shall be witnesses unto me" (Acts 1:8).

He has gone up yonder to intercede for us, but He wants us to shine for Him down here. "Ye are the light of the world" (Matthew 5:14).

So our work is to shine: not to blow our own trumpet so that people may look at us. What we want to do is to show forth Christ. If we have any light at all it is borrowed light. Someone said to a young Christian; "Converted! It is a moonshine!" He said, "I thank you for the illustration. The moon borrows its light from the sun, and we borrow ours from the Sun of Righteousness." If we are Christ's, we are here to shine for Him; therefore He will call us home to our reward.

I remember hearing of a blind man who sat by the wayside with a lantern near him. When he was asked what he had a lantern for, as he could not see the light, he said it was that people should not stumble over him. I believe more people stumble over the inconsistencies of professed Christians than from any other cause. What is doing more harm to the cause of Christ than all the skepticism in the world is this cold, dead formalism—this conformity to the world; this professing what we do not possess? The eyes of the world are upon us. I think it was George Fox who said every Quaker ought to light up the country for ten miles around him. If we were all brightly shining for the Master, those about us would soon be reached, and there would be a shout of praise going to heaven.

People say, "I want to know what is the truth." Listen: "I AM ... THE TRUTH" (John 14:6), says Christ. If you want to know what the truth is, get acquainted with Christ. People also complain that they have not life. Many are trying to give themselves spiritual life. You may galvanize yourselves and put electricity into yourselves, so to speak; but the effect will not last very long. Christ alone is the author of life. If you would have real spiritual life get to know Christ. Many try to stir up spiritual life by going to meetings. That may be well enough; but it will be of no use, unless they get into contact with the living Christ. Then their spiritual life will not be a spasmodic thing, but will be perpetual; flowing on and on, and bringing forth fruit to God.

Christ Is Our Keeper

A great many young disciples are afraid they will not hold out. "He that keepeth Israel shall neither slumber nor sleep" (Psalm 121:4).

It is the work of Christ to keep us, and if He keeps us there will be no danger of our falling. I suppose if Queen Victoria had to take care of the Crown of England, some thief might attempt to get access to it. But it is put away in the Tower of London, and guarded night and day by soldiers. The whole English army would, if necessary, be called out to protect it. And we have no strength in ourselves. We are no match for Satan. He has had six thousand years' experience. But then we remember that the One who neither slumbers nor sleeps is our keeper. In Isaiah 41:10, we read, "Fear thou not, for I am with thee; be not dismayed, for I am thy God: I will strengthen thee; yea, I will help thee; yea, I will uphold thee with the right hand of my righteousness."

In Jude also, verse 24 we are told that He is "able to keep us from falling." "We have an Advocate with the Father, Jesus Christ the righteous" (1 John 2:1).

But Christ is something more. He is our Shepherd. It is the work of the shepherd to care for the sheep, to feed them, and protect them.

309

1. "I am the good shepherd" (John 10:11).
2. "My sheep hear my voice" (John 10:27).
3. "I lay down My life for the sheep" (John 10:15).

In that wonderful tenth chapter of John, Christ uses the personal pronoun no less than twenty-eight times, in declaring what He is and what He will do. In verse 28 He says: "They shall never perish; neither shall any *[man]* pluck them out of my hand." But notice the word "man" is in italics. See how the verse really reads, "Neither shall ANY pluck them out of my hand"—no devil or man shall be able to do it. In another place the Scripture declares, "Your life is hid with Christ in God" (Colossians 3:3).

His Sheep Hear His Voice

Christ says, "My sheep hear my voice ... and they follow me" (John 10:27). A gentleman in the East heard of a shepherd who could call all his sheep to him by name. He went and asked if this was true. The shepherd took him to the pasture where they were, and called one of them by some name. One sheep looked up and answered the call, while the others went on feeding and paid no attention. In the same way he called about a dozen of the sheep around him. The stranger said, "How do you know one from the other? They all look perfectly alike." "Well," said he, "you see that sheep toes in a little; that other one has a squint; one has a little piece of wool off; another has a black spot; and another has a piece out of its ear." The man knew all his sheep by their failings, for he had not a perfect one in the whole flock. I suppose our Shepherd knows us in the same way.

An Eastern shepherd was once telling a gentleman that his sheep knew his voice and that no stranger could deceive them. The gentleman thought he would like to put the statement to the test. So he put on the shepherd's frock and turban, and took his staff, and went to the flock. He disguised his voice, and tried to speak as much like the shepherd as he could; but he could not get a single sheep in the flock to follow him. He asked the shepherd if his sheep never followed a stranger. He was obliged to admit that if a sheep got sickly it would follow anyone.

So it is with a good many professed Christians. When they get sickly and weak in the faith, they will follow any teacher that comes along; but when the soul is in health, a man will not be carried away by errors and heresies. He will know whether the "voice" speaks the truth or not. He can soon tell that, if he is really in communion with God. When God sends a true messenger, his words will find a ready response in the Christian heart.

Christ is a tender Shepherd. You may sometime think He has not been a very tender Shepherd to you: you are passing under the rod. It is written, "Whom the Lord loveth he chasteneth, and scourgeth every son whom he receiveth" (Hebrews 12:6). Just because you are passing under the rod is no proof that Christ does not love you.

A friend of mine lost all his children. No man could ever have loved his family more; but the scarlet fever took them away, one by one; and so the whole four or five, one after another, died. The poor stricken parents went over to Great Britain, and wandered from one place to another, there and on the continent. At length they found their way to Syria. One day they saw an Eastern shepherd come down to a stream, and call his flock to cross. The sheep came down to the brink, and looked at the water; but they seemed to shrink from it, and he could not get them to respond to his call. He then took a little lamb, put it under one arm; he took another lamb and put it under the other arm, and thus passed into the stream.

The old sheep no longer stood looking at the water. They plunged in after the shepherd; and in a few minutes the whole flock was on the other side, and they hurried away to newer and fresher pastures. The bereaved father and mother, as they looked on the scene, felt that it taught them a lesson. They no longer murmured because the Great Shepherd had taken their lambs one by one into yonder world, and they began to look up and look forward to the time when they would follow the loved ones they had lost. If you have loved ones gone before, remember that your Shepherd is calling you to "set your affection on things above" (Colossians 3:2). Let us be faithful to Him, and follow Him, while we remain in this world. And if you have not taken Him to be your Shepherd do so this very day.

WONDERFUL DESCRIPTION OF CHRIST

Christ is not only all these things that I have mentioned: He is also our Mediator, our Sanctifier, our Justifier; in fact, it would take volumes to tell what He desires to be to every individual soul. While looking through some papers I once read this wonderful description of Christ. I do not know where it originally came from, but it was so fresh to my soul that I should like to give it to you:

> *Christ is our Way; we walk in Him.*
> *He is our Truth; we embrace Him.*
> *He is our Life; we live in Him.*
> *He is our Lord; we choose Him to rule over us.*
> *He is our Master; we serve Him.*
> *He is our Teacher, instructing us in the way of salvation.*
> *He is our Prophet, pointing out the future.*
> *He is our Priest, having atoned for us.*

He is our Advocate, ever living to make intercession for us.

He is our Savior, saving to the uttermost.

He is our Root; we grow from Him.

He is our Bread; we feed upon Him.

He is our Shepherd, leading us into green pastures.

He is our true Vine; we abide in Him.

He is the Water of Life; we satisfy our thirst from Him.

He is the fairest among ten thousand; we admire Him above all others.

He is "the brightness of the Father's glory, and the express image of His person"; we strive to reflect His likeness.

He is the upholder of all things; we rest upon Him.

He is our Wisdom; we are guided by Him.

He is our Righteousness; we cast all our imperfections upon Him.

He is our Sanctification; we draw all our power for holy life from Him.

He is our Redemption, redeeming us from all iniquity.

He is our Healer, curing all our diseases.

He is our Friend, relieving us in all our necessities.

He is our Brother, cheering us in our difficulties."

Here is another beautiful excerpt. It is from Gotthold:

For my part, my soul is like a hungry and thirsty child; I need His love and consolation for my refreshment.

I am a wandering and lost sheep, and I need Him as a good and faithful shepherd.

My soul is like a frightened dove pursued by the hawk, and I need His wounds for a refuge.

I am a feeble vine. I need His cross to lay hold of, and to wind myself about.

I am a sinner, and I need His righteousness.

I am naked and bare and I need His holiness and innocence for a covering.

I am ignorant, and I need His teaching: simple and foolish; and I need the guidance of His Holy Spirit.

In no situation, and at no time, can I do without Him.

Do I pray? He must prompt, and intercede for me.

Am I arraigned by Satan at the Divine tribunal? He must be my Advocate.

Am I in affliction? He must be my Helper.

Am I persecuted by the world? He must defend me.

When I am forsaken, He must be my Support. When I am dying, He is my Life. When moldering in the grave, He will be my Resurrection.

Well then, I will rather part with all the world, and all that it contains, than with Thee, my Savior. And, God be thanked! I know that Thou too art neither able nor willing to do without me.

Thou art rich, and I am poor.

Thou hast abundance, and I am needy.

Thou hast righteousness, and I sins.

Thou hast wine and oil, and I wounds.

Thou hast cordials and refreshments, and I hunger and thirst.

*Use me then, my Savior for whatever purpose,
and in whatever way Thou mayest require.*

*Here is my poor heart, an empty vessel; fill it
with Thy grace.*

*Here is my sinful and troubled soul, quicken and
refresh it with Thy love.*

*Take my heart for Thine abode; my mouth to
spread the glory of Thy name; my love and all my
powers, for the advancement of Thy believing people;
and never suffer the steadfastness and confidence
of my faith to abate—that so at all times I may be
enabled from the heart to say, "Jesus needs me, and
I Him and so we suit each other."*

[Note: Christian Scriver, Born January 2, 1629 was a court preacher who had quite a friendship with Gotthold, whose first name he does not give, but from whose lips he heard and took down what he called "Gotthold's" emblems. They were well known in Martin Luther's day. Translated in U.S.A. in 1859.]

Chapter 9

BACKSLIDING

*"I will heal their backsliding; I will love them freely:
for mine anger is turned away"*—Hosea 14:4

There are two kinds of backsliders. Some have never been
converted. They have gone through the form of joining
a Christian community and claim to be backsliders, but they
never have, if I may use the expression, "slid forward." They
may talk of backsliding; but they have never really been
born again. They need to be treated differently from real
backsliders—those who have been born of the incorruptible
seed, but who have turned aside. We want to bring the latter
back the same road by which they left their first love.

In Psalm 85:5 we read: "Wilt thou be angry with us
forever? Wilt thou draw out thine anger to all generations?
Wilt thou not revive us again: that thy people may rejoice
in thee? Show us thy mercy, O Lord; and grant us thy
salvation."

Now look again: *"I will hear what God the Lord will
speak:* for he will speak peace unto his people, and to his
saints; but let them not turn again to folly" (verse 8).

There is nothing that will do backsliders so much good as to take them to the Word of God; and for them the Old Testament is as full of help as the New. The book of Jeremiah has some wonderful passages for wanderers. What we want to do is to get backsliders to hear what God the Lord will say.

Look for a moment at Jeremiah 6:10; "To whom shall I speak, and give warning, that they may hear? Behold, their ear is uncircumcised, and they cannot hearken, behold, the word of the Lord is unto them a reproach; they have no delight in it."

That is the condition of backsliders. They have no delight whatever in the word of God. But we want to bring them back, and let God get their ear. Read from the fourteenth verse to the seventeenth: "They have healed also the hurt of the daughter of my people slightly, saying, Peace, peace; when there is no peace. Were they ashamed when they had committed abomination? Nay, they were not at all ashamed, neither could they blush: therefore they shall fall among them that fall: at the time that I visit them they shall be cast down, saith the Lord. Thus saith the Lord, Stand ye in the ways, and see, and ask for the old paths, where is the good way, and walk therein; and ye shall find rest for your souls. But they said we would not walk therein. Also I set watchmen over you, saying, Hearken to the sound of the trumpet. But they said, we will not hearken."

That was the condition of the Jews when they had backslidden. They had turned away from the old paths. And that is the condition of backsliders. They have got away from the good old book. Adam and Eve fell by not hearkening to the word of God. They did not believe God's word; but they believed the Tempter. That is the way backsliders fall—by turning away from the word of God.

318

In Jeremiah 2:13 we find God pleading with them as a father would plead with a son.

"Thus saith the Lord, What iniquity have your fathers found in me, that they are gone far from me, and have walked after vanity, and are become vain ... Wherefore I will yet plead with you, saith the Lord; and with your children's children will I plead ... For my people have committed two evils—they have forsaken me the fountain of living waters; and hewed them out cisterns, broken cisterns, that can hold no water."

Now there is one thing to which we wish to call the attention of backsliders; and that is that the Lord never forsook them, but that they forsook Him! The Lord never left them, but they left Him! And this too without any cause! He says, "What iniquity have your fathers found in Me, that they are gone far from Me?" Is not God the same today as when you came to Him first? Has God changed? Men are apt to think that God has changed; but the fault is with them.

Backslider, I would ask you, "What iniquity is there in God, that you have left Him and gone far from Him?" You have, He says, hewed out to yourselves broken cisterns that hold no water. The world cannot satisfy the new creature. No earthly well can satisfy the soul that has become a partaker of the heavenly nature. Honor, wealth, and the pleasures of this world, will not satisfy those who, having tasted the water of life, have gone astray, seeking refreshment at the world's fountains. Earthly wells will get dry. They cannot quench spiritual thirst.

Again in the thirty-second verse: "Can a maid forget her ornaments, or a bride her attire? Yet my people have forgotten me, days without number." That is the charge that

God brings against the backslider. They "have forgotten me, days without number."

I have often startled young ladies when I have said to them, "My friend, you think more of your earrings than of the Lord." The reply has been, "No, I do not." But when I have asked, "Would you not be troubled if you lost one; and would you not set about seeking for it?" the answer has been, "Well, yes, I think I should." But though they had turned from the Lord, it did not give them any trouble; nor did they seek after Him that they might find Him.

How many once in fellowship and in daily communion with the Lord now think more of their dresses and ornaments than of their precious souls! Love does not like to be forgotten. Mothers would have broken hearts if their children left them and never wrote a word or sent any memento of their affection. God pleads over backsliders as a parent over loved ones who have gone astray, and He tries to woo them back. He asks, "What have I done that they should have forsaken Me?"

The most tender and loving words to be found in the whole of the Bible are from Jehovah to those who have left Him without a cause. Hear how He argues with such: "Thine own wickedness shall correct thee and thy backsliding shall reprove thee: know therefore, and see, that it is an evil thing and bitter, that thou hast forsaken the LORD thy GOD, and that my fear is not in thee, saith the LORD GOD of hosts" (Jeremiah 2:19).

I do not exaggerate when I say that I have seen hundreds of backsliders come back. I asked them if they have not found it an evil and a bitter thing to leave the Lord. You cannot find a real backslider, who has known the Lord, who will not admit that it is an evil and a bitter thing to turn away from Him. I do not know of any one verse more used to bring back wanders than that very one. May it bring you back if you have wandered into the far country.

A Bitter Thing to Turn Away

Look at Lot. Did not he find it an evil and a bitter thing? He was twenty years in Sodom, and never made a convert. He got on well in the sight of the world. Men would have told you that he was one of the most influential and worthy men in all Sodom. But alas, he ruined his family. And it is a pitiful sight to see that old backslider going through the streets of Sodom at midnight, after he has warned his children, and they have turned a deaf ear.

I have never known a man and his wife to backslide, without its proving utter ruin to their children. They will make a mockery of religion and will deride their parents: "Thine own wickedness shall correct thee; and thy backsliding shall reprove thee!"

Did not David find it so? Mark him, crying, "O my son Absalom, my son, my son Absalom! Would God I have died for thee; O Absalom, my son, my son!" (2 Samuel 18:33). I think it was the ruin, rather than the death, of his son that caused this anguish.

Consequences of Sin

I remember being engaged in conversation some years ago, with an old man. He had been for years wandering on the barren mountains of sin. That night he wanted to get back. We prayed, and prayed, and prayed, till light broke in upon him, and he went away rejoicing. The next night he sat in front of me when I was preaching; and I think that I never saw anyone look so sad and wretched in all my life. He followed me into the inquiry-room. "What is the trouble?" I asked. "Is your eye off the Savior? Have your doubts come back?" "No, it is not that," he said. "I did not go to work, but spent all this day in visiting my children. They are all married in this city. I went from house to house; but there was not one that did not mock me regarding my faith. It is the darkest day of my life. I woke up to what I have done. I have taken my children into the world, and now I cannot get them out." The Lord had restored unto him the joy of His salvation, yet there was the bitter consequence of his transgression.

You can run through your experience and you can find just such instances repeated again and again. Many who came to your city years ago serving God, in their prosperity have forgotten Him. And where are their sons and daughters? Show me the father and mother who have deserted the Lord and gone back to the beggarly elements of the world, and I am mistaken if their children are not on the high road to ruin.

As we desire to be faithful we warn these backsliders. It is a sign of love to warn of danger. We may be looked upon as enemies for a while; but the truest friends are those who lift up the voice of warning. Israel had no truer friend than Moses. In Jeremiah God gave His people a weeping prophet to bring them back to Him; but they cast off God. They forgot the God who brought them out of Egypt, and who led them through the desert into the Promised Land. In their prosperity they forgot Him and turned away. The Lord had told them what would happen (Deuteronomy 28). And see what did happen. The king who made light of the word of God, was taken captive by Nebuchadnezzar, and his children brought up in front of him and every one slain; his eyes were put out of his head; and he was bound in fetters of brass and cast into a dungeon in Babylon. (2 Kings 25:7). That is the way he reaped what he had sown. Surely it is an evil and a bitter thing to backslide, but the Lord would win you back with the message of His Word.

In Jeremiah 8:5 we read, "Why then is this people of Jerusalem slidden back by a perpetual backsliding? They hold fast deceit; *They refuse to return.*"

That is what the Lord brings against them.

He Wants You To Come Back

"I hearkened and heard; but they spake not aright. No man repented him of his wickedness, saying, what have I done? Every one turned to his course, as the horse rusheth into the battle. Yea, the stork in the heaven knoweth her appointed times; and the turtle and the crane and the swallow observe the time of their coming; but my people know not the judgment of the Lord" (Jeremiah 8:6-7).

Now look: "I hearkened and heard; but they spake not aright." No family altar! No reading the Bible! No closet devotion! God stoops to hear, but His people have turned away! If there be a penitent backslider, one who is anxious for pardon and restoration, you will find no words more tender than are to be found in Jeremiah 3:12: "Go, and proclaim these words toward the north, and say, Return, thou backsliding Israel, saith the Lord; and I will not cause mine anger to fall upon you- for I am merciful, saith the Lord, and I will not keep anger for ever."

Now notice: "Only acknowledge thine iniquity, that thou hast transgressed. Against the Lord thy God, and hast scattered thy ways to the strangers under every green tree, and ye have not obeyed my voice, saith the Lord. Turn, O backsliding children, saith the Lord; for I am married unto you" (Jeremiah 3:14)—think of God coming and saying, "I am married unto you"! —"And I will take you one of a city, and two of a family, and I will bring you to Zion."

"Only acknowledge thine iniquity." How many times have I held that passage up to a backslider! "Acknowledge" it, and God says I will forgive you. I remember a man asking, "Who said that? Is that there?" And I held up to him the passage, "Only acknowledge thine iniquity"; and the man went down on his knees, and cried, "My God, I have sinned"; and the Lord restored him there and then. If you have wandered, He wants you to come back.

He says in another place, "O Ephraim, what shall I do unto thee? O Judah, what shall I do unto thee? For your goodness is as a morning cloud, and as the early dew it goeth away" (Hosea 6:4).

His compassion and love is wonderful!

In Jeremiah 3:22: "Return, ye backsliding children, and I will heal your backslidings. Behold, we come unto thee; for thou art the Lord our God." He just puts words into the month of the backslider. Only come; and, if you will come, He will receive you graciously and love you freely.

In Hosea 14:1, 2, 4: "O Israel, return unto the Lord thy God; for thou hast fallen by thine iniquity. Take with you words, and turn to the Lord (He puts words into your mouth): say unto Him, Take away all iniquity, and receive us graciously: so will we render the calves of our lips ... I will heal their backsliding, I will love them freely: for mine anger is turned away from him."

Just observe that, Turn! *Turn!!* TURN!!! Rings all through these passages.

Now, if you have wandered, remember that you left Him, and not He you. You have to get out of the backslider's pit just in the same way you got in. And if you take the same road, as when you left the Master you will find Him now, just where you are.

Saying "Good-bye" to Jesus

If we were to treat Christ as an earthly friend we should never leave Him, and there would never be a backslider. If I were in a town for a single week I should not think of going away without shaking hands with the friends I had made, and saying "Good bye" to them. I should be justly blamed if I took the train and left without saying a word to anyone. The cry would be, "What's the matter?" But did you ever hear of a backslider bidding the Lord Jesus Christ "Good bye"; going into his closet and saying "Lord Jesus, I have known Thee ten, twenty, or thirty years: but I am tired of Thy service. Thy yoke is not easy, nor Thy burden light; so I am going back to the world, to the fleshpots of Egypt. Goodbye, Lord Jesus! Farewell"? Did you ever hear of that? No, you never did, and you never will. I tell you, if you get into your closet and shut out the world and hold communion with the Master you cannot leave Him. The language of your heart will be, "To whom shall we go," but unto Thee? "Thou hast the words of eternal life" (John 6:68).

You could not go back to the world if you treated Him in that way. But you left Him and ran away. You have forgotten Him days without number. Come back today, just as you are! Make up your mind that you will not rest until God has restored unto you the joy of His salvation.

A gentleman in Cornwall once met a Christian in the street whom he knew to be a backslider. He went up to him, and said: "Tell me, is there not some estrangement between you and the Lord Jesus?" The man hung his head, and said, "Yes." "Well," said the gentleman, "what has He done to you?" The answer to which was a flood of tears.

In Revelation 2:4-5, we read: "Nevertheless I have somewhat against thee, because thou hast left thy first love. Remember therefore from whence thou art fallen; and repent, and do the first works: or else I will come unto thee quickly, and will remove thy candlestick out of his place, except thou repent."

I want to guard you against a mistake that some people make with regard to doing "the first works". Many think that they are to have the same experience over again. That has kept thousands for months without peace, because they have been waiting for a renewal of their first experience. You will never have the same experience as when you first came to the Lord. God never repeats Himself. No two people of all earth's millions look alike or think alike. You may say that you cannot tell two people apart, but when you get well acquainted with them you can very quickly distinguish differences. So no one person will have the same experience a second time. If God will restore His joy to your soul let Him do it in His way. Do not mark out a way for God to bless you. Do not expect the same experience that you had two or twenty years ago. You will have a fresh experience, and God will deal with you in His own way. If you confess your sins and tell Him that you have wandered from the path of His commandments He will restore unto you the joy of His salvation.

Peter's Fall

I want to call your attention to the manner in which Peter fell; and I think that nearly all fall pretty much in the same way. I want to lift up a warning note to those who have not fallen. "Let him that thinketh he standeth, take heed lest he fall" (1 Corinthians 10:12).

Twenty-five years ago—and for the first five years after I was converted—I used to think that if I were able to stand for twenty years I need fear a fall. But the nearer you get to the Cross the fiercer the battle. Satan aims high. He went among the twelve and singled out the Treasurer—Judas Iscariot, and the Chief Apostle—Peter. Most men who have fallen have done so on the strongest side of their character. I am told that the only side upon which Edinburgh Castle was successfully assailed was where the rocks were steepest, and where the garrison thought they were secure. If any man thinks that he is strong enough to resist the devil at any one point, he need specially watch there for the tempter comes then.

Abraham stands, as it were, at the head of the family of faith, and the children of faith may be said to trace their descent to Abraham. Yet down in Egypt he denied his wife (Genesis 12). Moses was noted for his meekness, and yet he was kept out of the Promised Land because of one hasty act and speech, when he was told by the Lord to speak to the rock so that the congregation and their beasts should have water to drink. "Hear now, ye rebels; must we fetch you water out of this rock?" (Numbers 20:10).

Elijah Falters
Elijah was remarkable for his boldness, and yet he went off a day's journey into the wilderness like a coward and hid under a juniper tree, requesting for himself that he might die, because of a message he received from a woman (1 Kings 19). Let us be careful. No matter who the man is- he may be in the pulpit—but if he gets self-conceited he will be sure to fall. We who are followers of Christ need constantly to pray to be made humble, and kept humble. God made Moses' face

so to shine that other men could see it, but Moses himself knew not that his face shone, and the more holy in heart a man is the more manifest to the outer world will be his daily life and conversation. Some people talk of how humble they are; but if they have true humility there will be no necessity for them to publish it. It is not needful. A lighthouse does not have a drum beaten or a trumpet blown in order to proclaim the proximity of a lighthouse, it is its own witness. And so if we have the true light in us it will show itself. It is not those who make the most noise who have the most piety. There is a brook, or a little "burn" as the Scotch call it, not far from where I live, and after heavy rain you can hear the rush of its waters a long way off, but let there come a few days of pleasant weather, and the brook becomes almost silent. But there is a river near my house, the flow of which I never heard in my life, as it pours on in its deep and majestic course the year round. We should have so much of the love of God within us that its presence shall be evident without our loud proclamation of the fact.

Peter's Error of Self-Confidence

The first step in Peter's downfall was his self-confidence. The Lord warned him. The Lord said: "Simon, Simon, behold, Satan hath desired to have you, that he may sift you as wheat: but I have prayed for thee, that thy faith fail not" (Luke 22:31, 32).

But Peter said:
1. "I am ready to go with thee, both into prison and to death." (Luke 22:33).
2. "Though all shall be offended because of thee, yet will I never be offended" (Matthew 26:33).
3. "James and John, and the others, may leave you; but You can count on me!" "Peter said unto Him, Although all shall be offended, yet will not I" (Mark 14:29).

But the Lord warned him: "I tell thee, Peter, the cock shall not crow this day, before that thou shalt thrice deny that thou knowest me" (Luke 22:24). Though the Lord rebuked him Peter said that he was ready to follow Him to death. That boasting is too often, a forerunner of downfall. Let us walk humbly and softly. We have a great Tempter; and, in an unguarded hour, we may stumble and fall and bring a scandal on Christ.

The next step in Peter's downfall was that he went to sleep. If Satan can rock the Church to sleep he does his work through God's own people. Instead of Peter watching one short hour in Gethsemane he fell asleep, and the Lord asked him, "What could ye not watch with me one hour?" (Matthew 26:40).

The next thing was that he fought in the energy of the flesh. The Lord rebuked him again and said, "They that take the sword shall perish with the sword" (Matthew 26:52).

Jesus had to undo what Peter had done. The next thing—he "followed afar off." Step by step he gets away. It is a sad thing when a child of God follows afar off. When you see him associating with worldly friends, and throwing his influence on the wrong side, he is following afar off, and it will not be long before disgrace will be brought upon the old family name, and Jesus Christ will be wounded in the house of his friends. The man, by his example, will cause others to stumble and fall.

Peter's Denial

The next thing: Peter is familiar and friendly with the enemies of Christ. A damsel says to this bold Peter, "Thou also wast with Jesus of Galilee." But he denied before them all, saying, "I know not what thou sayest." And when he was gone out into the porch another maid saw him and said unto them that were there, "This fellow was also with Jesus of Nazareth." And again he denied with an oath, "I do not know the man." Another hour passed, and yet he did not realize his position; when another confidently affirmed that he was a Galilean for his speech betrayed him. And he was angry and began to curse and to swear, and again denied his Master: and the cock crew (Matthew 26:69-74).

He commences away up on the pinnacle of self-conceit, and goes down step by step until he breaks out into cursing and swears that he never knew his Lord.

The Master might have turned and said to him, "Is it true, Peter, that you have forgotten Me so soon? Do you not remember when your wife's mother lay sick of a fever that I rebuked the disease and it left her? Do you not call to mind your astonishment at the draught of fishes so that you exclaimed, 'Depart from me; for I am a sinful man, O Lord' (Luke 5:8)? Do you remember when in answer to your cry, 'Lord, save, or I perish,' I stretched out My hand and kept you from drowning? Have you forgotten when, on the Mount of Transfiguration, with James and John, you said to Me, 'Lord, it is good to be here ... let us make three tabernacles' (Matthew 17:4)? Have you forgotten being with Me at the supper-table, and in Gethsemane? Is it true that you have forgotten Me so soon?"

The Lord might have upbraided him with questions such as these, but He did nothing of the kind. He cast one look on Peter and there was so much love in it that it broke that bold disciple's heart; and he went out and wept bitterly.

And after Christ rose from the dead see how tenderly He dealt with the erring disciple.

"And Peter"

The angel at the sepulcher says, "Tell His disciples, *and Peter*" (Mark 16:7). The Lord did not forget Peter, though Peter had denied Him thrice; so He caused this kindly special message to be conveyed to the repentant disciple. What a tender and loving Savior to have!

Friend, if you are one of the wanderers, let the loving look of the Master win you back, and let Him restore you to the joy of His salvation.

Before closing, let me say that I trust God will restore some backslider reading these pages, who may in the future become a useful member of society and a bright ornament of the Church. We should never have had the thirty-second Psalm if David had not been restored: "Blessed is he whose transgression is forgiven, whose sin is covered"; or that beautiful fifty-first Psalm which was written by the restored backslider. Nor should we have had that wonderful sermon on the day of Pentecost when three thousand were converted—preached by another restored backslider.

May God may restore other backsliders and make them a thousand times more used for His glory than they ever were before.

CHRISTIAN LOVE

CHRISTIAN LOVE

The Word of God speaks in Galatians about love, the fruit of the Spirit being love, joy, peace, gentleness, long suffering, meekness and temperance. The way this writer has put it—and I think it is very beautiful—is that joy is love exultant, peace is love in repose, and long suffering is love enduring. It is all love, you see, gentleness is love in society, and goodness is love in action, and faith is love on the battlefield, and meekness is love at school, and temperance is love in training.

Now there are a great many that have got love and they hold the truth. I should have said they have got truth, but they don't hold it in love, and they are very unsuccessful in working for God. They are very harsh, and God cannot use them. Now let us hold the truth, but let us hold it in love. People will stand almost any kind of plain talk if you only do it in love. If you do it in harshness it bounds back and they won't receive it. So what we want is to have the truth and at the same time hold it in love.

Then there is another class of people in the world that have got the truth, but they love so much that they give up the truth because they are afraid it will hurt some one's feelings. That is wrong. We want the whole truth anyway. We don't

335

want to give it up, but hold it in love, and I believe one reason why people think God don't love them is because they have not this love. I met a lady in the inquiry-room today, and I could not convince her that God loved her, for she said that if He did love her He would not treat her as He had. And I believe people are all measuring God with their own rule, as I said the other day, and we are not sincere in our love, and we very often profess something we really don't possess. Very often we profess to have love for a person when we do not, and we think God is like us.

Now God is just what He says He is, and He wants His children to be sincere in love; not to love just merely in word and in tongue, but to love in earnest. That is what God does. You ask me why God loves. You might as well ask me why the sun shines. It can't help shining, and neither can He help loving, because He is love Himself; and any one that says He is not love does not know anything about love. If we have got the true love of God shed abroad in our hearts we will show it in our lives. We will not have to go up and down the earth proclaiming it. We will show it in everything we say or do.

Heart Love

There is a good deal of what you might call false love. People profess to love you very much, but then you find it is all on the surface. It is not heart love. Very often you are in a person's house, and the servant comes in and says such a person is in the front room, and she says; "Oh, dear, I am so sorry he has come, I can't bear the sight of him"; and she'll get right up and go into the other room and say, "Why, how do you do? I am very glad to see you!" There is a good deal of that sort of thing in the world.

I remember, too, I was talking with a man one day and an acquaintance of his came in, and he jumped up at once and shook him by the hand—why I thought he was going to shake his hand out of joint, he shook so hard—and he seemed to be so glad to see him and wanted him to stay, but the man was in a great hurry and could not stay, and he coaxed him and urged him to stay, but the man said no, he would come another time. After that man left my companion turned to me and said, "Well, he is an awful bore, and I am glad he's gone." Well, I began to feel that I was a bore, too, and I got out as quickly as I could. That is not real love. That is love with the tongue while the heart is not true. Now, let us not love in word and in tongue, but in deed and in truth. That is the kind of love God gives us, and He wants the same in return.

Now, there is another side to this truth. A man was talking to me out here the other day that he didn't believe there was any love at all; that Christians professed to have love, but he didn't believe men could have two coats, and I think he reflected on me, because I had on my overcoat at the time and he hadn't got any. I looked at him and said, "Suppose I should give you one of my coats, you would drink it up before sundown. I love you too much to give you my coat and have you drink it up."

A good many people are complaining now that Christians don't have the love they ought to have, but I tell you it is no sign of want of love that we don't love the lazy man. I have no sympathy with those men that are just begging twelve months of the year. It would be a good thing, I believe, to have them die off. They are of no good. I admit there are some that are not real, and sincere, and true, but there are many that would give the last penny they had to help a man who really needed help. But there are a good many sham cases—men that won't work, and the moment they get a penny they spend it for drink. To such men it is no charity to give. A man that won't work should be made to work. I believe there is a great deal more hope of a drunkard or a murderer or a gambler than there is of a lazy man.

Too Lazy to Be Converted

I never heard of a lazy man being converted yet, though I remember talking once with a minister in the backwoods of Iowa about lazy men. He was all discouraged in his efforts to convert lazy men, and I said to him, "Did you ever know a lazy man to be converted?" "Yes," he said; "I knew of one, but he was so lazy that he remained converted for only about six weeks." And that is as near as I ever heard of a lazy man being converted, and if there are any here today saying they don't love us because we don't give them any money, I say we love them too well. We don't give to them because it will ruin them.

Some years ago I picked up several children in Chicago and thought I would clothe them and feed them, and I took special interest in those boys to see what I could make of them. I don't think it was thirty days before the clothes had all gone to whisky and the fathers had drunk it all up. One day I met one of the little boys for whom I bought a pair of boots only the day before. There was a snowstorm coining up and he was barefooted. "Mike," I said, "how's this? Where are your boots?" "Father and mother took them away," he said. There is a good deal that we think is charity that is really doing a great deal of mischief, and the people must not think because we don't give them money to aid them in their poverty that we don't love them, for the money would go into their pockets with which to get whiskey.

Poverty Can Be a Blessing

It is no sign that we are all hypocrites and insincere in our love if we don't give money. I believe if the prodigal son could have got all the money he wanted in that foreign country he would never have come home, and it was a good thing for him that he did get hard up and to live on the husks that the swine ate. And it is a good think that people should suffer. If they get a good living without work, they will never work. We can never make anything of them. God has decreed that man shall earn his bread by the sweat of his brow, and not live on other people.

But I am getting away from the subject. I only wanted to touch upon this subject because a good many are complaining that Christian people don't help them. I have sometimes fifteen or twenty letters a day, coming from Kansas, and Europe even, asking us to take up a collection. They say, "Here is a poor woman. Just get the people to give a penny apiece." Suppose we began doing that sort of thing. We should have to have somebody to look up this man or this woman and find if they are worthy. If we took up one collection, we would have to take up five hundred. I never found a person true to Christ but what the Lord would take care of them. I think it is a good thing for people to suffer a little until they come back to God. They will find that God will take care of them that love Him. A great many say, "Oh, I love God." It is easy enough to say this, but if you do love God He knows about it, be assured. He knows how much you love Him. You may deceive your neighbors and think you love God, and assume a good deal of love, when there is really no love in your heart.

Now it says in Corinthians 8; "But if any man love God, the same is known of him." God is looking from heaven down into this world just to find that one man. God knows where he lives, the number of his house, and the name of the street he lives in. In fact, He has the very hairs of your head numbered, and He will take good care of you. He will not let any of His own children come to want, He will not let any of those that come to want suffer, He will provide for their wants if they are only sincere, but He doesn't want any sham work, When the Lord was here He was all the time stripping those Pharisees of their miserable self-righteousness. They professed great love for Him while their hearts were far from God. Let us not profess to love God with our tongue and lips, while our lives are far from it.

How to Know if You Really Love God
Another class say, "I don't know whether I love God or not. I am really anxious to know whether or not I love God." Now, if you are really anxious it won't take you long to find out. You cannot love God and the world at the same time, because they abhor each other. They are at enmity, always have been and always will be. It is the world that crucified God's Son; it was the world that put God's Son to death. Therefore, if we love the world it is pretty good evidence that the love of the Father is not in us. We may say our prayers and go through some religious performances, but our hearts are not right with God because we cannot love God and the world at the same time. We have got to get the world under our feet and the love of God must be first in our hearts or else we have not got the love of God.

The command we have is that he who loveth God loveth his brother also. Now, if we have got our heart full of enmity and jealousy and malice toward any of God's children it is a sure sign that the love of God is not in our hearts. To love a man that loves me doesn't require any goodness; the greatest infidel can do that. But to love a man that reviles me and lies about me and slanders me; that takes the grace of God. I may not associate with him, but I may love him. I may hate the sin, but love the sinner; and that is one of the tests by which to find out whether you have love in your heart. The first impulse of the young convert is to love everyone, and to do all the good he can. That is the sign that a man has been born from above, born of God, and that he has real love in his heart; and these tests God gives us that we may know.

Christian Love Opposite of Worldliness

The question is, do you love the world? Would you rather go to a theater than to prayer meeting? Would you rather go to a dance than to commune with the godly? If so, then it is a good sign that you have not been converted and not born of God. That is the test. People want to know whether they love God or not, let them turn to that test and they will find out. If your heart is set on the world and you would rather not be with God's people, it is a sure sign that you have not been born of God.

Well, there is another class of people who say, "I don't see that God really loves me and I love Him, why I am called upon to have so many afflictions and troubles." Just turn a moment to the 8th chapter of Romans, the 28th verse: "And we know that all things work together for good to them that love God, to them that are called according to his purpose." It is not a few things; not a part of them, but all work together for good. Give a man constant prosperity and how quickly he turns away from God, and so it is we have a little trouble here, and some prosperity there, and taken all together it is the very thing we need.

If you just take and read your Bibles you will find that God loves you. There is no one in this wide world, sinner that loves you as God loves you. You may think your father loves you, or your mother loves you, or a brother or a sister, but you can multiply it by ten thousand times ten thousand before it can equal God's love. "While we were yet sinners, Christ died for us" (Romans 5:8). Can you have greater proof of God's love and Christ's love? "Greater love hath no man than this, that a man lay down his life for his friends" (John 15:13). Christ laid down his life for his enemies. Ah, my friends, it will take all eternity for us to find out the height and breadth and length and depth of God's love.

Protected By the Flag

How men with an open Bible can say that God doesn't love them is more than I can understand. But the devil is deceitful and puts that into their heads. Let me beg you to go to Calvary and there you may just for a moment catch a glimpse of God's love.

There was a man came from Europe to this country a year or two ago, and he became dissatisfied and went to Cuba in 1867 when they had a great civil war there. Finally he was arrested for a spy, court-martialed, and condemned to be shot. He sent for the American Consul and the English Consul, and went on to prove to them that he was no spy. These two men were thoroughly convinced that the man was no spy, and they went to one of the Spanish officers and said, "This man you have condemned to be shot is an innocent man." "Well," said the Spanish officer, "the man has been legally tried by our laws and condemned, and the law must take its course and the man must die."

And the next morning the man was led out to be executed. The grave was already dug for him, and the black cap was put over his head. The soldiers were there ready to receive the order to fire, and in a few moments the man would be shot and be put in that grave. Just then, the American Consul rose up and took the American flag and wrapped it around him;

and the English Consul took the English flag and wrapped it around him, and they said to those soldiers, "Fire on those flags if you dare!" Not a man dared; there were two great governments behind those flags. And so God says, "Come under my banner, come under, the banner of love, come under the banner of heaven." God will take good care of all that come under His banner.

Oh, my friends come under the banner of heaven today. This banner is a banner of love. May it float over every soul here, is the prayer of my heart. God doesn't desire the death of any who will come under His banner of love. It is pure love, and sinner, may the love of God bring you into the fold is the prayer of my heart. I read once of a young man who left his father, and at last that father died and the boy came to the funeral. There was not a tear that flowed over his cheeks during the entire funeral. He saw that father laid down into the grave, and he did not shed a tear. When they came to break open the will, and the boy heard that the father had dealt kindly with him and had given him some property, he began to shed tears. When that boy heard his father's will read, his heart was broken and he came to his father's God.

O sinner, if you want to find out God's love, take this last will and testament of Jesus Christ. He showed his love by going to Calvary. He showed his love by His death agony there. He loves you with an everlasting love. He doesn't want you to perish. O, may you love Him in return.

PRACTICAL DIRECTIVES FOR PASTORS AND TEACHERS

QUESTIONS AND ANSWERS WITH D. L. MOODY

PRACTICAL DIRECTIVES FOR
PASTORS AND TEACHERS

QUESTIONS AND ANSWERS
WITH D. L. MOODY

Dwight L. Moody was a born teacher. He was also a great learner. His capacity for drawing out information from people with whom he came in contact was marvelous. If entering a new place, he never rested till he had found out all he could about the country and the people, especially their spiritual condition. When with a minister, he would have the best that that man could give him regarding the passages of Scripture, especially those in his mind at the time. Early in his public speaking he would gather around him Bible teachers, evangelists, and pastors, secure their best thoughts on some subject upon which he was to speak, and then go directly from such a conference to a meeting to deliver a heart-searching sermon, the actual material for which he had secured from his friends, absorbed, and made his own. In answer to an inquiry how far a young man was at liberty to use other men's thoughts, he replied:

"Always give due credit if you can, and if you can't, or if you don't want to mention the man's name, say, 'Some one has said.' Don't be afraid of using other men's thoughts. The chances are that the man you get it from read it in some other form. There is practically very little that is original, and it's better to give the best of others' thoughts than what is poor, even if it is original."

In Sunday school conventions, in Christian work, in revival meetings, in conferences, and in his schools he set apart times for answering questions. Sometimes he would sit on the platform and put a leading clergyman in the witness box and question him steadily for an hour, to the great edification and spiritual refreshment of the audience. Again, he would himself be the witness and let the audience try their hand at questioning. In order that the time might not be consumed with foolish questions, or with those that were asked for the sake of discussion rather than profit, he insisted that they should be submitted in writing. Frequently conferences were held at the close of each revival meeting, where Christian workers could find out how to carry on evangelistic work in their own churches.

The following practical questions and helpful answers illustrate this phase of his teaching:

Q. How can we make our prayer meetings more interesting?

A. Well, be more interesting yourself; that is one way. I have seen many meetings just murdered, the life taken out of them, by the leader. There is a way of going into a meeting by which you may do this. Go in with your coat buttoned up, looking at no one; do not use your natural voice, and be as stiff as you can. Begin by saying you have nothing to say, and then talk for half an hour. If the meeting isn't dead then, I am a false prophet. Then get up and scold the people for not taking part after you have thrown the meeting open.

For my own part, I don't know why we would even go into church in that cold, formal way. When we go to church, why not take someone by the hand, throw off the stiffness, and make everybody feel at home?

Q. If the pastor of a church does not favor evangelistic work, what can a layman do, besides praying, to promote the spiritual work?

A. I should do a great deal more than pray. I believe the time has come for the laymen to move; and by 'laymen' I mean men and women. If you can't work in the church, don't leave it, but go out and hold home meetings. In the country get the schoolhouse; that is a magnificent place to work. If the school board prohibits the use of the schoolhouse, hold meetings on a hilltop. That is what Christ did. Pray God to fill you with the Holy Ghost. Nothing can stop a man who is red hot and full of the Spirit of God. If we cannot get the people to come to church, let us go into their homes.

I believe that a man or woman who is filled with the Spirit of God can gain access to the hearts of the people, and can have conversions anywhere and everywhere. There is a class of people who don't believe in revivals and in what we call conversions. Don't quarrel with them, but go right to work and *have* conversions. A man who hides his talent under a napkin, and because his pastor is opposed to evangelistic meetings, goes through life praying for his church once a week, or once a month, to ease his conscience, is on the wrong track.

Q. Would you advise a pastor to hold an evangelistic meeting every Sunday night?

A. I would hold an evangelistic service fifty-two Sundays in the year. Sunday night is better than any other time, because a great many never get out except on Sunday night. Working men and don't have any other time, and if you don't reach them Sunday night you won't reach them at all. Most of the church audiences on Sunday morning are made up of Christian people, and that is the time when ministers ought to feed the flock and build up the church. If they are fed properly all the members become preachers themselves, and instead of the minister having one meeting Sunday night, there might be twenty. Within five miles of Round Top every Sunday night we have ten or twelve gospel meetings when we are in running order. I believe this can be done throughout the United States.

I heard of a minister who said to a judge in his congregation: "I am going out to a schoolhouse to preach. You have horses, and I would like for you to drive me out." The judge said that he would be very glad to do so. On the way the minister said: "Judge, I am going to ask you to speak."

"Oh," said the judge, "I couldn't do that."

"But," said the minister, "I was in the court the other day, and I never heard anything better than the charge you gave to the jury."

The minister had some tact, and when he went on to the platform he said: "Now, I am going to pray and read a portion of the Scripture, and then I am going to put the judge in the witness-box and examine him." He asked the questions, and the judge preached the whole sermon. Our judges and our lawyers are spoiling for work. It wouldn't take long to evangelize this country if we could only get the pews into the pulpit, but the ministers can never do it alone.

Q. Would you have a stated after-meeting every Sunday night?

A. Yes; every time I preached the Gospel I would look for results. There are three or four kinds of meetings. When we come around the Lord's Table, it is worship. When we expound the Bible, it is to feed the Church of God. But when we invite men to come to God, then we ought to expect that they will come right then and there.

Q. How would you conduct an after-meeting?

A. I never would conduct it fifty-two Sundays alike. There are very few men who could do that successfully. If the sermon is over at half-past eight, when the audience expected to stay until nine, they are in good mood to stay a half-hour longer.

There are two ways of inviting people to stay to an after-meeting. One is, to send them all home. The benediction is a polite invitation for people to go. I wouldn't pronounce any benediction at the first meeting, and I wouldn't say, "*If* any are concerned about their soul they are invited to stay." You stick an "if" four feet high before them, and it will take an earthquake to move them into an inquiry room. When I was converted it took three months to screw up my courage to be examined by a committee to be taken into the church. You might as well try to get a man to go before a justice of the peace. I would say, "Now, we are going to have a second meeting, and if any one must go, won't you just slip out while we are singing?" I would put it as though I expected no one to go.

Q. How can a minister have special meetings when he has failed to get an evangelist?

A. There is a plan that is working very well in England and in some parts of this country. Let a minister who has special evangelistic gifts give two weeks to a brother minister, and let that brother minister preach for him the Sunday between. Then that minister has two weeks in which he can go all through his church and invite people out that perhaps he wouldn't like to ask to come to hear himself. He can get his whole church to work in the same way. Then, if people are converted, the church members will be more likely to look after them than if there had been some great union meeting. That plan helps the minister who has been preaching, as well. He goes back to his own church all on fire, and preaches to his people with new interest.

A series of meetings is a good thing, because if a man is awakened on Sunday, and there is to be a meeting on Monday, he is likely to come; and the impression is deepened. On Tuesday it grows deeper, and Wednesday or Thursday he will attend the after-meeting. I think if that could be done, many a church would double its membership right off. It is perfectly feasible. Let a minister go away for ten days and preach the best sermons he has. He has nothing to do but to pray and meditate and study, while the other minister with his members is out gathering the people.

Q. Would you advise a young man to go into the ministry?

A. Never. If God calls a man, all right. But I have seen too many man-made ministers. If God calls a man, then he will succeed; but if man sends him, he will fail. I should advise every man to engage in Christian work, but not to give up all other occupations and live by the pulpit.

Q. Is it a good thing for a minister to study elocution?

A. Yes and no. It is a good thing to learn to read well. But when it comes to modern elocution, these studied gestures in the pulpit—my word, I am sick and tired of them! Some men remind me of a windmill, with their practiced gestures. How would Moses have succeeded if he had gone down into Egypt and tried elocution on Pharaoh? I like the oratory that moves men, but I have no use for the elocution where a man is showing off.

Q. What would you do if you were a pastor in a town where there are five churches and only room for one?

A. Get out mighty quick. No power on earth can make me believe it is God's will that a Methodist and a Baptist and a Congregational and a Presbyterian and an Episcopal church should be in one town where there is not room for more than one or two. There is scarcely any difference in their creeds, and it is waste of time to be preaching in such a town. I believe that sort of thing is the work of the devil.

Q. What would you do in a neighborhood of about one hundred families and no church, where there are no Christians except one godly family?

A. One godly family can evangelize one hundred families very easily. Let any man or woman who can read well get a good sermon by some prominent man, and let it be announced that this sermon is to be read on Sunday morning or evening. Then get the people together and read that sermon and pray that God may bless it. It may be just as effective as an original sermon. That has been done all through the mining districts. It is a sight in Colorado on Sunday to see the miners come out of the bowels of the hills and gather in the schoolhouses or under the trees while some old English miner stands up and reads one of Charles Spurgeon's sermons. They have conversions right along.

Q. How can we get hold of strangers in these great cities?

A. I believe that if you would have in the pews a blank card with a place for name and residence, and if the minister would say when strangers are present that he or his wife would be glad to visit them if they would write their name and address on the card, and leave it in the pew. I believe that if a minister would do that constantly, he would reach a great many people and bring them into the church.

353

In all the cities a great many people are lonesome or homesick, and want sympathy, but they don't know how to get it. I heard of a man who went to a church for six months without a single person speaking to him. Of course he was as much to blame as the church, but one morning the minister preached on recognizing friends in Heaven, and as the man went out he asked a deacon to ask the minister if he wouldn't preach on recognizing friends on earth, for he had been attending his church a half year and no one had spoken to him. It would be a good thing to have a committee at the door, and let no stranger get out without a word of welcome.

Q. If you are advertised to preach, and there is a small audience on account of the bad weather, is it best to turn it into a prayer meeting?

A. No, sir, I don't think so at all. If I expected five thousand people there and found only five, I would give them the best I could. Another thing, don't abuse the people who come for those that don't come. A rainy, stormy night is the time I expect the greatest blessing, because people have made a sacrifice to come. I was advertised to speak in Boston, and three thousand tickets had been given out. There came up the biggest blizzard they had had in Boston for eight or nine years. I had hard work to get to the city, and there I had to plough my way through deep snowdrifts. Less than one hundred people were in that big hall, and the leaders wanted to know if it would not be best to close the meeting and wait until the storm was over. 'No,' I said, 'not by a good deal.' I never preached so hard in my life as I did to that one hundred people. I put half a dozen sermons together, and threw them right at them. If a man ploughed through that snow to hear me I ought to do my best to pay him for coming. What we want is to turn defeat into victory. If a man can't do that he is a failure.

Q. Ought a man to be admitted into the church if he has not been regenerated?

A. No, you hurt the church and hurt the man. A great many churches think that by admitting a man you bring him under good influences that may lead to his conversion; but they often find it leads to just the reverse. He gets settled in his self-righteousness, and it grows harder and harder to reach him. The moment you begin to talk to him he runs up his lightning rod. "Oh, I am saved! I am a member of the church!" There he sticks.

Q. Is it right for any man or woman who has not been converted to have anything to do in an evangelical church?

A. I never set an unconverted man or woman to work, but Christian men need to be warmed up and then set to work to convert those who are not Christians.

Q. Would you tell a man whose speaking injures a meeting not to take part in a prayer meeting?

A. Yes, mighty quick. I would rather hurt the man's feelings than hurt the whole meeting. Some time ago I said to a man, "You ought not to have said what you did tonight, and, besides, your record is bad, and you ought not to take part at all."

"Sir," he said, "you hurt my feelings."

"Well," I said, "you hurt mine. I have feelings as well as you, and you hurt the feelings of five hundred other people besides."

Q. What would you do if members in your congregation are at "swords points" with others and won't reconcile?

A. I should keep at them until they did make up or left the church. No blessing can be expected to come to a church as long as the members go to the Lord's Supper and have an open quarrel. I believe the reason that there are so few conversions in many churches is because of these church feuds. God isn't going to bless a church in that condition."

Q. What can be done to influence young men in the church and Sunday school who are not Christians?

A. It depends altogether on what class of young men they are. It may be wise to begin by gathering them together for a social time. Ask them to your house to tea, and get acquainted with them. Find out something that they can do, something they would like to do. Another good way is to visit them personally. Men like to be treated as men. They like to have a man take an interest in them. If a minister calls on men in their office or store or on the farm, they will usually manage to go to hear him preach.

Q. How can a man who wants to preach overcome nervousness?

A. That is a practical question, my friend. Do you remember the first time you got up to preach, and how your knees went thump, thump? I'll tell you what to do. Get so full of your subject that you forget yourself. Be occupied with the subject, and you are all right. This opens the question of preaching. Let me say right here that I like to say "to speak" better than "to preach," because if I can only get people to think I am talking with them, and not preaching, it is so much easier to hold their attention. The other night I was walking home in the dark, and two people right behind me were talking about the meeting. One of them said, "Did Moody preach tonight?" The other said, "No, he didn't preach, he only talked."

"Did you ever hear him before?"

"Yes."

"How do you like him?"

"Well, we don't like him. He never has the church service, and he doesn't have on any robes; and then his preaching— why, he doesn't preach at all, he just talks."

I thought that was quite a compliment. I am glad if I can make people think I am talking with them. I think sometimes we almost preach the people to death—it is preach, preach, preach. If you can get the idea out of their minds that you are going to preach, and just let them think that you are going to talk, you are more likely to reach them.

Another thing: be yourself. I detest the kind of people that take a religious tone when they begin to talk to you on the subject of religion, and have a peculiar whine that makes you think they are not sincere. Be natural. Talk on this subject as you would on any other.

Q. How can a young man hold the people's attention?

A. Get hold of their curiosity. If you take up Dr. Guthrie's sermons, you will find that he begins a thousand miles away from his text, apparently, and you wonder how he is ever going to get back to his theme. When he has the curiosity of the congregation excited, he comes back to his text. You will find he almost invariably begins in that way. Another point: If you have got a good thing to say, say it in the beginning. Don't get into ruts; strike out a path of your own.

Don't say, "Firstly," and "Secondly," and "Thirdly," and then "Finally," "In conclusion," and "Lastly," and all that. Take the whole truth or the whole text and throw it right at them; then try to drive it home.

It is said of Cicero, the great Roman orator, that when he had spoken every one would go out of the building saying, "what a magnificent address! What an orator!" But when Demosthenes, the Greek orator, had finished, the people would say, "Let us go and fight Philip!" He had fired them up with the cause; and what we want is to get the attention of the people away from ourselves and on to the subject.

Q. Suppose you see a man asleep in the audience?

A. It is a good thing to stop and say, "Won't you open the window and let in a little air? Here is a gentleman who has gone to sleep." That'll wake up every one of them. You can't reach a man when he is asleep. Men may talk in their sleep, but you can't talk to a man when he is asleep. An interruption like that won't do any harm, especially if it makes the people think it wasn't your preaching, but the bad air, that put the man to sleep. Very often you will wake a man up by pointing right down to him. Sometimes I have seen a man just going to sleep, and I would stamp my foot. One man asleep will publish to the whole audience that you are a dry preacher.

Q. How long should a sermon be?

A. It is very much better to get a reputation for being brief than to have people say that you preach long sermons. Say what you have got to say in just as few words as you can. Then stop when you get through. Some men go on and feel around for a good stopping place. I'd rather stop abruptly than do that. Don't waste any time. Remember, we are living in an intense age. Men think quicker than they used to. The time was when if a man wanted to do a little business in Boston, he would write half a dozen sheets of foolscap and send them by mail. Now he puts it all in a telegram of ten words. What we want in our preaching is to condense. Get a reputation for being short, and people will want to hear you.

Q. What would you do if the choir disturbed you?

A. I remember preaching once at Limerick when our hymn books were new. A young man came in and joined the choir. There were three or four hundred people on the stage, and he took a front seat. He took up a hymnbook just as I began to preach, and turned over the leaves. Beginning with the first hymn, he went on as if he were going to examine every page in the book. I thought to myself, "Have I got to preach until he gets all through that book before I can get the attention of the people?" What to do I didn't know.

Finally I used him as an illustration. Speaking of a young man in America, I said, "He was about the age of this young man reading a hymn book." The result was that when I asked all those in the house who wanted us to pray for them to rise, he rose. That young man was the first soul God gave me in Limerick. If he had gone on reading the hymnbook, it would have been almost impossible for me to get hold of him or the people. Get the attention of your audience somehow. If you are going to be a public speaker, train yourself for that.

Q. What should be done after the attention is gained?

A. Aim at the heart. Just keep thundering away at the man's heart and you will get it, and if you get his heart, you will get his head and his feet and everything—you get the whole man. The story of the Prodigal Son will melt any man's heart. So will the story of the Good Samaritan. Or take any of the miracles of healing—how Christ saw a man blind or paralyzed and came to him and had compassion on him. Just open the heart of Christ to the people and draw the multitude around I him. If you want to get hold of an audience, aim at the heart; and there is nothing that will warm up the heart like the Gospel of Jesus Christ.

EFFECTIVE
EVANGELISM

EFFECTIVE EVANGELISM

Personal dealing is of the most vital importance. No one can tell how many souls have been lost through lack of following up the preaching of the Gospel by personal work. It is deplorable how few church members are qualified to deal with inquirers. And yet that is the very work in which they ought to aid the pastor most efficiently. People are not usually converted under the preaching of the minister. It is in the inquiry meeting that they are most likely to be brought to Christ.

It would be a good thing if people would interrupt the minister now and then in the middle of some metaphysical sermon and ask what he means. The only way to make sure that people understand what he is talking about is to let them ask questions. I don't know what some men who have the whole thing written out would do if some one should get up and ask, "What must I do to be saved?" Yet such questions would do more good than anything else you could have. They would wake up a spirit of inquiry.

Some people say, "All you want to do is to make the preaching so plain that plain people will understand it." Well, Christ was a plain preacher, and yet he asked, *"Have ye understood all these things?"* (Matthew 13:51.) He

363

encouraged them to inquire. I think sometimes, when the minister is preaching over their heads, people would be greatly relieved if he would stop and ask whether they understood it. His very object is to make the Word of God clear. Christ was a plain preacher, but when He preached to Saul the man was only awakened. Christ could have convicted and converted him, but He honored a human agency, and sent Ananias to tell the word whereby he was to be saved.

Philip was sent away into the desert to talk to one man in the chariot. We must have personal work—hand-to-hand work—if we are going to have results. "I admit you can't lay down rules in dealing with inquirers. There are no two persons exactly alike. Matthew and Paul were a good way apart, and the people we deal with may be widely different. What would be medicine for one might be rank poison for another. In the fifteenth of Luke the elder son and the younger son were exactly opposite. What would have been good counsel for one might have been ruin for the other. God never made two persons to look alike. If we had made men, probably we would have made them all alike, even if we had to crush some bones to get them into the mold. But that is not God's way. In the universe there is infinite variety. The Philippian jailer required peculiar treatment. Christ dealt with Nicodemus one way and with the woman at the well another way. It is difficult to say just how people are to be saved; yet there are certain portions of Scripture that can be brought to bear on certain classes of inquirers.

I think it is a great mistake, in dealing with inquirers, to tell your own experience. Experience may have its place, but I don't think it has its place when you are talking with them. The first thing the man you are talking to will do will be to look for your experience in his case. He doesn't want your experience; he wants one of his own. No two persons are converted alike. Suppose Bartimaeus had gone to Jerusalem to the man that was born blind and said, "Now, just tell us how the Lord cured you." The Jerusalem man might have said, "He just spat on the ground and anointed my eyes with the clay." "Ho!" says Bartimaeus, "I don't believe you ever got your sight at all. Who ever heard of such a way as that? Why, to fill a man's eyes with clay is enough to put them out!" Both men were blind, but they were not cured alike. A great many men are kept out of the Kingdom of God because they are looking for somebody else's experience—the experience their grandmother had, or their aunt, or someone in the family.

Always use your Bible in personal dealing. Do not trust to memory, but make the person read the verse for himself. Do not use printed slips or books. Therefore, if convenient, always carry a Bible or New Testament with you.

"It is a good thing to get a man on his knees, but don't get him there before he is ready. You may have to talk with him two hours before you can get him that far along. But when you think he is about ready, say, "Shall we not ask God to give us light on this point?"

Sometimes a few minutes in prayer have done more for a man than two hours in talk. When the Spirit of God has led him so far that he is willing to have you pray with him, he is not very far from the Kingdom. Ask him to pray for himself. If he doesn't want to pray, let him use a Bible prayer; get him to repeat, for example, "Lord help me!" Tell the man, "If the Lord helped that poor woman, He will help you if you make the same prayer. He will give you a new heart if you pray from the heart." Don't send a man home to pray. Of course he should pray at home, but I would rather get his lips open at once. It is a good thing for a man to hear his own voice in prayer. It is a good thing for him to cry out, "God be merciful to me, a sinner!"

Urge an immediate decision, but never tell a man he is converted. Never tell him he is saved. Let the Holy Spirit reveal that to him. You can shoot a man and see that he is dead, but you cannot see when a man receives eternal life. You can't afford to deceive any one about this great question. But you can help his faith and trust, and lead him aright.

Always be prepared to do personal work. When war was declared between France and Germany, Count von Moltke, the German general, was prepared for it. Word was brought to him late at night, after he had gone to bed. "Very well," he said to the messenger, "the third portfolio on the left!" and he went to sleep again.

Do the work boldly. Don't take those in a position in life above your own, but as a rule, take those on the same footing. Don't deal with a person of opposite sex if it can be otherwise arranged. Bend all your endeavors to answer for poor, struggling souls that question of such importance to them, "What must I do to be saved?"

To summarize this important subject:

1. Have for constant use a portable reference Bible, a Cruden's Concordance, and a Topical Text-book.
2. Always carry a Bible or Testament in your pocket, and do not be ashamed of people seeing you read it on trains, etc.
3. Do not be afraid of marking it or making marginal notes. Mark texts that contain promises, exhortations, warnings to sinners and to Christians, gospel invitations to the unconverted, and so on.

4 Set apart at least fifteen minutes a day for study and meditation. This little time will have great results and will never be regretted.

5 *Prepare your heart to know the way of the Lord and to do it.* (Ezra 7:10.)

6 Always ask God to open the eyes of your understanding that you may see the truth, and expect that He will answer your prayer.

7 Cast every burden of doubt upon the Lord. *'He will never suffer the righteous to be moved.'* Do not be afraid to look for a reason for the hope that is in you.

8 Believe in the Bible as God's revelation to you, and act accordingly. Do not reject any portion because it contains the supernatural or because you cannot understand it. Reverence all Scripture. Remember God's own estimate of it: *Thou hast magnified Thy Word above all Thy Name.*

9 Learn at least one verse of the Scripture each day. Verses committed to memory will be wonderfully useful in your daily life and walk. *Thy Word have I hid in mine heart that I might not sin against Thee.* Some Christians can quote Shakespeare and Longfellow better than the Bible.

10 If you are a preacher or a Sunday school teacher try at any cost to master your Bible. You ought to know it better than anyone in your congregation or class.

11 Strive to be exact in quoting Scripture.

12 Adopt some systematic plan of Bible study: either topical or by subjects, like "The Blood," "Prayer," "Hope," etc., or by books, or by some other plan outlined in the preceding pages.

13 Study to know for what and to whom each book of the Bible was written. Combine the Old Testament with the New. Study Hebrews and Leviticus together, the Acts of the Apostles and the Epistles, the Prophets and

the historical books of the Old Testament.

14 Study how to use the Bible so as to 'walk with God' in closer communion, also so as to gain a working knowledge of Scripture for leading others to Christ. An old minister used to say that the cries of neglected texts were always sounding in his ears, asking why he did not show how important they were.

15 Do not be satisfied with simply reading a chapter daily. *Study* the meaning of at least one verse.

GEMS FROM
D. L. MOODY

GEMS FROM D. L. MOODY

AFFLICTION

A great many people wonder why it was that Christ did not come at once to Martha and Mary, whom He loved, whenever He heard of their affliction. It was to try them, and it is the same with His dealings toward us. If He seems not to come to us in our affliction, it is only to test us and make us better.

If you have had some great affliction, if any of you have lost a loving father, mother, brother, husband, or wife, come to Christ, because God has sent Him to heal the broken-hearted.

Christ never preached any funeral sermons.

Take your stand on the Rock of Ages. Let death, let the judgment come: the victory is Christ's and yours through Him.

ASSURANCE

I believe that Satan is deceiving hundreds of Christian people, and that they do not have assurance of salvation just because they are not willing to take God at His word.

It is our privilege to know that we are saved.

Now, I find a great many people who want some evidence that they have accepted the Son of God. My friends, if you want any evidence, take God's word for it. You can't find better evidence than that. You know that when the Angel Gabriel came down and told Zachariah he would have a son he wanted a further token than the angel's word. He asked Gabriel for it and he answered, "I am Gabriel, who stands in the presence of the Lord." He had never been doubted, and he thundered this out to Zachariah. But he wanted a further token, and Gabriel said, "You shall have a token. You shall be unable to speak until your son is born."

There is no knowledge like that of a man who knows he is saved, who can look up and see his "title clear to mansions in the skies."

There is no doubt about assurance in the Word of God. A person said to me some time ago: "I think it is great presumption for a person to say she is saved." I asked her if she was saved. "I belong to a church," she sobbed. "But are you saved?" "I believe it would be presumption in me to say that I was saved." "Well I think it is a greater presumption for anyone to say: 'I don't know if I believe in the Lord Jesus Christ because it is written, He that believeth on me hath everlasting life.'" It is clearly stated that we have assurance.

My friends, there is one spot on the earth where the fear of death, sin, and judgment, need never trouble us—the only safe spot on earth where the sinner can stand—Calvary.

BIBLE READING AND MEDITATION

When we find a man meditating on the words of God, my friends, that man is full of boldness and is successful.

Set yourself more and more on the Bible. Then troubles in your Christian life will pass away like a morning cloud. You will feed and live on the Word of God, and it will become the joy of your soul.

If you will show me a Christian living on the Word of God, I will show you a joyful man. He is mounting up all the time. He has got new truths that lift him up over every obstacle, and he mounts over difficulties higher and higher.

The greatest truths are found by digging deep for them.

Take the Bible; study it; leave criticism to the theologians; feed on the Word; then go out to work. Combine the two— study and work—if you would be a full-orbed Christian.

When a man is filled with the Word of God you cannot keep him still. If a man has the Word, he must speak or die.

There are over two hundred passages in the Old Testament that prophesied about Christ, and every one of them has come true.

Let us have one day exclusively to study and read the Word of God. If we can't take time during the week, we will have Sunday uninterrupted.

Now, as old Dr. Bonner of Glasgow said, "The Lord didn't tell Joshua how to use the sword, but He told him how he should meditate on the Lord day and night, and then he would have success."

I have never found a man who has read the Bible from front to back carefully who has remained an infidel.

One thing I have noticed in studying the Word of God, and that is, when a man is filled with the Spirit he deals largely with the Word of God, whereas the man who is filled with his own ideas refers rarely to the Word of God. He gets along without it, and you seldom see it mentioned in his discourses.

Now I am no prophet, nor the son of a prophet, but one thing I can predict; that every one of our new converts that goes to studying his Bible, and loves this book above every other book, is sure to hold out. The world will have no charm for him. He will get the world under his feet, because in this book he will find something better than the world can give him.

What can botanists tell you of the lily of the valley? You must study this book for that. What can geologists tell you of the Rock of Ages, or mere astronomers about the Bright Morning Star? In those pages we find all knowledge unto salvation; here we read of the ruin of man by nature, redemption by the blood, and regeneration by the Holy Ghost These three things run all through and through them.

THE BLOOD OF CHRIST

The most solemn truth in the gospel is that the only thing Christ left down here is His blood.

A man who covers up the Cross though he may be an intellectual man, and draw large crowds will have no ilk there, and his church will be but a gilded sepulcher.

There is either of two things we must do. One is to send back the message to heaven that we don't want the blood of Christ to cleanse us of our sin, or else accept it.

Into every house where the blood was not sprinkled, the destroying angel came. But wherever the blood was on doorpost and lintel, whether they had worked much, or whether they had worked none, God passed them over.

A man who has not realized what the blood has done for him has not the token of salvation. It is told of Julian, the apostate, that while he was fighting he received an arrow in his side. He pulled it out, and, taking a handful of blood threw it into the air and cried, "Galilean, Galilean, thou hast conquered."

Look at that Roman soldier as he pushed his spear into the very heart of the God-man. What a hellish deed! But what was the next thing that took place? Blood covered the spear! Oh! Thank God, the blood covers sin. There was the blood covering that spear—the very point of it. The very crowning act of sin brought out the crowning act of love; the crowning act of wickedness was the crowning act of grace.

It is said that old Dr. Alexander, of Princeton College, when a young student used to start out to preach, always gave them a piece of advice. The old man would stand with his gray locks and his venerable face and say, "Young man, make much of the blood in your ministry? Now, I have traveled considerable during the past few years, and never met a minister who made much of the blood and much of the atonement that God hasn't blessed his ministry, and souls were born into the light by it.

COMFORT

No matter how low down you are; no matter what your disposition has been, you may be low in your thoughts, words, and actions; you may be selfish; your heart may be overflowing with corruption and wickedness; yet Jesus will have compassion on you. He will speak comforting words to you; not treat you coldly or spurn you, as perhaps those of earth would, but will speak tender words, and words of love and affection and kindness. Just come at once. He is a faithful friend—a friend that sticketh closer than a brother.

CONFESSION

If Christ comes into our hearts we are not ashamed.

I wish we had a few more women like the woman of Samaria, willing to confess what the Lord Jesus Christ had done for their souls.

Believing and confessing go together; and you cannot be saved unless you take them both. "With the mouth confession is made unto salvation." If you ever hope to see the kingdom of heaven you have to take this path.

Satan puts straws across our path and magnifies it and makes us believe it is a mountain, but all the devil's mountains are mountains of smoke; when you come up to them they are not there.

I can't help thinking of the old woman who started out when the war commenced with a poker in her hand. When asked what she was going to do with it she said: "I can't do much with it, but I can show what side I'm on." My friends, even if you can't do much, show to which side you belong.

I may say with truth that there is only about one in ten who professes Christianity who will turn round and glorify God with a loud voice. Nine out of ten are still born Christians. You never hear of them. If you press them hard with the question whether they are Christians they might say, "Well, I hope so." We never see it in their actions; we never see it in their lives. They might belong to the church you go to, but you never see them at the prayer meetings or taking any interest in the church affairs. They don't profess it among their fellows or in their business, and the result is that there are hundreds going on with a half hope, not sure whether their religion will stand them or not.

DELIVERANCE

If you believe on the Lord Jesus Christ you are free.

There is no sin in the whole catalogue of sins you can name but Christ will deliver you from it perfectly.

We are led on by an unseen power that we have no strength to resist, or else the loving Son of God leads us.

The trouble is, people do not know that Christ is a Deliverer. They forget that the Son of God came to keep them from sin as well as to forgive it.

You say, "I am afraid I cannot hold out." Well, Christ will hold out for you. There is no mountain that He will not climb with you if you will. He will deliver you from your besetting sin.

Satan rules all men that are in his kingdom. Some he rules through lust. Some he rules through covetousness. Some he rules through appetite. Some he rules by their temper, but he rules them. And none will ever seek to be delivered until they get their eyes open and see that they have been taken captive.

If you receive Him it will be well; if you reject Him and are lost it will be terrible.

When Christ was on the earth there was a woman in the temple that was bowed almost to the ground with sin. Satan had bound her for eighteen years, but after all these years of bondage Christ delivered her. He spoke one word and she was free. She got up and walked home. How astonished those at home must have been to see her walking in

One day I saw a steel engraving that I liked very much. I thought it was the finest thing I ever had seen, at the time, and I bought it. It was a picture of a woman coming out of the water, and clinging with both arms to the Cross. There she came out of the drowning waves with both arms around the Cross perfectly safe. Afterwards, I saw another picture that spoiled this one for me entirely; it was so much lovelier. It was a picture of a person coming out of dark waters; with one arm clinging to the Cross and with the other she was lifting some one else out of the waves. That is what I like. Keep a firm hold upon the Cross, but always try to rescue another from the drowning.

EVANGELISM

There is joy in the service of Christ that the world knows nothing of, and you never will until you taste it.

We shall draw the world to Christ when we are filled with religion.

What makes the Dead Sea dead? Because it is all the time receiving, never giving out anything. Why is it that many Christians are cold? Because they are all the time receiving, never giving out anything.

Oh, little children, if you find Jesus tell of Him to your fathers and mothers. Throw your arms around their necks and lead them to Jesus.

The greatest pleasure of living is to win souls to Christ.

I believe in what John Wesley used to say, "All at it, and always at it," and that is what the Church wants today.

If we were all of us doing the work that God has got for us to do, don't you see how the work of the Lord would advance?

There is no man living that can do the work that God has got for me to do. No one can do it but myself. And if the work isn't done we will have to answer for it when we stand before God.

What makes the Dead Sea dead? Because it is all the time receiving, never giving out anything. Why is it that many Christians are cold? Because they are all the time receiving, never giving out anything.

I do not know anything that would wake up Chicago better than for every man and woman here who loves Him to begin to talk about Him to there friends, and just to tell them what He has done for you. You have a circle of friends? Go and tell them of Him.

FAITH

God will honor our faith.

There is nothing on this earth that pleases Christ so much as faith.

Faith is the foundation of all society. We have only to look around and see this.

I believe there is no man in the world so constituted that he cannot believe in God's word. He simply tells you to believe in Him, and He will save you.

When I was converted twenty years ago I felt a faith in God, but five years after I had a hundred times more faith; and five years ago I had even more, because I became better acquainted with Him. I have read up the Word, and I see that the Lord has done so and so, and then I have turned to where He has promised to perform it, and when I see this I have reason to believe in Him

All you have got to do is to prove that you are a sinner, and I will prove that you have got a Savior.

"Lord, you don't really mean that we shall preach the Gospel to those men that murdered you, to those men that took your life?" "Yes," says the Lord, "go and preach the Gospel to those Jerusalem sinners." I can imagine Him saying, "Go and hunt up that man that put the cruel crown of thorns upon My brow, and preach the Gospel to him. Tell him he shall have a crown in My kingdom without a thorn in it."

FRIENDSHIP WITH CHRIST

A rule I have had for years is to treat the Lord Jesus Christ as a personal friend. His is not a creed, a mere empty doctrine, but it is He himself we have. The moment we have received Christ we should receive Him as a friend. When I go away from home I bid my wife and children good-by, I bid my friends and acquaintances good-by, but I never heard of a poor backslider going down on his knees and saying: "I have been near You for ten years; Your service has become tedious and monotonous; I have come to bid You farewell; good-by, Lord Jesus Christ." I never heard of one doing this.

GRACE

We must not limit the mighty grace of God.

Grace means undeserved kindness. It is the gift of God to man the moment he sees he is unworthy of God's favor.

A man does not get grace till he comes down to the ground, till he sees he needs grace. When a man stoops to the dust and acknowledges that he needs mercy, and then it is that the Lord will give him grace.

If you are ready to partake of grace you have not to atone for your sins—you have merely to accept of the atonement. All that you want to do is to cry, "God have mercy upon me," and you will receive the blessing.

"The grace of God hath power to bring salvation to all men," and if a man is unsaved it is because he wants to work it out. He wants to receive salvation in some other way than God's way, but we are told that "he that climbeth up another way, the same is a thief and a robber."

When we get full of this grace we want to see every one blessed—we want to see all the churches blessed, not only all the churches here, but in the whole country. That was the trouble with Christ's disciples. He had hard work to make them understand that His gospel was for everyone, that it was a stream to flow out to all nations of the earth. They wanted to confine it to the Jews, and He had to convince them that it was for every living being.

HEAVEN

There is no knowledge like that of a man who knows he is saved, who can look up and see his "title clear to mansions in the skies."

"But," a man said to me, "no one has come back, and we don't know what is in the future. It is all dark, and how can we be sure?" Thank God! Christ came down from heaven, and I would rather have Him, coming as he does right from the bosom of the Father, than any one else. We can rely on what Christ says, and He says, "He that believeth on Me shall not perish, but have everlasting life." Not only that we are going to have it when we die, but right here today.

Take your stand on the Rock of Ages. Let death, let the judgment come: the victory is Christ's and yours through Him.

How different is death for a believer in Christ! For him not only is the present life filled with the peace of God, but the future is bright with hope. He knows that for him death is only the exchanging of a shifting tent for an enduring mansion.

One of two things you must do; you must either receive Him or reject Him. You receive Him here and He will receive you there; you reject Him here and He will reject you there.

There are a great many people who forget that there are eleven commandments. They think there are only ten. The eleventh commandment is: "Lay up for yourselves treasures in heaven." How many of us remember—ah! How many people forget the words of the Lord now in his wonderful sermon on the mount: "Lay not up for yourselves treasures upon earth, where moth and rust doth corrupt, and where thieves break through and steal; but lay up for yourselves treasures in heaven, where neither moth nor rust doth corrupt, and where thieves do not break through and steal." How few of our people pay any heed to these words. That's why there are so many broken hearts among us; that's why so many men and women are disappointed and going through the streets with shattered hopes; it's because they have not been laying up treasures in heaven.

A little child, whose mother was dying, was taken away to live with some friends because it was thought she did not understand what death is. All the while the child wanted to go home and see her mother. At last, when the funeral was over, and she was taken home, she ran all over the house, searching the sitting room, the parlor, the library, and the bedrooms. She went from one end of the house to the other, and when she could not find her mother, she wished to be taken back to where they came from. Home had lost its attractions for the child when her mother was not there. My friends, the great attraction in heaven will not be its pearly gates, its golden streets, or its choir of angels, but it will be Christ. Heaven would be no heaven if Christ were not there. But we know that He is at the right hand of the Father, and these eyes shall gaze on Him by-and-by; and we shall be satisfied when we awake with his likeness.

HOLY SPIRIT

When the Spirit came to Moses, the plagues came upon Egypt, and he had power to destroy men's lives; when the Spirit came upon Elijah, fire came down from heaven; when the Spirit came upon Gideon, no man could stand before him; and when it came upon Joshua, he moved around the city of Jericho and the whole city fell into his hands. But when the Spirit came upon the Son of Man, He gave His life; He healed the brokenhearted.

LOVE

Christ is a loving, tender hand, full of sympathy and compassion.

The only man who ever suffered before Christ was that servant who had his ear cut off. But most likely in a moment afterward he had it on, and very likely it was a better ear than ever, because whatever the Lord does He does it well. No man ever lost his life with Him.

THE OVERCOMING LIFE

He that overcometh shall inherit all things. God has no poor children.

If you are under the power of evil, and you want to be under the power of God, cry to Him to bring you over to His service. Cry to Him to take you into His army. He will hear you! He will come to you, and if need be, He will send a legion of angels to help you to fight your way up to heaven. God will take you by the right hand and lead you through this wilderness, over death, and take you right into His kingdom. That's what the Son of Man came to do. He has never deceived us. Just say here, "Christ is my deliverer."

Thanks be to God, there is hope today; this very hour you can choose Him and serve Him.

Now just think a moment and answer the question, "What shall I do with Jesus who is called Christ?"

PEACE

There cannot be any peace where there is uncertainty.

There is no sin in the whole catalogue of sins you can name but Christ will deliver you from it perfectly.

POWER

Do you believe that He would send those men out to preach the gospel to every creature unless he wanted every creature to be saved? Do you believe He would tell them to preach it to people without giving people the power to accept it? Do you believe the God of heaven is mocking men by offering them his gospel and not giving them the power to take hold of it? Do you believe He will not give men power to accept this salvation as a gift? Man might do that, but God never mocks men. And when he says, "Preach the gospel to every creature," every creature can be saved if he will.

Lift your eyes from off these puny Christians—from off these human ministers, and look to Christ. He is the Savior of the world. He came from the throne to this earth. He came from the very bosom of the Father. God gave Him up freely for us, and all we have to do is to accept him as our Savior Look at Him at Gethsemane, sweating as it were great drops of blood. Look at Him on the Cross, crucified between two thieves; hear that piercing cry, "Father, Father, forgive them, they know not what they do." And as you look into that face, as you look into those wounds on His feet or His hands, will you say He has not the power to save you? Will you say He has not the power so redeem you?

PRAISE

Praise is not only speaking to the Lord on our own account, but it is praising Him for what He has done for others.

If we have a praise church we will have people convened.

I don't care where it is, what part of the world it's in, if we have a praise church we'll have successful Christianity.

Every good gift that we have had from the cradle up has come from God. If a man just stops to think what he has to praise God for, he will find there is enough to keep him singing praises for a week.

We have in our churches a great deal of prayer, but I think it would be a good thing if we had a praise meeting occasionally. If we could only get people to praise God for what He has done, it would be a good deal better than asking Him continually for something.

PRAYER

All should work and ask God's guidance.

The world knows little of the works wrought by prayer.

Let us pray, and as we pray, let us make room for Jesus in our hearts.

Unless the Spirit of God is with us, we cannot expect that our prayers will be answered.

David was the last one we would have chosen to fight the giant, but he was chosen of God.

Every one of our children will be brought into the ark, if we pray and work earnestly for them.

The impression that a praying mother leaves upon her children is life-long. Perhaps when you are dead and gone your prayer will be answered.

I would rather go into the kingdom of heaven through the poor house than go down to hell in a golden chariot.

I believe there are more young men who come to Boston who are lost because they cannot say no, than for any other reason.

It isn't necessary to leave the things of this life when you follow Him. It is not necessary to give up your business, if it's a legitimate one, in order to accept Christ. But you must not set your heart on the old nets by a good deal.

A great many people want to bring their faith, their works, their good deeds to Him for salvation. Bring your sins, and He will bear them away into the wilderness of forgetfulness, and you will never see them again.

SALVATION

There was never a sermon that you have listened to but in it Christ was seeking for you. I contend that a man will find in every page of this book that Jesus Christ is seeking him through His blessed Word. This is what the Bible is for to seek out the lost.

The mightiest man that ever lived could not deliver himself from his sins. If a man could have saved himself, Christ would never have come into the world.

He came to deliver us from our sinful dispositions, and create in us pure hearts, and when we have Him with us it will not be hard for us. Then the service of Christ will be delightful.

I hold to the doctrine of sudden conversion as I do to my life, and I would as quickly give up my life as give up this doctrine, unless it can be proved that it is not according to the word of God. Now, I will admit that light is one thing and birth is another. A soul must be born before it can see light. A child must be born before it can be taught; it must be born before it can walk; it must be born before it can be educated.

There is no other way to the Kingdom of God but by the way of the Cross, and it will be easier for you to take it now than it will be afterward.

Do you believe the Lord will call a poor sinner, and then cast him out? No! His word stands forever, "Him that cometh unto Me I will in no wise cast out."

If God put Adam out of this earthly Eden on account of one sin, do you think He will let us into the Paradise above with our tens of thousands sins upon us.

The only charge they could bring against Christ down here was, that He was receiving bad men. They are the very kind of men He is willing to receive.

I believe in my soul that there are more at this day being lost for want of decision than for any other thing.

No man in the world should be so happy as a man of God. It is one continual source of gladness. He can look up and say, "God is my Father, Christ is my Savior, and the Church is my mother."

Dear sinner, Jesus is ready and willing to carry you over the mountains of sin, and over your mountains of unbelief. Give yourself to Him.

BIBLIOGRAPHY

Fitt, Arthur Percy, *The Life of D. L. Moody*, The Bible Institute Colportage Society, 1900.

Goodspeed, Rev. E. J., *Wonderful Career of Moody and Sankey in Great Britain and America*, C. C. Wick & Co., 1876.

McClure, J. B., *Anecdotes and Illustrations of D. L. Moody*, Rhodes & McClure, 1881.

Moody, Dwight, L., *The Overcoming Life*, Fleming H. Revell, 1896.

Moody, Dwight, L., *The Way To God*, Fleming H. Revell, 1884.

Moody, Dwight, L., *Brilliants*, H. M. Caldwell, 1894.

Moody, Dwight, L., *Great Joy*, William Nicholson and Sons, 1892.

Moody, Paul, D., *My Father, An Intimate Portrait of Dwight Moody*, Little Brown and Company, 1938.

Moody, William, R., The Life of Dwight L. Moody By His Son, Fleming H. Revell, 1900.

THE OVERCOMING LIFE
STUDY GUIDE

CHAPTER 1: THE CHRISTIAN'S WARFARE

1. What is Christian warfare? When do we enter the battle? Against who and what is the battle waged?

2. Is salvation a free gift from God, or is there something we have to do to receive it?

3. Christ is the foundation of our faith, but the structure we then build on that foundation has eternal significance. What kind of structure are you building? (Read 1 Corinthians 3:11-15)

4. In what sense are we "co-workers" with God?

5. How is it that the believer is Christ is able to overcome the world, sin, flesh and the devil? (Read, 2 Corinthians 5:7; Ephesians 6:16; Hebrews 11)

6. Why do so many Christians fail to overcome in this life?

7. Are you overcoming the world, or is the world overcoming you?

CHAPTER 2: INTERNAL FOES

1. What are our internal enemies?

2. Can a person sin who has become a Christian? (Read Romans 7; Galatians 5:17)

3. What's the difference between "reigning sin" and "remaining sin" in our lives?

4. Do you lead a self-examined life?

5. Can man overcome the internal foes of temper, pride, covetousness, and appetite in his own power? If not, by what power is he enabled?

CHAPTER 3: EXTERNAL FOES

1. What are our external enemies?

2. When we refer to the enemy of "the world," what do we mean? (Read 1 John 2:15-17; John 15:18,19; 16:33)

3. What does it mean when our Lord instructs us to live "in" the world, but not be "of" the world?

4. How can the Christian be an example of Christ-likeness in the world?

5. How do the Christian and the unbeliever deal differently with persecution. What positive affects does persecution have for the believer?

6. What are the eight "overcomes" found in the book of Revelation? How do they apply to you in your life?

CHAPTER 4: TRUE REPENTANCE

1. What are the five effects of true repentance?

2. What is the difference between guilt and conviction?

3. What are the three things that lead to godly conviction?

4. By what power are people able to experience conviction of the heart? (Read John 14:16-17)

5. How does contrition lead to repentance?

6. How is true confession of sin exercised? (John 14:6: Matthew 5:23,24; 1 John 1:9)

7. True repentance must lead to conversion. What two things does conversion mean in the Bible?

8. Confession of Jesus Christ as Lord and Savior is the culminating work of true repentance. Have you confessed Him in your heart and by your lips?

CHAPTER 5: TRUE WISDOM

1. How does godly wisdom set apart the Christian amidst a world of sinners?

2. Leading a surrendered life is vital to receiving wisdom from God. How can we better lead a surrendered life?

CHAPTER 6: "COME THOU AND ALL THY HOUSE INTO THE ARK"

1. The Noahic Flood is an actual event in the world's history used by God to bring judgment upon sinful man. How does the message of this event relate to what is happening in the world today, and when Christ comes again?

2. Do people today hear the message of judgment, or do they continue in ignorance just like the people of Noah's day?

3. Are we listening to the voice of God as revealed in His Word, in the circumstances of our lives, and in our private prayer and meditation closets?

4. Can the Christian know the time of Christ's return? (Read Mark 13:32; Matthew 25:13)

CHAPTER 7: HUMILITY

1. What does it mean to possess godly humility?

2. Does meekness mean weakness?

3. Augustine said that humility is first of all the Christian graces. What did he say was the second and third?

4. Describe the difference between false humility and genuine humility.

5. Look upon your own life and attitudes (Read John 3:30). How can I decrease that Christ may increase?

6. What does it mean to be filled with the Holy Spirit? How is our experience different from that of the Apostles in Acts 2?

CHAPTER 8: REST

1. What is the promise of rest as described in Hebrews 4:1?

2. How do you "enter into His rest" as found in Hebrews 4:1-11?

3. What does it mean when the Lord instructs us to "Keep the Sabbath"?

4. Can true rest be found in this world? Where can we come to find true rest?

5. What factors bring unrest in our hearts and lives?

THE SEVEN "I WILLS" OF CHRIST

1. What are the seven "I Wills" of Christ and how are applying them to your Christian walk?

THE WAY TO GOD, AND HOW TO FIND IT

CHAPTER 1: "LOVE THAT PASSETH KNOWLEDGE"

1. What does it mean, "God is Love"? (Read 1 John 4:8.)
2. If God is love, how do we as Christians explain to the unbelieving world why bad things happen?
3. How does God most profoundly express His love for us?
4. How is the power of God's love manifested in our lives?
5. Is God's love unconditional? How are we expressing God's love to others?
6. Is God's love unfailing?

CHAPTER 2: THE GATEWAY INTO THE KINGDOM

1. What does it mean to be Born-again? (Read John 3.)
2. Is it God who acts first, or man, in the process if salvation. (Read John 6:44; Romans 9.)
3. What is regeneration? What is it not?
4. Do we have a part in our salvation? (Read Phil 2:12; James 2.)

CHAPTER 3: THE TWO CLASSES

1. What are the two classes of people? (Read the story of the Pharisee and the Publican contrasted in Luke 18:9-14.)
2. The sin of Adam is passed onto the human race. What is the anecdote to the curse of original sin?

3. Examine the three essential elements of faith? Knowledge, assent and appropriation.

4. "Feeling has nothing to do with believing," says Moody. What does he mean by this?

CHAPTER 4: WORDS OF COUNSEL

1. There are sudden conversions and there are gradual conversions. How was your call by God?

2. What is denominationalism? Is it biblical? Discuss the pros and cons.

3. How are we to deal with things in the Bible we do not understand? (Read Deuteronomy 29:29)

4. Sound doctrine is vital to faithful application of God's Word in our lives. (Read 2 Timothy 3:16; John 7:17)

CHAPTER 5: A DIVINE SAVIOR

1. The Holy Trinity—Father, Son, and Holy Spirit—is central to the Christian faith. How can we know that Jesus Christ is God? (Read John 16:15; 17:3; John 1:1-5; 1 John 5:20)

2. Could Jesus, who claimed to be God incarnate, be a mere "good man" or a "prophet" as some say? What's wrong with this thinking?

CHAPTER 6: REPENTANCE AND RESTITUTION

1. What is repentance? What is *not* repentance?

2. What is restitution?

CHAPTER 7: ASSURANCE OF SALVATION

1. Can we know for sure that we are children of God?
2. Is it possible for someone to lose salvation once it is given and received?
3. What types of people should not be assured of salvation?
4. What are the five things in 1 John 3 that give us assurance?
5. How does confession bring forgiveness?
6. What is the difference between Justification and Sanctification?

CHAPTER 8: CHRIST ALL AND IN ALL

1. Is Christ limited in what He can be to us? Do we limit Him?
2. How can we know Christ more intimately?
3. How is Christ our Redeemer? What does that mean to you?
4. How are feelings different than faith?

CHAPTER 9: BACKSLIDING

1. Describe the two types of backsliders?
2. How are we to restore those who are backsliders?
3. If you are a backslider, what is it that has drawn your affections away from God? The consequences are serious and eternal. What sins are you clinging to? Are you open to restoration?
4. Beware the error of self-confidence. How can you know you have fallen into this error?

CHRISTIAN LOVE

1. How does God show His love towards you? How do you show your love for God?

2. How do you show your love for one another?

3. Are we called as Christians to love unbelievers? If so, how? If not, why not?

4. What is "heart love"?

5. The blessing of trials is often God expression of love towards His people.

6. How can I know if God really loves me?

7. How is the Christian's love different than the world's love?

INDEX

A

Absalom 136, 273, 321

Achan 79

affliction 55, 91, 314, 371

ambition 22, 91, 175

Ananias and Sapphira 79

appetite 73, 74, 240, 378, 394

ark 125, 126, 127, 128, 129, 130, 131, 132, 133, 134, 135, 136, 140, 388

assurance 281, 282, 283, 290, 292, 371, 372, 399

of Salvation vi, 281, 399

Atonement, the 265

Augustine 90, 142, 157, 396

B

backslider 320, 321, 323, 324, 325, 331, 381, 399

baptized 209

Blood, the 174, 297, 299, 303, 374, 375, 376

Bonar, Dr. Horatius 34

born

of God 61, 72, 293, 341

of the Spirit vii, 208, 210, 211, 213, 227, 255, 281. *See also* New Birth

Pure Gold Classics

AN EXPANDING COLLECTION OF THE BEST-LOVED CHRISTIAN CLASSICS OF ALL TIME.

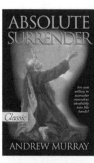

ABSOLUTE SURRENDER
Classic
ANDREW MURRAY

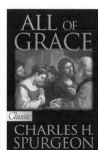

ALL OF GRACE
Classic
CHARLES H. SPURGEON

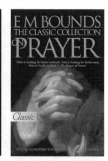

E M BOUNDS
THE CLASSIC COLLECTION OF PRAYER
Classic

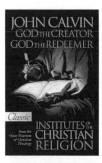

JOHN CALVIN
GOD THE CREATOR
GOD THE REDEEMER
Classic
from the Opus Magnum of Christian Theology
INSTITUTES OF THE CHRISTIAN RELIGION

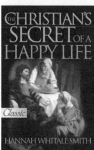

THE CHRISTIAN'S SECRET OF A HAPPY LIFE
Classic
HANNAH WHITALL SMITH

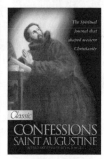

The Spiritual Journal that shaped western Christianity
Classic
CONFESSIONS SAINT AUGUSTINE

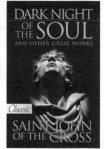

DARK NIGHT OF THE SOUL
AND OTHER GREAT WORKS
Classic
SAINT JOHN OF THE CROSS

EVENING BY EVENING
Classic
CHARLES H. SPURGEON

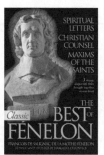

SPIRITUAL LETTERS
CHRISTIAN COUNSEL
MAXIMS OF THE SAINTS
Classic
THE BEST OF FÉNELON
FRANÇOIS DE SALIGNAC DE LA MOTHE-FÉNELON

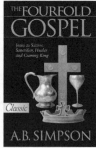

THE FOURFOLD GOSPEL
Jesus as Savior, Sanctifier, Healer and Coming King
Classic
A.B. SIMPSON

FOXE'S BOOK OF MARTYRS
Updated up to the 21st Century
Classic
JOHN FOXE

GOD OF ALL COMFORT
Classic
HANNAH WHITALL SMITH

THE GREATEST THING IN THE WORLD
Classic
HENRY DRUMMOND

THE HOLY SPIRIT POWER
10 Includes additional Timeless Messages
Prologue by Charles Wesley
Classic
JOHN WESLEY

HUMILITY
The deepest humility is the secret of the truest happiness, of a joy that nothing can destroy, Andrew Murray
Classic
ANDREW MURRAY

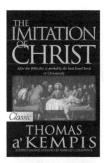
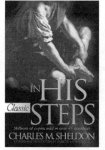
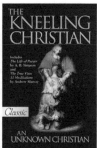

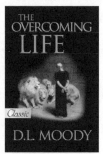

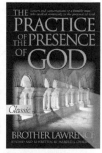
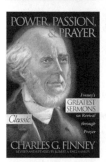

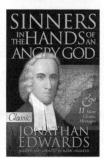

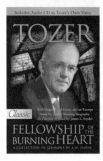
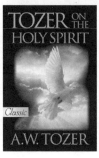
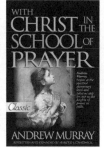
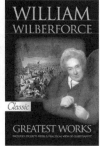

Pure Gold Classics

CHRISTIAN CLASSICS

A classic is a work of enduring excellence; a Christian classic is a work of enduring excellence that is filled with divine wisdom, biblical revelation, and insights that are relevant to living a godly life. Such works are both spiritual and practical. Our Pure Gold Classics contain some of the finest examples of Christian writing that have ever been published, including the works of John Foxe, Charles Spurgeon, D.L. Moody, Martin Luther, John Calvin, Saint John of the Cross, E.M. Bounds, John Wesley, Andrew Murray, Hannah Whitall Smith, and many others.

The timeline on the following pages will help you to understand the context of the times in which these extraordinary books were written and the historical events that must have served to influence these great writers to create works that will always stand the test of time. Inspired by God, many of these authors did their work in difficult times and during periods of history that were not sympathetic to their message. Some even had to endure great persecution, misunderstanding, imprisonment, and martyrdom as a direct result of their writing.

The entries that are printed in green type will give you a good overview of Christian history from the birth of Jesus to modern times.

The entries in red pertain to writers of Christian classics from Saint Augustine, who wrote his *Confessions* and *City of God*, to Charles Sheldon, twentieth-century author of *In His Steps*.

Entries in black provide a clear perspective on the development of secular history from the early days of Buddhism (first century) through the Civil Rights Movement.

Finally, the blue entries highlight secular writers and artists, including Chaucer, Michelangelo, and others.

Our color timeline will provide you with a fresh perspective of history, both secular and Christian, and the classics, both secular and Christian. This perspective will help you to understand each author better and to see the world through his or her eyes.

1714-1770 George Whitefield, Calvinist evangelist known for powerful preaching and revivals in England and America. Friend of John Wesley.

1720-1760 "The Great Awakening" in America. Numerous revivals result in widespread Church growth.

1741 Handel's *Messiah* composed.

1756-1763 Seven Years War in Europe, Britain defeats France.

1759-1833 William Wilberforce, British abolitionist and author of *A Practical View of Christianity*.

1775-1783 American Revolutionary War.

1779 Olney Hymns published, John Newton's *Amazing Grace*.

1789 French Revolution begins.

1792-1875 Charles Finney, American evangelist. Leads Second Great Awakening in 1824.

1805-1898 George Mueller, English evangelist & founder of orphanages; author, *Answers to Prayer*.

1813-1855 Soren Kierkegaard, Danish philosopher & theologian; author, *Fear and Trembling*.

1816-1900 J.C. Ryle, author of *Practical Religion* and *Holiness*.

1820-1915 "Fanny" Crosby, though blind, pens over 8,000 hymns.

1828-1917 Andrew Murray, author of *Humility, Abide in Christ, With Christ in the School of Prayer*, and *Absolute Surrender*.

1828 Noah Webster publishes a dictionary of the English Language.

1829 Salvation Army founded by William and Catherine Booth.

1832-1911 Hannah Whitall Smith, author of *The Christian's Secret to a Happy Life* and *God of All Comfort*.

1834-1892 Charles H. Spurgeon, author of *Morning by Morning* and *The Treasury of David*.

1835-1913 E.M. Bounds, author of *The Classic Collection on Prayer*.

1836-1895 A.J. Gordon, New England Spirit-filled pastor; author, *The Ministry of the Spirit*.

1837-1899 Dwight L. Moody, evangelist and founder of Moody Bible Institute in Chicago. Author of *Secret Power* and *The Way to God*.

1843-1919 A.B. Simpson, founder of Christian and Missionary Alliance, author of *The Fourfold Gospel*.

1844 Samuel Frank Morse invents the telegraph.

1847-1929 F.B. Meyer, English Baptist pastor & evangelist; author, *Secret of Guidance*.

1857-1858 Third Great Awakening in America; Prayer Meeting Revival.

1851-1897 Henry Drummond, author of *The Greatest Thing in the World … Love*.

1856-1928 R.A. Torrey, American evangelist, pastor and author.

1857-1946 Charles Sheldon, author of *In His Steps*.

1859 Theory of evolution; Charles Darwin's *Origin of Species*.

1861-1865 American Civil War.

1862-1935 Billy Sunday, American baseball player who became one of the most influential evangelists in the 20th century. *Collected Sermons*.

1867 Alexander Graham Bell invents the telephone.

1869-1948 Mahatma Gandhi makes his life's work India's peaceful independence from Britain.

1881-1936 J. Gresham Machen, "Old School" Presbyterian leader, writes *Christianity and Liberalism*; forms the new Orthodox Presbyterian Church in 1936.

1886-1952 A. W. Pink, evangelist & biblical scholar; author, *The Sovereignty of God*.

1897-1963 A.W. Tozer, author of *Fellowship of the Burning Heart*.

1898-1900 Boxer Rebellion in China deposes western influence, particularly Christian missionaries.

c. 1900-1930 *The Kneeling Christian* (Written by The Unknown Christian.)

1901 American Standard Version of Bible published.

1906 Azusa Street Revival, Los Angeles, instrumental in rise of modern Pentecostal Movement.

1906-1945 Dietrich Bonhoeffer spreads Christian faith to Germans in opposition to WWII Nazism.

1914-1918 World War I.

1917 Bolshevik Revolution in Russia.

1925 Scopes Monkey Trial pits Bible against theory of evolution.

1929 US Stock Market crashes, 12 years of Great Depression.

1939-1945 World War II. Holocaust in eastern Europe under Hitler.

1947 Dead Sea Scrolls found in caves in Judean desert.

1948 State of Israel reestablished.

1949 Communist revolution in China; religion suppressed.

1952 RSV Bible first published.

1960s Civil Rights movement in the United States.

4-6 BC Jesus of Nazareth is born.

30 Christ crucified and risen.

30 Pentecost.

32 Stephen becomes the first Christian martyr.

35 Paul's conversion.

46-48 Paul's missionary work begins.

47 Term "Christian" first used.

58 Emperor Ming-Ti introduces Buddhism to his country.

64 Fire destroys Rome. Emperor Nero blames the Christians.

65 Martyrdom of the Apostle Paul in Rome.

66 First Jewish revolt against Rome.

68-70 Dead Sea Scrolls buried in Qumran caves. Found between 1947 and 1956.

70 Titus destroys Jerusalem and its Temple. Dispersion of the Jews.

95 Apostle John writes the Book of Revelation.

105 Paper invented in China.

150 "The First Apologist," Justin Martyr, advances Christian efforts against competing philosophies.

190 First "official" date of Easter.

231 Origen's Polyglot Bible.

300 Persecution of Christians under Diocletian.

313 Constantine issues *Edict of Milan*, granting legal rights to all Christians in the Roman Empire.

325 First Council of Nicea.

367 Athanasius compiles earliest known list of New Testament canon in current form.

395 Roman Empire divided between East and West, setting stage for division of the Christian Church.

397 Augustine of Hippo converts to Christianity, later writes his *Confessions* and *City of God*.

400 Vulgate Latin text becomes standard Bible of Christianity.

410 Fall of Roman Empire to the Visigoths, led by Alaric.

430 Patrick brings Christianity to pagan Ireland.

450 Bodhidharma founds Zen Buddhism in India; takes to China.

451 Council of Chalcedon affirms apostolic doctrine that Christ is "truly God and truly man."

451 The Romans and Visigoths defeat Atilla the Hun at Chalons.

478 First Shinto religious shrines erected in Japan.

529 Benedictine order establises rule for monastic life.

542-594 Bubonic plague cuts population of Europe in half.

622 Birth of Islamic religion.

640 Library of Alexandria with 30,000 manuscripts completely destroyed.

732 Battle of Poitiers: Muslim forces defeated in France; kept Islam out of Europe.

800 "By the sword and the Cross" Charlemagne restores social and religious order to medieval Europe.

871-901 King Alfred preserves Christianity amidst opposition within and outside the Church.

988 Vladimir converts; brings Christianity to Russia.

1000 Viking Leif Erikson discovers North America.

1000 Chinese perfect the use and production of gunpowder.

1050 First agricultural revolution of Europe begins.

1054 Permanent separation between the Roman Church in the West and Eastern Orthodox Church.

1066 Norman conquest of England under William fuses French and English cultures. As a result, English language evolves into Middle English.

1085 Christians conquer Toledo; discover works of Aristotle and Plato.

1090-1153 Bernard of Clairvaux.

1096 First of eight Christian Crusades begins in effort to prevail over Muslim invaders.

1140-1217 Peter Waldo, founder of the Protestant Waldenses.

1182 Magnetic compass invented.

1182-1226 Francis of Assisi.

1207 Genghis Khan conquers Asia.

c. 1225-1274 Thomas Aquinas, Italian theologian and author of *Summa Theologica*.

1270 Last Christian Crusade.

1280 Eyeglasses are invented.

1298 Marco Polo writes *The Travels of Marco Polo*

1329-1384 John Wycliffe, translator of the Bible into English. It's condemned and forbidden by the Archbishop.

1337-1453 Hundred Year War between France and England.

1342-1400 Geoffrey Chaucer, who wrote *The Canterbury Tales* in 1386

1347 Black death kills 25 million and halts economic growth in Europe for 200 years.

1350-1527 Approximate dates of the Renaissance

CHRISTIAN HISTORY   CLASSIC AUTHORS   SECULAR HISTORY   SECULAR AUTHORS & ARTISTS

1368 Chinese Ming Dynasty continues through 1644.

1369-1415 John Huss, Czech religious reformer before the Reformation. Burned at the stake for his bold stand against corrupt clergy.

1378-1417 Great Schism brings competing popes to the Church.

1380-1471 Thomas à Kempis, who published *The Imitation of Christ* in 1427.

1386-1466 Donatello, Florentine sculptor who created first freestanding statues in the Renaissance.

1420 Huss followers, "Hussites," revolt under John Zizka.

1431 Joan of Arc burned at the stake.

1450 Johannes Gutenberg invents the printing press.

1452-1519 Leonardo da Vinci, Italian sculptor, architect, painter, inventor, engineer, and scientist.

1453 Constantinople falls to the Turks; renamed Istanbul.

1455 Gutenberg Bible printed. Availability and affordability of Bibles becomes a key factor in the ensuing Protestant Reformation.

1469-1527 Niccolo Machiavelli, Italian philosopher and author of *The Prince*.

1471-1528 Albrecht Durer, German, Christian artist

and sculptor of The Praying Hands.

1473-1543 Nicolaus Copernicus, Polish astronomer, founds modern astronomy.

1475-1564 Michelangelo, Florentine sculptor and painter: The Pieta, Moses, David and the Sistine Chapel ceiling.

1477 First book printed in England.

1478 Spanish Inquisition begins.

1483-1546 Martin Luther.

1492 Columbus lands in America.

1494-1536 William Tyndale, Protestant reformer and scholar who translated the Bible into Early Modern English. Martyred in 1536.

1497 Italian explorer settles in England, takes the name John Cabot, sails in the name of the Royal Crown and discovers Newfoundland.

1500s Spanish conquer Aztec, Inca civilizations in New World.

1505-1572 John Knox, reformer of Scotland.

1509-1564 John Calvin, French theologian, author. Pens *Institutes of Christian Religion* in 1536.

1515-1582 St. Teresa of Avila, major figure in Catholic Reformation; author, *Interior Castle*.

1516-1587 John Foxe, author of *Book of Martyrs*.

1517 Protestant Reformation begins. Martin Luther posts

his 95 Theses against the selling of indulgences.

1531 King Henry VIII breaks with the Church of Rome.

1533-1584 Ivan the Terrible rules Russia.

1542-1591 St. John of the Cross, Carmelite priest, major figure in Catholic Reformation; author, *Dark Night of the Soul*.

1545 Council of Trent convenes to refute accusations of heresy made by Protestants. Beginning of Tridentine Church, today's Roman Catholic Church.

1553 Mary "Bloody Mary" Tudor begins her reign.

1555-1556 Leading early reformers Cranmer, Latimer and Ridley burned at stake.

1560 Geneva Bible, the first complete Bible to be translated into English from Hebrew and Greek.

1564-1616 William Shakespeare.

1564 Birth of Puritanism.

1598 *Edict of Nantes* grants Huguenots religious freedom.

1611 Authorized *King James Version* of the Bible produced.

1614-1691 Brother Lawrence, author of *The Practice of the Presence of God*.

1618 Synod of Dort refutes Arminianism in favor of Calvinism.

1620 Pilgrims land at Plymouth.

1628-1688 John Bunyan, author of *The Pilgrim's Progress*.

1642-1727 Isaac Newton discovers color in light; laws of gravity, motion.

1647-1748 Isaac Watts, who wrote over 700 hymns and 25 books.

1648 Westminster Confession of Faith. Reformed doctrines of the Church clarified.

1648-1717 Madame Guyon, author of *Experiencing Union with God Through Inner Prayer*.

1651-1715 Francois Fenelon, author of *Maxims of the Saints, Spiritual Letters and Christian Counsel*.

1662 The Act of Conformity forces over 2,000 Puritan pastors out of the Church of England.

1662-1714 Matthew Henry, author of *Commentary on the Whole Bible*.

1667 John Milton publishes *Paradise Lost*.

1686-1761 William Law, English devotional writer; author, *A Serious Call to a Devout and Holy Life*.

1703-1758 Jonathan Edwards, great American theologian and author. Sermons include *Sinners in the Hands of an Angry God*.

1703-1791 John Wesley, founder of modern day Methodist church, authors many landmark sermons, including *The Holy Spirit and Power*.